D0781141

Place, Ecology and the Sacred

ALSO AVAILABLE FROM BLOOMSBURY

Public Religion and the Urban Environment, Richard Bohannon
Religions and Environments, Richard Bohannon
Religion in Environmental and Climate Change,
edited by Dieter Gerten and Sigurd Bergmann

REGIS COLLEGE LIBRARY
100 Wellesley Street West
Toronto, Ontario
Canada M5S 2Z5

WITHDRAWN

Place, Ecology and the Sacred:

The Moral Geography of Sustainable Communities

Michael S. Northcott

BF
353
N67
2015

B L O O M S B U R Y

LONDON • NEW DELHI • NEW YORK • SYDNEY

Bloomsbury Academic

An imprint of Bloomsbury Publishing Plc

50 Bedford Square	1385 Broadway
London	New York
WC1B 3DP	NY 10018
UK	USA

www.bloomsbury.com

BLOOMSBURY and the Diana logo are trademarks of Bloomsbury Publishing Plc

First published 2015

© Michael S. Northcott, 2015

Michael S. Northcott has asserted his right under the Copyright, Designs and Patents Act, 1988, to be identified as Author of this work.

All rights reserved. No part of this publication may be reproduced or transmitted in any form or by any means, electronic or mechanical, including photocopying, recording, or any information storage or retrieval system, without prior permission in writing from the publishers.

No responsibility for loss caused to any individual or organization acting on or refraining from action as a result of the material in this publication can be accepted by Bloomsbury or the author.

British Library Cataloguing-in-Publication Data

A catalogue record for this book is available from the British Library.

ISBN:	HB:	978-1-4411-9964-5
	PB:	978-1-4411-3406-6
	ePDF:	978-1-4411-1537-9
	ePub:	978-1-4411-1457-0

Library of Congress Cataloging-in-Publication Data

A catalog record for this book is available from the Library of Congress.

Typeset by RefineCatch Limited, Bungay, Suffolk

Printed and bound in India

CONTENTS

REGIS COLLEGE LIBRARY
100 Wellesley Street West
Toronto, Ontario
Canada M5S 2Z5

ACKNOWLEDGEMENTS

The essays in this book reflect some years of learning to grow food in Durisdeer, a small village in Southwest Scotland. Durisdeer means 'gate of the forest' and is set in the Lowther Hills of Dumfrieshire. As I have dwelled and dug here on weekends and holidays, its buildings, hills, inhabitants and soils have revealed a gathering of forces aesthetic, ecological, historical and spiritual, which mark the village as what George McLeod, founder of the Iona Community, called a 'thin' place. An account of these forces in the phenomenology of place is woven into the Introduction as a frame for the book. The essays that follow also reflect teaching and research at New College on the Mound in Edinburgh, situated close by Edinburgh Castle, which stands as forbidding sentinel above the rocky crags that overshadow Princes Street Gardens. I am grateful to successive cohorts of students on my course Ecology, Ethics and Religion, which I have also taught at Dartmouth College and Duke University, who have stimulated my thinking. I am grateful to the publishers of previously published material incorporated into the book, and to book publishers and journal editors for permission to reproduce my work here in revised form. I am very grateful to my friends Jolyon Mitchell and George Reiss who read earlier drafts of the whole book and made very helpful suggestions on improving it. A version of Chapter 3 was previously published as 'Artificial persons against nature: environmental governmentality, economic corporations, and ecological ethics', *Annals of the New York Academy of Sciences,* 1249 (2011), 104–117; a version of Chapter 4 was previously published as 'Sabbaths, shamans and superquarries in Scotland: environment and religion in a contested landscape' in Fred Gale and Michael M'Gonagle (eds), *Nature, Production, Power: Towards an Ecological Political Economy* (Cheltenham: Edward Elgar, 2000), 17–34; a version of Chapter 5 was previously published as 'Wilderness, religion, and ecological restoration in the Scottish Highlands', *Ecotheology* 10 (2005), 382–399. Chapter 2 originated as a presentation at the conference 'Green as a Leaf' sponsored by the Department of Theology and Religious Studies of Nottingham University and Southwell Minster, and held in the Minster in April 2010; Chapter 6 was given as a paper at the CAFOD seminar on 'Climate, Consumption and the Common Good' held at Kings College London in May 2014, and I am grateful to participants for comments on the paper; parts of Chapter 8 were presented at the symposium 'Landscapes of Hope: Towards the Imaginary Reconstruction of Society' at the Institute for Advanced Studies in the Humanities of the University of Edinburgh, 27 February 2014. Finally I am very grateful to the UK Arts and Humanities Research Council for funding the research project 'Caring for the Future Through Ancestral Time: Engaging the Cultural and Spiritual Presence of the Past to Promote a Sustainable Future' (AH/K005456/1), which enabled me to bring this book to completion.

Introduction

There is a growing disconnect in contemporary life between people and the land, or what moderns call 'nature' or the nonhuman 'environment'. This disconnect originates with rapid urbanisation, which began after 1800 with the industrial revolution, and the Enclosures, in England.[1] Globally the majority of human beings now live in cities or suburban areas. This population shift also marks the withdrawal of most of the human population from participation in agriculture. In the UK and North America fewer than 2 per cent of the population are now involved in formal agriculture. The resultant disconnect between people and the earth has effects both on human beings and on other creatures.

It might be expected that, with the withdrawal of human beings from rural occupations and from rural dwelling, the number of species would increase. Those formed in the Romantic aesthetic of nonhuman wilderness as sublime, and intrinsically valuable apart from its use to humans, assume that human beings inevitably reduce biodiversity through their food growing, fuel gathering and other consumption and production activities.[2] But on the contrary the withdrawal of most human beings from rural pursuits and engagement in farming has been accompanied by a *decline* in the abundance of species, and in the quality of rural habitats. Key to this decline is the use of fertilisers, herbicides, pesticides and heavy machinery, and the growing numbers of domesticated animals, sponsored by industrial agriculture. These practices displace human labour on the land, but at the same time they erode living soils and uncultivated areas, and hence the base of the food webs on which insects, birds and small mammals rely. Traditional mixed farms and smallholdings by contrast sustain a much larger range of species, and they produce more *human* food per hectare than modern industrial farming methods. What they do not produce is quantities of grains and oils sufficient to supply the industrial-scale facilities, including cattle, chicken and pig sheds and feed lots, in which the majority of the 5 billion globally domesticated animals and birds are cruelly incarcerated, and the industrial food factories that manufacture packaged and 'refined' foods beloved of supermarkets and food scientists, and increasingly associated with a range of human dietary disorders and diseases.

The great disconnect between people and the land is promoted not only by industrial agriculture and rural depopulation but by planners and development companies, who devote a growing proportion of urban and urban-edge land to commercial spaces – such as freeways, industrial 'parks', private residential estates, shopping malls and 'big box stores' – designed for private mechanical transportation and to maximise spaces for consumption. The resultant contrast between older and contemporary urban spaces can be seen most clearly from the air. Both London and Kuala Lumpur – cities I have lived in – have an inner core of public buildings interspersed with large parks and public squares, while older residential areas show extensive space given to trees and grass, as in London's Georgian residential squares. But suburban housing areas from the 1960s onwards are mostly built on land that has been entirely denuded of trees, and common space is devoted instead to tarmac roads between houses, and to parking spaces. This design trend of contemporary urban areas reduces land given over to green places such as parks, waterways, flood meadows, food growing areas, copses, and other 'unbuilt' features that were normal features of pre-industrial towns and cities. In contrast to the increasingly overbuilt modern urban environment the pre-industrial town was not only much smaller in scale but it was an 'edible landscape', since most of the space around dwellings and workshops was given over to food growing, including fruit trees, perennial herbs and beds for staple foods such as root crops and brassicas.[3]

Another source of the contemporary disconnect between people and nature is the growing surveillance of children's play, and the reduced time spent by children in educational and domestic settings in unsupervised play outdoors. Even when children live in rural areas or near woodlands, they are now less likely to wander beyond the front door than they did in the past, or to play outdoors for extensive periods unsupervised by adults. The raised quotient of time spent by children indoors is devoted instead to interactions with screens, games machines and other electronic devices instead of interactions with other living beings, including other children, adults or domestic animals and plants. One manifestation of this disconnect is that a growing proportion of children in cities in both developed and less developed countries no longer know where their food comes from. Most British children do not know that butter comes from cows or that eggs come from chickens.[4] Similarly many have never encountered farm animals, or visited farmed fields, orchards, vineyards or wild places such as forests, lakes, moorlands or mountains. Outdoor education trainers also report that when they take urban children outside the city, many of them express feelings of anxiety and fear at potential threats from unfamiliar surroundings.[5]

The great and growing disconnect between nature and contemporary humans represents a phenomenological equivalent to the ideational nature–culture divide that is observed by environmental philosophers since the Enlightenment as a principal cause, and symptom, of the ecological crisis. This divide is harmful to nature, since it fosters harmful consumption practices: if urban people do not know food comes from soils and water they may be untroubled by early signs that industrial civilisation is responsible for extensive soil erosion and a growing water crisis. Analogously, lack of knowledge of the environment, and reduced engagement in wild or at least non-urban places, reduces engagement in and political support for ecological conservation. If contemporary young adults have less knowledge of, and engagement with, the nonhuman environment, they are less likely as adults to engage in behaviours, or to support policies, that reduce the growing impacts of industrial production methods and consumer practices on the health of the planet. But the disconnect between people and nature, or the phenomenological nature–culture divide, is also bad for people, as a growing array of evidence indicates. Interaction with nonhuman species is an important but under-investigated source of child development and mental and physical health, and also plays a significant role in adult wellbeing. Hence there is epidemiological evidence that hospital patients who can see trees and not buildings from their beds recover faster from operations.[6] There is related evidence that childrens' play on grass and in planted areas is more constructive, imaginative and sociable than on barren areas such as tarmac, and that play in richer environments promotes better learning outcomes in the classroom.[7] But there is a greater body of evidence that shows harmful effects on children and adults of reduced interaction with the outdoors and nonhuman species, and of the growing disconnect between people and nature.

There is a rising tide of psychological and physical ill health, and rising rates of self-harm, suicide, eating disorders and obesity among young people in Australia, Britain and North America.[8] Mainstream psychologists and educationalists seem unable to explain the reasons for this rise.[9] Wilkinson and Pickett find a plausible correlation between rising economic inequality and rising mental anxiety and illness.[10] One factor in this may be the awareness among young people of the risks of falling into extreme poverty and unemployment post-school, and the related focus among parents and teachers on school performance as a strategy to prevent this. Richard Louw argues that the key to rising levels of psychological ill health in young people is lack of interaction with nature. He coins the phrase 'nature deficit disorder' in order rhetorically to counter the idea that children who will not sit still for hours on end in indoor educational settings suffer from a medical condition, often called 'attention deficit disorder', and treatable with drugs such as Ritalin.[11]

Children are developing mammals and like all young mammals they need embodied physical play with other mammals, and in outdoor places, in order to properly develop motor and mental skills. This need is not confined to pre-schoolers: young humans have the longest developmental period of any mammal, and do not reach physical maturity until their teenage years. Mental maturity may come even later. The enduring need of young people for embodied play is insufficiently met by short school breaks on concrete or tarmac playgrounds, or by one or two hours a week of 'Physical Education' principally in indoor settings such as school halls. Yet British and other governments have sold, for housing and commercial development, large areas of land once devoted to school playing fields, while the time given to physical education in school curricula has also been reduced by growing governmental regimentation of classroom curricula. The disconnect of children from the outdoors is also promoted by the rise of a risk-averse culture, known in Britain by the phrase 'health and safety,' so that any activity that carries a perceived risk – tree climbing, playing in dirt, interaction with nonhuman animals – is discouraged. Another factor is the growing regulatory demands on teachers for paperwork that evidences learning performance to educational managers: teachers therefore have much less time and energy to devote to 'extra-curricular' activities such as supervising school sports and outings.

As a child I attended schools with large playing fields, and my boarding school campus included ancient oak trees, an outdoor swimming pool, rugby fields, tennis courts and an unkempt wooded river valley. Both schools devoted three full afternoons a week to outdoor activities. When not boarding, I lived on a wide leafy road in a London suburb that was until 1963 a bumpy dirt track with brambles on its edge and so very safe for children to play around since cars could not drive above 10 miles an hour. Tragically a neighbour's child, whom I knew, was killed on the road within five years of it being turned into tarmac. We also lost a much loved dog, Susan, to a car on the same road and hence I do not find plausible utilitarian cost-benefit calculations suggesting that new or faster roads increase human wellbeing. In this relatively un-trafficked semi-rural environment I was permitted extensive time outdoors, much of it spent on a bicycle, and this included day cycles down country lanes into North Kent that today children would not undertake unsupervised because of the number of motor vehicles. We also went for annual summer holidays to stay on a small mixed farm in Pembrokeshire where we became familiar with farm animals and farm fields.

As an adult, and in particular a working academic, I have begun to experience something of the disconnect between urban living and nature that is the lot of a growing number of children, and a hint even of its harmful effects. I have been 'working' as a theologian on the human–nature relationship for many years. But I have been a city dweller most of my working life, and for most of each week I am indoors in a library or office, often looking at a screen such as the one on which I write this book. As an academic, and before that a clergyman, I have lived and worked over thirty-five years in the large cities of Manchester, Birmingham, Kuala Lumpur, and Edinburgh. I began to experience an increasing disconnect between my writing on and about the earth, in the general areas of environmental theology and ethics, and my urban lifestyle. I would often go walking in the Scottish Highlands with colleagues and friends at the weekend. During the week I cycle to work, and part of my route is along a tree-lined former rail line. But I had a growing sense of disconnect between my writing and my lifestyle, which was also, with hindsight, clearly connected to spending insufficient time outside and with nonhuman species.

My initial response was to think about moving with the family to a more rural location but this would have committed us to commuting, and driving the children around, and this seemed inappropriate and unsustainable. As the children became more independent – as they could in a city that has an excellent bus service and a low crime rate – I began to spend periods of time writing and walking at a friend's cottage on Applecross in the Western Highlands, in a hamlet called Fernamore. The house, or 'bothy', has views across the sea to Raasay and Skye, and across Loch Torridon to the Torridon Mountains, which are stunningly beautiful. But my times there made me think I wanted to do more than put my toe in the water of rural living. I wanted to dig, to plant, to grow roots in a place other than the city, and in so doing to *make* something beyond essays, books, learning experiences, liturgies and the occasional piece of furniture knocked up in our small back garden. I yearned in other words for a place that is more than a 'machine for living', or a 'consumption space'. While convenient for a short cycle to work, mostly through Edinburgh's Georgian New Town, and while having been a wonderful place to bring up a family – being close to a local park and school – our Edinburgh house is nonetheless packed in among other houses, and it seemed to offer no prospect of reconnecting with land via a tiny back garden overshadowed by a twelve foot wall that for most of the day shades it from the sun. I could have joined the ten-year waiting list for a local allotment, since we are not alone as urban residents wanting to reconnect with the land and grow some food. A move to East Lothian was another possibility, particularly with the children moving into tertiary education. But this hinterland is Scotland's sunniest cereal growing area, and those houses that do come up for sale tend to have quite small gardens, so in effect this would be a move to a 'deep suburb', requiring extended daily time given over to commuting, without prospect of a significant alteration in garden size or engagement with the land.

I was effectively among that growing proportion of modern humanity who are 'landless people', and who suffer from what the forester, academic and ecological pioneer Aldo Leopold called 'land pathology'. The pathology originates in the characteristically modern failure to include land in the organism that moderns call society: Leopold's solution is to include the 'economic and esthetic' functions of land into the way every acre of the earth is used. For Leopold the problem with modern conservation is that many of its advocates do not differ from bureaucrats, developers and politicians in thinking that economics is the principal consideration for the majority of land uses, while aesthetics is primarily about a small proportion of land that has been set aside from productive use, such as gardens, parks and protected wilderness areas.[12] Leopold purchased over a hundred acres in Wisconsin to address the reconnection of these two things and over thirty years devoted himself to replanting trees, and enabling soils to recover on the overused land of his 'sand county'. The repair to my own land pathology arose in the opportunity to purchase a former shepherd's cottage garden in a remote village in Southwest Scotland, some sixty miles from Edinburgh, but which happened to be just a mile from a direct bus route. The village where the house is located is remote from places of work – the nearest possible place of regular work is Dumfries over twenty miles away – and it lacks up-to-date telecommunications facilities of the kind that make teleworking possible. Houses here are therefore a hard and long sell, and friends urgently needed to dispose of a holiday cottage and its substantial garden in the midst of the 2008 global financial crisis.

The house is among the oldest in the tiny hamlet of Durisdeer, which is set in the Lowther Hills, ten miles south of the source of the River Clyde and thirty miles north of the Solway Firth, which is the body of water to the North of the famously beautiful English Lake District. As the cover photograph of the book partly reveals, the village nestles in a cirque of hills and is protected from the North wind by a grove of ancient beech trees that sustains a large rookery, as well as providing roosts to owls, buzzards and, occasionally, a red kite. Above the village, in the 'Lang Glen', memorialised in Robert Burns' *Scottish Ballad*, dwelled Roman legionnaires in the first century of the Christian era, in a fortlet, the earthworks of which are still visible.[13] Here they presided over a long straight track on which their colleagues brought lead from the 'lead hills' ten miles north down through the ancient forests to the large Roman settlement on the River Nith, which runs below Durisdeer through Dumfries to the Solway Firth. There are however few trees on the hills today, which instead are grazed by sheep, rabbits, mountain hares, deer and feral goats.

At the centre of the village of traditional cottages and houses, nestled around a village green, sits a church and tower on an embankment above a small river, which has a history going back to the Celtic roots of Christianity in Scotland. The church is located on the medieval pilgrims' route from Melrose Abbey to Whithorn, and close to the modern Southern Upland Way. The present day church and tower provide a pleasing visual focus to the place for visitors to the village, and an enduring house of worship for local people.

The garden when we got into it was much under weeds, and half of it fenced off and untended for decades. It is beautifully situated with hills and large trees all around, and parts of it sheltered from the wind by dry stone walls. The most difficult weeds to eradicate are buttercup and ground elder; the latter – *Aegopodium podagraria* – was introduced by the Romans, who sowed the plant along their roads for legionnaires to eat, as it prevented them getting scurvy and will grow almost anywhere. It is a rhizome and so every portion of root will grow, and total eradication is unlikely. It is also the only plant I know of that acquired a new name at the Reformation, since it was formerly known as bishop's weed, bishops and abbots being among the principal landowners in medieval Britain. The mostly weekend work of digging out weeds, laying paths with bricks from an old pigsty, and creating raised beds with old roof rafters has been hard physical work, and cultivating the soil so that it is fertile for vegetables equally so. But it is incredibly satisfying and we are now seeing food growing year round. The soil tends to be clayey and acidic and contains quite a lot of stone. We began with double digging, and then introduced variously sea weed, wood ash, compost from our bins, leaf mould from the churchyard, and we continue to rake out stones and weeds. After six years, when I raked and turned the soil in the warm spring of 2014, I could feel it was different across almost the whole acre: no longer clayey or full of pebbles and small rocks, but a moist, fibrous growing medium. And the plants know it too and grow more securely and productively. Gardening organically, we are also seeing more birds, butterflies, moths and bees in the garden, and toads come every year to produce a new batch of tadpoles in the pond.

Some of the joy of gardening here comes from its setting in the hills. The village is blessed with a palpable sense of place. This is in part because the Roman track from the lead hills was never metalled. The present single-track road into the village ends at a gate into the glen, while the modern A702 trunk road from Dumfries to Edinburgh takes another way through the mountain pass. Consequently, the village is remarkably peaceful, there is no danger from speeding vehicles, and traffic noise hardly encroaches, except on the busiest of weekends, into the village environs. But, more than the absence of a through road, there is something about the presence of the houses and the church at a bend in a river flowing south towards the Solway Firth and below ancient trees and a cirque of hills dotted with sheep, and covered with grass, bracken, heather and the occasional rowan tree or copse of beech, that is pleasing to the senses and to the soul. The Chinese would say the village has good *feng shui*. This is because it is located below hills to the north on more gently sloping land facing south, on a bend in a river where water slows from upland channels, and where the sun's rays warm the soils.[14] In Chinese philosophy such a place represents a gathering of natural forces including the heavens, high land, a plateau, vegetation, trees, plants and animals, and water. Such gatherings of forces into eddies where their flow is held or slowed are generative of organisms, and organisms themselves represent such gatherings in microcosm. The abundance of forces in such a place represents an accumulation of surplus energy, which from the beginning of life on earth has characterised the gradual rise of speciation from the humblest assemblages of cells in the ocean to that most complex of all living organs, the brain of *Homo sapiens*.[15]

Gardening here is satisfying and fulfilling, and we have a sense of tending 'God's acre' that is really rewarding, especially when we start eating and sharing the produce, or survey the garden on a midge-free summer's evening. But Durisdeer and its surroundings, while a beautiful place, is not Paradise. In some ways the village comes close to Oliver Rackham's portrayal of the *Deserted Village* in his classic lament at the depeopling effects of the Enclosures on the English countryside.[16] Durisdeer once supported hundreds of families in a variety of trades; in the early 1900s the village had many families with children and there was a public house as well as tanneries, blacksmith and slaters in addition to shepherds and others working the land. But there are now just seventeen habitable houses within half a mile of the village square, and two of these are rarely occupied holiday lets. Most of the farm land near the village is managed by just two tenant farmers, with the help of part-time shepherding hands and a vast array of machinery. Consequently, if not completely deserted, on a winter's evening with the rain pouring down and the winds whistling through the trees, and only the occasional light in a window, it certainly does not feel like a flourishing community.

The land beyond the village boundaries is, moreover, sparse in trees and other vegetation. The highland above the village is partly given over to grazing of sheep, which eat everything that pushes above the grass, and hence it is treeless outside of a few copses on particularly steep or wet land. The rest of the high land is known as 'grouse moor', and is managed for bird shooting by the Queensberry Estate, which belongs to the Duke of Buccleuch who is Europe's largest private landowner. The moor is burned into a patchwork to keep the heather from getting too dense and deep, and hence providing too much cover for the birds from the shooters. Partridges are reared within a mile of the village in open pens, which provide protection from buzzards and crows, and contain food hoppers and water. There are few raptors other than buzzards, and the occasional pair of red kites, since gamekeepers have for two hundred years actively eradicated them. While it is illegal to kill raptors now, Southwest Scotland continues to have the largest rate of recorded wildlife crime in the UK, and there are large bird traps on the hill that, though 'legal' and meant for crows, are not exactly raptor friendly. I have also encountered a bedraggled fox that had beaten a circular path in the grass because caught in an illegal wire trap a few hundred yards from my front door. Lacking a gun I could not put it out of its misery.

The hills are also infested with rabbits, and they eat what the sheep do not. Moreover their warrens eventually collapse, and this leaves ugly scree scars on already quite bare hills. On the steeper contours the erosion of rain over decades on treeless slopes is clearly marked, with rivulets forming deep eroded gullies and washing the soil off the hill down to the rock. The estate also maintain ugly shooting tracks to transport shooters up to the high land so they do not have to walk in. They bulldozed a new one close by the village after we moved in. It is an unsightly scar on the land but Scots law permits estate owners to lay tracks without planning permission. And this is just one of many ways in which there is one law for the landowner around here and one for the rest. Any householder who adds a few bricks to his or her home without planning permission risks being asked to take them down again. Landowners in Scotland are also exempt from capital gains and inheritance taxes, and from business rates, though they claim their shooting estates are businesses that bring 'productive' use to wild land. At the same time they receive large public subsidies for land maintenance activities from the European Union.[17]

The grouse moor, though remote and beautiful in its own way, and especially when under frost and snow in winter, or when the purple heather is in flower, is a reminder of the principal cause of the great disconnect between people and land in Scotland. This is that just 432 individuals own half the private land of Scotland, which is the highest concentration of private land ownership in the world. Scotland also has an under-employed industrial workforce in the inner and outer housing areas of its largest towns and cities, including Dumfries just south of Durisdeer, and in Dundee, Edinburgh and Glasgow. Many of the ancestors of the presently under-employed were cleared off ancestral lands, their cottages' roofs burned by nineteenth-century estate factors, so that the 'lairds' could take all the use of the land for themselves, principally for sheep and sport. Scotland also imports more food than any other country in Europe and while its nationalist government aspires to capture more sovereign powers from its Union with England, it shows less initiative in bringing the land back into productive use for the benefit of the Scots people, as I discuss more fully below.

Britain's long history of land eviction, from the sixteenth-century Dissolution of the Monasteries to the eighteenth-century English Enclosures and the nineteenth-century Scots Clearances, gives Britain the longest history of urbanisation of all modern nation-states. There were a number of great Benedictine and Cistercian monasteries in the region of Southwest Scotland that were sacked and destroyed by the Protestant reformers with terrible consequences for the local population, many of whom were tenants of the monks. The Dissolution began a process of enforced migration from peasant places to urban spaces that extended across the British Empire and now continues through economic globalisation around the world. Evidence of this process can sometimes be seen on gravestones in the region, which indicate both the place of birth and death of the inhabitant, and the city in the Empire where they worked in the armed forces or colonial service. One inscription in Galloway reads 'sometime of Bombay', referring to the city where the deceased couple had spent most of their working life.[18]

I can find no record of monastic life in Durisdeer although much of the land around here would have been owned by the Church in the Middle Ages, and one of the local farms is still known as Chapel Farm after the monastic chapel built on it. The takeover of Church land by the aristocracy at the Dissolution of the Monasteries is, however, commemorated in quite a striking way by a building known as the 'Queensberry Aisle'. This monumental building stands on the site of the north aisle of the old Catholic church of Durisdeer, and now forms one part of the cruciform shape of the post-Reformation building. The aisle is the family mausoleum of the Queensberry family who are the ancestors of the present landowner, the Duke of Buccleuch. The Buccleuch and Queensberry families intermarried with the Tudors, Stuarts and Hanoverians and so knitted themselves as kin to the authors of the first great modern state. From the Tudor Dissolution of the Monasteries to the Hanoverian era of English Enclosures and Highland

Clearances, the State amassed to the court and the aristocracy land, money and military power on a vast scale. In the process the Buccleuchs not only became the largest landowners in Scotland but held great offices of state and court. William Douglas, the first Duke of Queensberry, was Lord-High Treasurer of Scotland from 1682 until he was deposed for maladministration. In that capacity he acquired significant quantities of money, which he utilised in building Scotland's largest continuously inhabited dwelling – Drumlanrig Castle. The castle is set in the midst of sculpted Versailles-style gardens, on a plateau of land above the River Nith, first settled by the Romans four miles from Durisdeer.

The mausoleum was built at the same time as the castle, not in the castle grounds but in the oldest seat of ecclesiastical authority in the Nith Valley, since historical records indicate that Durisdeer was the principal parish church in the area going back to Celtic times. The castle, then, is built on an outpost of Roman empire. The mausoleum is built in the symbolic centre of the Roman Catholic Church in the area, and both are testaments in stone to the feudal nature of landownership that has dominated this region since the Dissolution of the Monasteries. The mausoleum, like the castle, is roofed in the expensive material of lead, and it contains a richly decorated tomb capped by a marble canopy in the style of Bernini's black marble canopy over the altar of St Peter's in Rome. This adds a peculiar ecclesiastical flourish to the transfer of land from Catholic monks to a feudal Lord who, far from putting aside Catholic symbolism and hierarchy, claimed in stone the symbolism of Saint Peter's itself – the ultimate shrine to the centralised power structure of the Roman Catholic Church – in honour of the new landowner.

In Durisdeer I find in our garden a way to reconnect myself as a producer, and not merely a consumer, to a small and precious place on earth. In so doing I make a small contribution, as a son of Adam, a son of the soil, to tending, caring and beautifying God's creation. But just a few yards from our garden gate stands a monumental symbol to the root of the gradual evisceration of good land and sacred place in this island and the transformation of land, and labour, from God-given land for the use and sharing of all to commodified space. The form of commodification in the capture of the land by the aristocracy was land record, and the Queensberry Estate Books record in great detail the fields, buildings, sheep, hay, grain and game gathered on Estate lands.[19] The books reflect the tendency of the wealthy to classify and map their wealth in a way that underscored their possession of it, and that also provided a surplus for them to spend as they saw fit in their pursuits of building country houses, holding balls and shoots and weekend house-parties and going on expeditions and grand tours and so on. Michel Foucault identifies this turn of wealth towards classification as one of the defining marks of the modern era of disciplinary power and the modern tendency to surveillance as manifest in the panopticon.[20] The estate book is one such panopticon, and as well as the history of the capture of the land by Parliament, these books also chart the capture of species.

The exclusion of peasant owner-farmers from the land, and its enclosure by parliament and large landowners, was preceded by a systematic effort by both the Stuart and Tudor States to classify and eradicate 'vermin', as I describe below. In the course of the centralising state-making project the large estates in many places took over the functions of the parishes and played the central role of financing the killing. Hence at the outset of the nation-state project, the classification and eradication of nonhuman species paved the way for the monopolisation by the State, acting through its officers drawn largely from the ruling families, of the powers of parish and people. Cartography gave mathematical form and scientific justification to this new, state-controlled order of both space and time, which gradually drew both the land and labouring bodies of men and women into its orbit. As Foucault puts it, this new order was 'of the same type as that which was being established between living creatures', and this new 'classified time' is characterised by both a 'squared and spatialised development'[21]:

> The new mechanism of power is more dependent on bodies and what they do than upon the Earth and its products. It is a mechanism of power which permits time and labour, rather than wealth and commodities, to be extracted from bodies.[22]

The spatial classification and control of place, and of species in place, is the origin of modern biopower and biopolitics, which for Foucault are the characteristically modern forms of sovereignty and power relations.

In this book I argue that the seminal origin of the modern disconnect between land and people, and the related and growing pathologies of the landless, is the turning of *place* into *space* by the new corporate owners of the land, both private and Statist. Unlike the medieval Church, whose monopoly over the land was less oppressive and for the most part guarded the use rights of peasant farmers, aristocratic and corporate ownership of land has commodified it as the private property of far fewer hands. The productive powers of land, and place, are thereby extracted into a store of private wealth that eviscerates the ability of people in communities of place to govern themselves, and to sustain a resilient land-based economy. The related weakening of the distinctive identity and ecology of places is underwritten by a series of State-making and corporate development processes, which include the titling of land and mapping, and the substitution of cash-oriented land uses – sheep and beef principally in Dumfriesshire – for the previously more diverse and employment-rich local economy of horticulture, crafts and trades. In the twentieth century new forms of mechanical transportation and telecommunications underwrote the centralising tendencies of corporate and State power. The resultant flows of goods, machines, people and wealth promote the cultural homogenisation of place so that places increasingly resemble one another, whether in the form of the convergent organisation of human work and religious rituals, or the growing sameness of forms of entertainment, shopping outlets and hospitality spaces.[23]

If placelessness is a central feature of the modern condition, cartography and surveying are the key technical devices that underwrite it. Cartographers and surveyors, working initially at the behest of landowners annexing the farms of ancestral tenants, have extended their geometric grids from the enclosed lands of England and Germany across the whole surface of the earth as tribes and peoples and regions are drawn into the orbit of modern State-making. The project reaches its zenith in Google Earth, which offers both cartographic and photographic images of virtually every place on earth in software that combines mathematical and grid-based representation with captured satellite images in the ultimate evisceration of place by space. And the project continues in other places, including the deep ocean floor, whose contours are yet to be fully explored, and in extraterrestrial places, including the moon, the sun, Mars and Jupiter. This shift of mapping from earth to space symbolises the larger philosophical move from place to space that the rise of cartography affirms and materialises on paper and screen, and which occurs almost without resistance in European philosophy and science between the twelfth and the eighteenth centuries.

Modern cartography in Scotland originated with the Union of Scotland and England, and the bloody defeat of the Highland Rising at Culloden in 1745. A Highland Survey was sponsored by the English military and its intent was to graphically map the mainland of Scotland, and so assert the control and reach of the newly unified state on the peoples and places of Scotland, including the 'remote' places – remote that is from Edinburgh and London, though not to their inhabitants – of the Highlands.[24] The Survey meant that the glens and fields of the Highlands and Lowlands could be securely recorded and hence legally titled, as accompaniment to the eviction of Scots smallholders and tenant farmers from their land and its theft by the lairds in the Clearances. As surveyors journeyed to ever more remote places, and drew then into a highly detailed and graphic representation of the newly united kingdom, land factors of the large estates whose lands were being mapped began turning the people out of their houses and away to the new slums and factories of Lowland Scotland, or to the new settler colonies of Canada, Nova Scotia, the Carolinas and New Caledonia. Mapping begins as a colonial project and continues today as an instrument of spatial control over the lives of peoples and species on ever larger areas of the planet.

In the twentieth century the Military Survey of Scotland turned into a mapping exercise, the Ordnance Survey, of all the lands and islands of Britain and Northern Ireland. The Ordnance Survey is the first modern project of detailed surveying and mapping of the whole terrain of a nation. As it happens Durisdeer and its surrounding hills were the last place to be surveyed. On the wall of the vestry of the present church is a framed plaque that commemorates the completion of the first full Ordnance Survey of Great Britain in 1959. The plaque includes a photograph of the ceremony that was held at the War Memorial of Durisdeer, which stands on a site where, before the Reformation, a Maypole would once have been erected on Whitsunday – symbol of celebration and the cycle of life – in the village square next to the church yard.[25] This setting is peculiarly apt since it places the end of the military mapping project precisely at the point in this particular place where the culture of war and the monopoly of violence and blood sacrifice, which are the defining apparatus and cult of the nation-state, are symbolically memorialised.[26] The ceremony was presided over by the then Duke of Buccleuch.

I went to Durisdeer to find a place on earth in a country not my own. To cultivate gardens and fields, and to construct and repair dwellings that endure, while being both productive and peaceable, is a way of becoming native to a place even if one is not *from* there. For the American agrarian Wes Jackson, to become native to a place requires that the one who would dwell there should cultivate that place by learning from the forces of soil, sun, wind and water that shape its topography and its climate, and hence consult the genius of place.[27] In so doing I have found that the soils of the place respond to careful tending by sustaining food year round, despite the high land in which it is situated. But I have also found here a peculiarly powerful microcosm of the historic forces that have turned Scotland, Britain, and now most of the lands and seas of the earth, into subdued and commodified space.

Like all places, this place is a repository of human and evolutionary time, and to really know the place is to drill down into the intergenerational forces that have made it what it is. The anthropologist, the archaeologist, the ecologist, the geologist, the historian and the theologian all do this through their respective disciplines when they seek to trace the life worlds that are displayed, or subliminally signalled, in the gatherings and rituals of animals, birds, copses, dwellings, fields, gardens, graves, households, machines, moorland, paths, plants, roads, rocks, soils, signs, temples and trees that constitute particular places. But there are other kinds of disciplining knowledge – I have so far referred briefly to cartography, surveying, legal title and economic commodification – that as they record place, draw power from place into the spatial orbit of universalising and centralising institutions and practices, and a space–time continuum that corrodes the ancestral origins of the present in the past. Under the power of these forms of disciplining knowledge, the precious chains of memory and the fragile networks of mutually dependent persons and species, which give to a place its peculiar depth and distinctiveness, are subdued and gradually erased.

In this book I explore the crisis of the disconnect between people and place from a number of angles. In Chapter 1 I unfold the genealogy of place in Jewish and Christian traditions, the influence of these traditions on the history of place in Europe and the gradual loss of place, and rise of placelessness, in modernity. I examine the attempted repair of the loss of place in twentieth-century philosophy through phenomenological and theological accounts of place, including those of Mircea Eliade and Martin Heidegger. Both anticipated a growing turn back to place in the human sciences. I conclude that this late modern return to place has opened up a cleavage in social science between the *micro-politics* of place and the *macro-economics* of space. In Chapter 2 I explore the impacts and the roots of the disconnect between people and place on ecological diversity in contemporary Britain. I review attempts by the Romantics, environmental philosophers and conservationists to repair the tendencies in modern culture and practices to destroy diversity in place. I argue that these attempts fail without a more profound critique of the centralising powers of the modern State and the modern production and consumption economy, and that repair is potentially resourced by a utopian turn toward 'parochial ecology'. In Chapter 3 I examine the role of economic corporations in underwriting and taking further the Statist evisceration of the ecology of place. I argue there is something vampiric in the nature of these intergenerational fictional 'persons', and that attempts to conserve biodiversity in terms corporations understand – i.e. by ascribing economic value to natural 'resources' – underwrite the corporate quest to transform the wealth of nature into growth in turnover and stock value. In Chapter 4 I describe resistance to corporate power exercised by people who are still in touch with a distinctive culture of place, such as that which endures in the distinctive religious culture of the Hebridean isles of Harris and Lewis. I suggest that resistance to corporate power is an essential tactic in the recovery of place, and that religious tradition is a potentially powerful source of such resistance. In Chapter 5 I explore the practice of ecological restoration through the lens of a particular Scottish Highland estate that has been brought into ownership by a conservation organisation. I note how the attempts to remove the historic trace of the human mark on the land is informed by, and perpetuates, the idea that there is an inevitable conflict between the ecology of place and human dwelling. In Chapter 6 I show that the human food economy is key to recovering a more harmonious, productive and resilient relationship between ecological diversity and human dwelling, but only when that human economy is both socially just and environmentally sustainable. In Chapters 7 and 8 I return to the pathology of landlessness and its potential repair by the recovery of the moral geography of sustainable communities. This repair, I show, is essential for reimagining and redesigning urban as well as rural habitats in ways that facilitate, and are governed by, resilient human communities of place that are politically just, economically productive and ecologically sustainable.

1

Losing and finding sacred place

In 1967, at the dawn of environmentalism as a mass political movement in North America, the United States historian of technology Lynn White Jr argued that the Christian doctrine of creation, and the Genesis ascription of 'dominion' to humanity, was a crucial historic root of the ecological crisis because it destroyed belief in the animistic powers that dwell in forests and wild species, and so opened up the land to human exploitation.[1] He propounded this thesis through a reading of European history, but his essay is better understood as a North American, rather than an indigenous European, reading of the Christian use of land and human–nature relationships. George Grant evidences this when he tells how European colonists, just because they did not recognise the indigenous gods and spirits of the places they encountered in North America, saw these places as infertile and 'wild'.[2] By failing to honour the myths and rituals of these places, they treated them as unredeemed and sought to redeem them by obliterating native uses, and instead imposing their tilling, mining and other European-derived land use practices. In the process they killed most natives, extinguished native species, and degraded the fragile human and species interactions that had sustained American ecosystems before the colonists arrived. Hence in the case of prairie land, they turned rich soils they did not understand into the dustbowls of the 1920s and 1930s. Until today most descendants of the colonists farm prairie land in ways that export topsoil into the Mississippi Delta, and unsustainably drain historic groundwater from the Ogallala Aquifer; venerated by the Sioux tribe, this great subterranean reservoir of historic water is today treated as an expendable resource.[3]

White's reading of the Genesis narrative is from a place and a time in which human dominion over the land had been asserted against the native history of place with disastrous results for native peoples and species. But in the place and time in which the Genesis narrative was generated, the account of Adam and Eve as having power over other species that risked their own and others' flourishing had real ecological value. There is increasing agreement among archaeologists and anthropologists that the Jordan Valley, and the surrounding region of the Southern Levant, is the place in which humans first domesticated cereals and legumes and so invented agriculture. Around 10,000 years ago the Mediterranean region developed a more strongly seasonal climate than previously. This led to long arid periods in which it would have been beneficial for humans to store foods such as cereals and root vegetables.[4] The story of the Garden of Eden, and of Genesis more broadly, maps intriguingly on this development. The earliest chapters of Genesis record the transition from a mode of obtaining food by gathering from existing plants to growing food by tillage, weeding and plant selection. The potential moral and social power involved in plant selection is evident in the story of the fruit of a forbidden tree, which Adam and Eve were not supposed to gather. Exile from the life of an original food gatherer is depicted in the third chapter of Genesis as a punishment involving the raising of cereals 'by the sweat of the brow' and in contest with other non-domesticated plants. If Genesis begins by ascribing dominion over plants and animals to Adam and Eve, then it ends in the Joseph saga, which describes what happens when large-scale agriculture makes possible not only dominion over plants and animals but dominion by one ruler over farmers turned feudal slaves.[5] In essence the Genesis saga, from the first ascription of dominion to Adam and Eve to its declension through the Joseph story into centralised food storage and feudal land ownership in Egypt, represents an origin myth designed to warn the first agriculturalists that becoming agrarians put them in the position of those who are like gods in relation to other species, and that this power is both dangerous and open to significant abuse. The narrative does not so much commend dominion as narrate what happens when human power over the land and other species becomes too domineering. This power was the root of new, more hierarchical and highly unequal forms of social life, and the institution of slavery, as Exodus goes on to describe.[6]

The invention of agriculture marked a new and portentous phase in the evolving relationship between humans and other species, in which humans had gained the upper hand. In the Jordan Valley humans had become the shapers of the environment for the first time, and they had in effect taken over the power to shape the future of life from the other forces – heavenly and earthly – which had brought life to this point. In the place and time of the Jordan Valley after the invention of agriculture, the ascription in the Genesis saga of dominion is not so much a charge to humanity to dominate as it is a narrative of the new responsibilities, and risks, that arise from the practice of domesticating plants and animals and so becoming the prime shaping influence over the environment. The Genesis Creation story while it emerged in the Levant became a central and shaping story in the history of the Mediterranean region, first among the people of Israel, and then among the followers of Christ in the Christian era before modernity. In the Hebrew Bible and the history of Israel the Genesis sagas set the stage for the mission of Israel as a small and distinctive nation who were called to do agriculture, politics and religion differently from the other peoples of the Ancient Near East. Freedom from slavery, and the calling to be a small nation, are connected with the story of the migration of the Hebrews back from Egypt, via the wilderness of Sinai, to the Jordan Valley. Once in the valley the law is designed to guide them towards a more deliberative form of agriculture, with a set of mandated practices – including dietary restrictions, restraints on overuse of land and animals, and restraints on debt and land accumulation – which, if followed, would have restrained inequality, conserved soil and prevented the recurrence of debt bondage, landlessness and slavery in the Jordan Valley under Hebrew occupation.[7]

In the Jewish and Christian traditions, and hence in the cultures of Europe that they particularly shaped, the calling of Israel to dwell in the land around the Jordan Valley as a people constituted to be a nation by a divinely revealed law and the gift of good land is the origin of the idea and practice of sacred place.[8] The original call of Israel takes place at the Jewish festival known as Shavuot, which occurred forty nine days after the Exodus from Egypt. Shavuot commemorates the original giving of the law to Israel by Moses (Exodus 34: 22), and their constitution as a nation. The first commandment of Moses is the origin of the conception of sacred place in this tradition for it commanded that the Israelites honoured the name of Yahweh as holy above all other names and so acknowledged their dependence on the dominion of Yahweh to whom the land to which they were journeying belonged. The festival of Shavuot is an agrarian festival marking the time of the wheat harvest in the Jordan Valley, when the Israelites would take the first fruits of their harvest of the seven species of the land – wheat, barley, grapes, figs, pomegranates, olives, and dates (Deuteronomy 8: 8) – together with two loaves of bread, to the Temple in Jerusalem.[9]

The mapping of the call of Israel onto the agricultural year reflects a pattern of mirroring between the cult of Israel and the divinely given order of creation and human work in the ritual pattern of place and time in the Hebrew Bible. The place in which the agricultural and religious rituals of Israel were focused was the Temple in Jerusalem. Yahweh had promised to be present among the people of God, first in the portable Tabernacle, and subsequent to settlement of the land in Solomon's Temple. The Temple being built of wood carved with flowers, fruits and vegetables evoked the Garden of Eden.[10] Israel was henceforth called to order her agricultural practices around the Temple in Jerusalem. Her farmers were required to bring all meat to be eaten for sacrificial slaughter in the Temple, which would have been a considerable restraint on the practice of meat eating. They were also required to bring the first fruits of the annual harvest of the seven species that grew in the land before she occupied it. Yet the land was not only a place of blessing but potentially also of curse.[11] The fruitfulness of the land and the guarantee of Yahweh's blessing on it depended upon Israel's covenantal faithfulness in honouring the name of Yahweh above all other gods, and in keeping the time of the Sabbath, which acted as a restraint on overuse of the land and its creatures. But the history books of the Hebrew Bible record that Israel under the kings went after other gods, and neglected the moral and ritual regulations that emanated from the Holy of Holies to all the fields of the given land. Consequently, the land was invaded by other peoples, the Israelites lost their sacred place, the Temple in Jerusalem was ultimately destroyed and many of the people were sent into exile in the cities of Assyria and Babylon.

During the Exile the Hebrew Prophets developed theological accounts of a holy place beyond the Jordan Valley and the destroyed Temple in Jerusalem. The most influential was Ezekiel's, whose image of the heavenly man inspired the Romantics in their efforts to create a new aesthetics of nature as the sublime in the post-Christian Enlightenment. Ezekiel responded to the destruction by fire of Solomon's Temple by reimagining the Holy of Holies in which resided the *shekinah* of God as the temple of creation. The four faces of the heavenly man therefore look to the four points of the compass, and the two cherubim that guarded the Temple entrance in Jerusalem are transformed into 'four living creatures' in the elemental forms of air (humanity), fire (lion), earth (ox) and water (eagle) and representing the universal elements of creation.[12] Instead of the divine presence that was said to hover above the Mercy Seat in the Holy of Holies, the presence of God in Ezekiel's vision hovers above the four living creatures:

> And above the firmament over their heads there was the likeness of a throne, in appearance like sapphire; and seated above the likeness of a throne was the likeness as it were of human form.
>
> EZEKIEL 1: 26

Through his vision Ezekiel gave hope to his fellow exiles that the Temple in Jerusalem was merely a form of the transcendent temple of divine presence that would henceforward be manifest throughout the cosmos and that no army could destroy. In the wheeled mobility of the four living creatures (Ezekiel 1: 20), God as Spirit was no longer confined to the Holy of Holies but instead was constantly moving between the four walls of the universe, which had previously been symbolised by the cuboid shape of Solomon's Temple.[13]

If Ezekiel described the sacred presence of God throughout the places of the cosmos, then Isaiah described an equally radical vision of the call of God to a people to be a holy nation as no longer confined to the people of Israel in the place of the Jordan Valley. In Third Isaiah the Prophet presents a vision of nationhood as a divine calling that extends from Israel and Jerusalem to all the peoples of the earth[14]:

> The sons of the stranger, that join themselves to the LORD, to serve him, and to love the name of the LORD, to be his servants, every one that keeps the Sabbath from polluting it, and takes hold of my covenant; them

will I bring to my holy mountain, and make them joyful in my house of prayer: their burnt offerings and their sacrifices shall be accepted upon my altar; for my house shall be called an house of prayer for all people. The Lord GOD, which gathers the outcasts of Israel says, Yet will I gather others to him, beside those that are gathered to him.

ISAIAH 56: 7–8

This prophecy of the universalisation of the calling of Israel is taken up in the New Testament. Christ himself invoked it when he swept the Temple precincts of trading stalls and reminded those who watched him that 'my house shall be a house of prayer' (Matthew 21: 13). There is also an echo of Isaiah in Christ's announcement to the Samaritan woman that henceforward true worship would no longer be confined by geography or place since 'the hour comes, when you shall neither in this mountain, nor yet at Jerusalem, worship the Father' (John 4: 22). Instead, 'true worshippers shall worship the Father in spirit and in truth' for 'God is a Spirit: and they that worship him must worship him in spirit and in truth' (John 4: 23–4). But most signally Isaiah's prophecy finds its fulfilment on the day of Pentecost, in which the Spirit is not only poured out on the Apostles, but the Apostles preach the gospel to a crowd in Jerusalem that included Jewish converts from 'every nation under heaven' (Acts 2: 5).

The universalisation of the calling of Israel to dwell in a particular sacred place was an innovation that challenged the whole geographical basis of the Jewish tradition. In adopting this post-holy land orientation, Christianity, unlike most traditional religions, lacks an authoritative account, and practices, of sacred place and place-making. For Mircea Eliade places such as Bethel, where Jacob wrestled with an angel, and the mountain on which Moses encountered the burning bush, were holy places because they were places of hierophany, where an 'irruption of the sacred' 'results in detaching of a territory from the surrounding cosmic milieu and making it qualitatively different'.[15] Traditional societies are characterised by a duality with respect of place in which their inhabited territory – forests, fields, homes, rivers or shoreline – constitutes a 'world (more precisely our world), the cosmos; everything outside is no longer a cosmos but a sort of "other world", a foreign, chaotic space, peopled by ghosts, demons, foreigners'.[16] The home world is consecrated, much as in the story of Jacob's ladder, and of Israel's occupation of the Jordan Valley, by the decision to inhabit, settle and organise a community in a place, and by the construction of a ceremonial place, such as an altar or temple, which sets apart from the unknown world the inhabited place as sacred cosmos, and makes it the centre of the world; on this account place-making, community-building, home-making are cosmogonic activities through which meaning is created and sustained, and places declared sacred, and so to be cared for, conserved and honoured, while space beyond the sacred cosmos is beyond the sphere of care and rendered peripheral, profane, secular. Hence the post-traditional culture of industrial societies secularises the world because it treats cities and towns as interchangeable places of habitation, and the home as merely a 'machine for living'.

If religion is the way in which premodern peoples find the sacred and ascribe meaning and purpose to inhabiting particular places, as Eliade argues, this raises the question of the relationship between Christianity and place. Christ tells his disciples that 'where two or three are gathered together in my name there am I in the midst of them' (Matt 18: 20). But if all places are potentially places of meeting between Christians and their God, how does Christianity generate meaning in particular places, and sustain communities, local gatherings, of beings? Eliade's account of place-making as cosmogonic suggests that perhaps Christianity is, as Lynn White argued, the cause of the modern ecological crisis. For Christianity the whole earth potentially becomes a sacred cosmic space. Its doctrine of a creator who does not inhabit a particular place in creation, combined with a primordial human – Adam – who bears the divine image and is charged to 'have dominion' over the earth, suggests that Christianity's global expansion did indeed dissolve pagan beliefs and rituals which set apart fields, groves, mountains and rivers as sacred. Thus, Christianity may indeed be said to have rendered the whole earth profane, secular and available for human reordering and exploitation.

It is not enough, in answer to White's charge, to recount the place-conserving character of the Genesis story in warning the first agrarians of the potential ecological, moral and spiritual risks in their newfound dominant and shaping influence over life. It is still possible that this story of the exaltation of the first agrarian as divine representative on an earth where God no longer dwells in any part would have underwritten the anthropocentric and desacralising tendencies of which Christianity is accused. A fuller answer to the question requires an account of the interpenetration of Christianity and place in the Mediterranean world and beyond from the first century of the Christian Era to the present. Those studies that exist of Christianity and place primarily focus on biblical texts and doctrines,[17] and the practices of pilgrimage and sacramental worship.[18] But there are no systematic studies available on Christian *dwelling* and Christian engagement with the common practices of dwelling in place such as agriculture, building, craft, fishing, forestry and so on.[19]

Susan Power Bratton's substantial research monograph *Christianity, Wilderness and Wildlife,* while not a systematic study of Christianity and place, nonetheless covers a sufficiently wide range of Jewish and Christian dwelling in natural environments in East and West as to go some way to filling this lacuna. Bratton begins with an ethnographic account of a wilderness experience while walking with a friend in the Great Smoky Mountains in Tennessee on Christmas Eve: a hill top view of a sunset over the creek of Goshen Prong led to a vivid sense of God speaking and 'the presence of the divine filled the mountain'.[20] Bratton pairs her wilderness experience with biblical accounts of theophanies in wild places, from the Garden of Eden and Jacob's ladder to the Hebrew prophets. She notes that the isolation offered by wilderness was a common factor to most of these stories and that in many of them a traditional sacred object – a cave, a forest glade, a mountain, an oasis or spring, a tree – is identified as a sanctuary in the course of, or subsequent to, the experience. Bratton also notes that wilderness experiences are associated with moments of transition – with a calling to live in a new place, or adopt a new way of life, or, in the case of the Exodus wilderness experiences, to be a new people. Like Strachan, Bratton notes that in the later Hebrew prophets a new note emerges, in which the people of God are called away from their established sanctuaries and dwelling places in the land of Israel to reinhabit wilderness:

> Behold I am doing a new thing;
> now it springs forth,
> do you not perceive it?
> I will make a way in the wilderness
> and rivers in the desert.
> The wild beast will honour me,
> the jackals and the ostriches;
> for I give water in the wilderness,
> rivers in the desert,
> to give a drink to my chosen people.

ISAIAH 43: 19–20

The later Prophetic move away from the land of Israel and the Temple, as the defining sacred places of God's theophanic presence to the people of God, recalls the meetings with God in wilderness of Israel's nomadic patriarchs, and is an instance of the creative historiography of Hebrew thought, which is able to see the hand of God in historic events and draw from Israel's past in reimagining her future.[21]

In the New Testament Bratton notes another and possibly related change and this is that individuals, including John the Baptist, Christ and Saint Paul, are described purposefully seeking out time in wilderness for spiritual discernment, revelation, testing and transformation. John the Baptist is described as living 'in the wilderness' until he takes up his ministry of repentance and baptism also 'in the wilderness' on the banks of the Jordan (Luke 1: 80; Mark 1: 4).[22] Christ first appears for the commencement of his public ministry in the wilderness with John where the dove, representing the divine Spirit, descends upon him at his baptism. He is then said to depart from John into the wilderness where he was 'tempted by the devil', dwelled 'with the wild beasts' and was 'ministered to by angels' (Mark 1: 12–13). Unlike the people of Israel in their forty years of wilderness wanderings, Christ does not succumb to temptation in the forty days of his wilderness sojourn. He proceeds from the sojourn to perform miracles and engage in public preaching in synagogues and, when made unwelcome there, teaches in open air venues such as agricultural fields, grazing land, hill tops and lake shores. Christ also frequently leaves crowds and the disciples for wild places, including lake shores and mountains, to pray and to recover his strength for his public ministry. Bratton observes that the Baptist and Christ express wilderness engagement that is ascetic, contemplative and restorative: Christ also rested and slept, as well as prayed, when he withdrew to wild places, for he was fully human.[23]

The marked change in the relation of the people of God and place that is anticipated by the Hebrew Prophets in Exile reaches its fulfilment in the founding of a new religion, Christianity, by the events of the life, death and resurrection of the founder, Jesus Christ. Before his death, Christ predicted more than once the downfall of the Herodian Temple in Jerusalem and he indicated that his own body was analogous to, and a new spiritual form of, the Temple (John 2: 19). Charged with blasphemy against the Temple (Mark 14: 58), Christ was exiled from Jerusalem at Golgotha, the place of the skull, where he was crucified. At his death Christ descended into the place of the dead, where he released souls to the resurrection. He then appeared to the disciples in a number of places, both wild and urban. He also promised his disciples that 'where two or three are gathered together in my name, there am I in the midst of them' (Matthew 18: 20).

Christianity represents a new stage in the theophany of God to humanity: Christ in his preaching and teaching announced that henceforth God was present potentially to people in every place, and hence before his final departure from earth at the ascension, Christ commissioned the disciples to preach the good news and baptise people from 'all the nations' (Matthew 28: 19). Throughout the Christ events as recorded in the New Testament wild places played a significant role, and they continued to do so in early Christian history as recorded in the Book of Acts, most notably in the conversion of Saint Paul and in the conversion of the Ethiopian eunuch. However, the first churches were all established in cities and Christianity was primarily an urban movement, first in Jerusalem, and then in the cities to which Saint Paul travelled in his three missionary journeys as recorded in the Book of Acts. But if cities were the first places where the gospel took root we should expect the claim that Christianity establishes a new relationship to place in Western religious history to be evident in the urban environment. However, soon after its rise, Christianity was subject to persecution and the places of meeting of Christians were therefore by no means public places but instead rooms in private houses, or the underground catacombs where Christians also preserved the bones of the dead saints in anticipation of their imminent resurrection. Hence there is not in the first hundred years of the Christian era any indication of a new orientation to place analogous to the tradition of sacred place in the Old Testament. And this lacuna in early Christianity might be said to indicate that Christianity lacks a doctrine of sacred place.

While the life, death and resurrection of Christ in Palestine in a significant way affirmed the land of Israel as the 'holy land', Christians have a different understanding of the relationship of redemption to place from their Israelite forebears. For Christians dwelling, place and land are no longer *means* of redemption. Instead, the God who is in Jesus meets Christians – Gentile and Jew alike – wherever and whenever they turn their minds and hearts to God. Hence Oliver O'Donovan argues that for Christians place is not the medium of salvation that it once was for Jews, and that it is in many other religious traditions.[24] In this argument O'Donovan reflects the opposition of the Protestant Reformers to pilgrimages, shrines and other holy places as idolatrous. But against the Protestant dismissal of sacred place in Christianity, Philip Sheldrake and John Inge argue that the events of Christ's life, and seminal events in the lives of the saints, did have the effect of making the places where these events occurred holy. Veneration of such places is therefore not inappropriate, and is a vital means for Christians to recover the homogenising collapse of local places to global space in the present era. Pilgrimage to Jerusalem, and to other places associated with events in the lives of the saints, is for Sheldrake and Inge a vital means by which place is made holy in the Christian tradition.[25]

As I argue elsewhere, the claim that pilgrimage is an essential means for the recovery of place in the Christian tradition is stronger if made in relation to *journeying* than in terms of the sites towards which pilgrims journey.[26] The road as site of conversion, and of moral and spiritual encounter, is affirmed a number of times in the New Testament. Many of Christ's miracles and seminal encounters occur when he is on the road. Christ is also described as journeyer, and even as homeless for 'the Son of Man has nowhere to lay his head' (Luke 9: 58). Christ is the wayfarer rather than the occupier. He has no home of his own during his ministry, staying with friends in Capernaum, borrowing rooms, sleeping in the hills or on the floor of a boat. Christ's most well known parable concerns a journey. In the Parable of the Good Samaritan, the road is the key place of encounter, since it is on the road from Jerusalem to Jericho that the man who is set upon by thieves is encountered and ministered to by the Samaritan who recognised him – on the road – as his neighbour. The parable is particularly ironic for neighbour is typically paired with neighbourhood as indicating persons who dwell near others. And yet in this original parable of moral obligation in place, those who experience this obligation and its fruits are not dwelling at all: they are wayfarers, travellers, and the road itself becomes the place of their meeting and of the acts of compassion and care that the story records.[27]

Two significant conversion stories in the New Testament are also located on roads. The first takes place during a chariot journey from Jerusalem to Gaza of an Ethiopian courtier who, while reading the Hebrew scriptures, is met by Philip who explains them in relation to Jesus Christ. The Ethiopian then receives the Holy Spirit and is baptised by Philip in the Jordan River (Acts 8: 26–39).[28] The second journey is that of Saul of Tarsus who is blinded by a bright light in the sky, hears a commanding voice from heaven, and subsequently receives the Holy Spirit and is baptised in Damascus

(Acts 9: 3–18). Both stories indicate the gradual move of the gospel from the Jewish church in Jerusalem to other peoples and lands. Saint Paul's conversion is the crucial event in the gradual divergence of Christianity from the Holy Land, since it is Paul on his missionary journeys who takes the Gospel from Jerusalem to the Gentile cities of Corinth, Galatia, Philippi, Ephesus, Thessaloniki and beyond. The journeys of Saint Paul as told in Acts represent a narrative map in which the Mediterranean – literally the sea in the midst of the earth – and the principal cities of the Roman Empire are gradually infiltrated by followers of the way of Jesus Christ and the churches they founded.

Through the missionary journeys of Paul and others, Christianity turns from a Jewish sect based in Jerusalem to a world religion that reaches throughout the Roman Empire. But this missionary reach is not without respect for place. The phrase 'contextual theology' has always struck me as being too vague, and also too sociological as a way of describing non-western theology. It seems to indicate that only in the colonial and postcolonial eras do issues of context arise in ways that give variant shape to Christian doctrine, life and worship. But much of what is at issue in the quest for a 'contextual' or a 'postcolonial' theology concerns locality, place and region as much as it does social context. The question of what happens when the gospel takes *root* in a new place goes back to the missionary journeys of Saint Paul. As Roland Allen argues, these missionary journeys are unique in mission history, not only in that Paul was the first missionary to the Gentiles, but also in the extent to which Paul trusted that after a period of months at a new place he could leave the gospel to germinate there, confident that the Spirit would give life and substance to the seeds he planted there.[29] This required both a sense for the potential ubiquity of the gift of the Spirit conferred on the church at Pentecost, and trust in the potential of each place to be a place of redemption, a new holy place where the people of God will become 'living stones' (1 Peter 2: 5) in a temple not built with hands but constituted by the Spirit.[30]

Trust in the potential of place to be redemptive finds analogy in the secular practices of conservation biology, ecological restoration and urban neighbourhood design. In order to repair the reductive effects of industrial development on biodiversity and ecosystems, conservationists seek to set aside areas of habitat from hunting and over-extraction as game or marine reserves. They also seek to restore damaged habitats by eradicating non-native species, and replanting or reintroducing native species. But, as I argue below, these practices are ambiguous if they lead to the ecological exclusion of people from place. When conservationists exclude local people from local uses of their habitats they act like landowners and corporations who also exclude traditional and customary uses as they seek to enhance their own property. This problem with the project of ecological restoration reflects the nature–culture split that infects modern scientific civilisation. It also reflects an incipient misanthropy, which infects those in the ecological movement who argue that humanity has become a plague on the health of the earth and that the only hope for planet earth is for the numbers of humans to decline, or even for the human species to be wiped out altogether, so giving the earth or 'gaia' a chance to restore herself.

Against the misanthropic tendencies of some varieties of modern environmentalism, ecological restoration in the Old Testament invariably connects the re-flourishing of plants and trees in wilderness with the recovery of justice, and land, by the poor who find in wilderness a home while the cities of the wealthy collapse or are destroyed. The biblical account of humans as the 'crown' of creation indicates that they are pivotal to the flourishing, or not, of the whole creation. Ecological restoration that exiles humans mirrors the exile of Adam and Eve from the Garden of Eden, and exacerbates the alienation between people and land that is in many cases the root of ecological destruction. By contrast, a biblically informed approach to ecological restoration involves redeeming the human–nature relationship in such a way as to recover just and peaceable relations between peoples, and between peoples and species. This approach is reflected in the support the churches in Scotland gave to the cause of land reform in the 1990s, which issued in a land reform law in the new Scottish Parliament in 2002, the intent of which was to enable communities of people in place to buy back their land and use rights from large estates and absentee landlords. Against the Romantic or conservationist valorisation of Scotland as empty 'wild' space, which merely colludes with the 'heritage industry' fostered by the sporting estates, the places where land reform has occurred – such as the isles of Eigg and Gigha, and around Loch Assynt – have experienced the sensitive re-peopling of emptied out places in the Highlands and Islands and Scottish Borders. This re-peopling is often accompanied by an increase in biodiversity and in the ecological values of place and is an important political tactic of resistance to those global and national forces that have seen the powers of people in their local places eviscerated.

In the twentieth century a small group of philosophers, including Martin Heidegger and Claude Merleau-Ponty, argued that the European Enlightenment, and its sponsorship of influential cultural universals such as rationality, economy and civil society tended to suppress the significance of place, and of dwelling in place, in the constitution of human identity and political community.[31] They proposed that a full understanding of the nature of flourishing, both human and nonhuman, revealed the importance of place attachment, and of relationships in place. For nonhuman creatures the importance of attachment to place is more obvious than it is for humans given our greater mobility. Many creatures have a limited range area, the habitat they require to maintain body temperature is climate sensitive, and their nutritional needs can only be met by certain species. Hence deforestation in tropical forests destroys habitat for tree dwelling creatures such as orang utans who, without the availability of particular fruit trees, are unable to survive. Analogously, the Capercaillie moorland bird lives on high land in

Scotland but requires an alpine climate for its foraging and other bodily functions. Hence changes in temperature in the Scottish Highlands, associated with anthropogenic climate change, threaten its habitat.

Human beings are apparently less dependent on such biological parameters of place because they mostly live in dwellings they have constructed that provide shelter from varying temperatures. They have also developed means of preserving, storing and transporting food and water over large distances, so that the non-availability of these on land adjacent to their dwellings does not threaten their survival, provided they have monetary or other means with which to procure them. However, there is a growing body of evidence that when humans live in entirely artificial environments, spend less time outdoors and interact little with nonhuman creatures such as trees, grasses or small animals and birds, they suffer psychological and physiological ill effects that may be harmful to their development to adulthood. Conversely, extended time outdoors, including interaction with other creatures, has been shown to have positive effects on children's psychological well-being and their capacity for independent agency and thought.[32]

Lacunae about place, and nature or the nonhuman, in modern Western understandings of human development and identity are a consequence of cultural transformations associated with the Enlightenment account of rationality as the core developmental capacity that sets humans apart from other animals, and in part a function of the increasingly artificial environments in which modern urbanised people dwell. The phenomenological repair of these lacunae involves not only acknowledgement of the role of place in creaturely wellbeing, but attention to the ways in which creatures, and especially persons, constitute places.[33] There are few landscapes on earth that have not been modified by humans given their spread and the global reach of their technologies and capacities in habitat modification. What is often called a sense of place is therefore created by a combination of natural or ecological forces and human cultural processes, which include the history and present arrangement of dwellings and landscapes. Attention to the succession of human events in a particular place is therefore essential to understanding the cultural processes that have constituted it inter-generationally as a place of dwelling.

Graves are one of the most foundational and paradigmatic markers of human dwelling places, and they are also the oldest built remains of human dwelling. The oldest remaining substantial built structure in the Middle East is an Egyptian pyramid that was constructed at great cost to house the remains of deceased persons. The oldest archaeological remains of human constructions in Europe are also in the main Neolithic burial sites, including burial cairns on Orkney in Scotland, and the extensive and even older site of Gobekli Tepe near the Euphrates in Turkey. These early built remains indicate that as soon as human beings developed capacities to construct dwellings from carved stone they hallowed their places of dwelling with graves and memorials for their ancestors. This desire to keep the dead near them, and to honour them, is unique to humans and indicates that there is a spiritual, as well as biological and cultural, dimension to place. Places that humans have over centuries and millennia come to value for their life-giving properties are invariably also places in which humans have constructed memorials to the souls of the departed.[34]

The turn to place among a small group of European philosophers is reflected in an analogous turn among theologians. John Inge and Philip Sheldrake argue that in the Christian tradition place is hallowed by events and performances, and in particular the sacramental worship of Jesus Christ, and the cult of the saints. Sheldrake argues, like Eliade, that in the Christian tradition it is events of revelation and witness in the lives of Christians that give to particular places a sacred quality.[35] Hence the Holy Land, and especially the places in which Christ dwelt, preached, was crucified and risen, acquired the status of sacred places for Christians. In this approach it is not the land as such that is redemptive or holy. Instead it is the *events* of Christ's life, death and resurrection that make it so. Analogously, Sheldrake and Inge argue that the event of eucharistic worship repeated week by week in Christian churches confers on Christian buildings an analogous sense of holiness to the holy places of the Christ events.

Those who advocate the role of the body, events and narratives in constituting the holiness of place risk missing a more fundamental sense of the holiness of place in the Jewish and Christian traditions that arises from the continuing creativity of the Creator Spirit throughout the living earth. In order to be faithful to a truly Trinitarian account of the relation of God to the Creation, it is necessary to acknowledge the sustaining presence of the Spirit of life to all species and in all habitats and ecosystems. Habitats and ecosystems of particular species richness are places that are also especially hallowed by the Creator Spirit. Species richness is also often a characteristic of those places where natural powers seem to gather the forces of nature together in particularly powerful combinations. As already suggested, such places include waterfalls, the meeting point of two rivers, estuaries and coastal zones, inland lakes, deep valleys, cirques of hills, and hilltops or cliffs overlooking savannah or ocean.[36] They also include edge zones, between one kind of ecosystem and another, between cultivated and uncultivated habitats, and between urban and rural areas.[37]

It was to such edge zones that Christian ascetics and holy men and women were drawn from the second century in their quest to mimic the ascetic, contemplative and transformative relation to wilderness that the New Testament ascribed to John the Baptist and to Christ. The area with the largest number of monasteries and hermitages dating back to the second century of the Christian era is the edge land between the holy river of Quadisha in North Lebanon and Mount al-Makmel, close to the last stands of preserved cedar of Lebanon in the 'Forest of the Cedars of God'.[38] Monasteries in this precious region over the centuries guarded the ancient cedar groves from pillage and eventual destruction by builders from Egypt and Syria.[39] The origins of Christian monasticism in wilderness dwelling reveal a long-standing association between Christian spirituality and love of nature, which long precedes Saint Francis in the thirteenth century. Against those who argue, following Lynn White, that Christians, and monks in particular, lack a deep appreciation of the ecological and spiritual value of nature, there is significant evidence of their love for wilderness and wild creatures, including predators, and of monastic efforts to restore and make fertile the often arid and desert-like environments to which early Christian monastics were drawn.[40] The first known Christian monastic is St Antony, who took up dwelling on a mountain in southern Egypt after 271. Athanasius, in his *Life of Antony*, records that the saint loved the place on first reaching it, with its clear spring of water and date palm trees, having tried the ascetic life in other locations closer to population centres.[41] In this desert place Antony established the first long-term Christian monastic cell, and he tilled and sowed a patch of land so as not to be dependent on his Saracen neighbours, who at first supplied him with bread; he later grew vegetables in order to be able to offer hospitality to the many visitors who started coming to him.[42] As Bratton notes, Antony's was a subsistence livelihood, but when he found wild animals coming to eat the food he grew he did not hunt them but instead persuaded them, as Jerome records, to avoid his food while still sharing his water source.[43] Antony had no library in this original monastic cell but, when asked how he managed without, he told a visitor that his book was 'the nature of created things'.[44]

Antony, like Jerome and other Christian monastics after him, is said to have communicated effectively with wild animals and so to have overcome the fear between humans and other animals that had been among the ecological consequences of sin in the Garden of Eden.[45] These two tropes – of tilling and sowing wilderness, and of peaceable relations with predators – both indicate that at the origins of Christian monasticism was the belief that Christ had come to call his followers to recreate Paradise on earth, and not only in heaven.[46] But as in the life of Christ, the desert was not only a place of contemplation and restoration but also of temptation and testing. Temptation and testing is a key theme in the writings of the fourth-century monastic John of Cassian, who was an important influence on Benedict in his composition of his monastic rule. Cassian describes how one of his desert brothers encountered troops of demons, and the prince of demons, when he took refuge in a cave one night, and similar experiences by others including St Antony.[47] Struggle against demons and temptation was heightened for the monastics by their isolation from other people. But they did not associate wild places or beings with such struggle but rather saw spiritual attacks as coming direct from Satan. Instead, as Bratton comments, the desert fathers saw nature as composed of lower beings than humans, towards which they expressed care and concern, as in the many stories of desert fathers healing wild animals and their progeny, or sharing water or food with them.[48] The reciprocal relations that the monks are said to have had with wild animals are unlike any account of human–animal relations in classical literature, and are read by them as the fulfilment of Isaiah's prophetic announcement that the messianic age would see a new peace between humans and other animals.

The desert fathers are, along with the life of Christ, the deep origin in Christian history of a sacred sense of place. They found in the desert and their relations with other creatures a new spirituality of wilderness that built on and enhanced the wilderness experiences of the Hebrew Patriarchs and Prophets and of Christ himself. And through these experiences they developed a deep identification with and love of wilderness: as Bratton puts it 'the monks were as the desert, and the desert was as the monks'.[49]

The lives and cenobitic practices of the desert fathers were the root of Christian monasticism that gradually spread northwards from the deserts of Egypt and the caves of Cappadocia through Gaul to the forests, lakes and islands of France, Germany, Britain and Ireland from the fourth century on. Long before the Benedictines established religious houses in Northern Europe, Patrick travelled to Ireland in the fifth century and Columba to North Britain in the sixth; both established monastic cells and churches and took up the practices they had read of in *The Life of Saint Antony*. But the Celtic Christians differed in their orientation to place since they had a closer link to the land than their counterparts in the deserts of North Africa and Anatolia. The Celtic monks were more of the place than their cenobitic forbears and often participated in familial links to land. They also established churches as well as monastic cells, and they often built them on places that the Celts had long considered holy, and often with the stones of earlier sacred structures. Hence the Celts experienced a stronger sense of place, and were less withdrawn from local society, than the desert fathers.[50] As Christopher Dawson observes, the blending of Celtic Christian with pre-Christian Celtic culture meant that:

> there was no sudden break between the old barbaric tradition and that of the Church, such as occurred elsewhere, and a unique fusion took place between the Church and the Celtic tribal society entirely unlike anything else in Western Europe.[51]

Celtic Christian literature, even more than that of the desert fathers, is a mixture of history, hagiography, miracle and myth but, as Bratton argues, the orientation and beliefs it displays are valuable evidence of Christian practices and beliefs in relation to nature and place.[52] Like the desert fathers, there are many stories of Celtic monks interacting peaceably with predatory animals, including feeding hungry wolves and rescuing deer from hunters. Church land is sometimes said to be encumbered with a ban on killing or hunting of animals or fish, and there are stories of otters, stags and sea eagles assisting saints. One example is St Cuthbert who, after soaking in the sea, which was a practice of mortification adopted by a number of the Celtic saints, took up a night prayer vigil on the shore of the island of Lindisfarne; as he went ashore two sea otters followed him, licked his feet, and warmed them with their breath.[53] Other created elements could also assist the saints: the ocean once provided St Cuthbert with a timber beam exactly the size he needed for his cell roof, and trees are said to have parted the way for St Coemgen when he was carried through a thick wood.[54] The Irish St Molua was said to have 'never killed a bird or any other living thing', and birds are said to have expressed appreciation for their protection by the monks, for example by ceasing singing as St Cellach lay dying.[55] The Celtic monks also resisted the cutting of forests and rarely themselves cut trees to create a place for dwelling.

Like their desert forbears, the Celtic saints preferred wild places to life in the town and they are often described praying and worshipping in wild places including forests, small islands and lake shores. They also sought to establish monasteries in such places, and hence Coemgen's choice of Glen da Loch, south of Dublin, as site for his monastery, and Columba's choice of Iona off the west coast of Scotland for his.[56] But another consideration was whether the land around a monastic site was suitable for growing food, since as well as loving wild nature they wished to be self-sufficient. Hence they often chose an oak grove for its rich soils and protection from the wind, or a lake shore for its supply of fresh water.

When Patrick was asked by the daughters of the Irish King of Connaught what God he worshipped, and where he dwelled, he replied:

> he has his dwelling round heaven and earth and sea, and all that in them is. He inspires all, he quickens all, he dominates all, he sustains all. He lights the light of the sun; he furnishes the light of the light.[57]

Patrick's sense for the immanence of the Creator in creation is close to that of the Hebrew Psalmists and reflects a belief in the underlying unity of all beings, which reflects their being inspired by God.[58] It was this belief in nature as a realm of divinely inspired beings that gave the Celtic saints their love for, and desire to protect, animals, birds and trees, and their preference for wild places and a vegetarian diet. As Jacques Chevalier comments, Celtic Christianity was 'animated throughout by the love of nature, and of native country, by a winning familiarity with our "unknown brothers," animals or angels, and by ardent passion for spirituality'.[59]

Celtic Christianity shaped a love of God, and of *places* around the islands of Britain and Ireland, that was distinctive in the extent to which it imbued a love of nature, and hallowed the common life and practices of rural dwellers and peasants. The monasteries practised agricultural work of all kinds and eschewed animal labour when they could substitute their own.[60] This association between the religious life and work with creatures and on the land fostered a hallowing of food growing and making, from the tending of flocks and crops to the baking of bread and the provision of hospitality.

For the Celts, as for the desert fathers, this work was not primarily for mortification of the flesh but a post-Edenic recreation of a paradisiacal state in the wild lands where they created self-sufficient dwellings. They did this not by destroying what was there before, but instead by refashioning monastic gardens out of the existing peasant ways and traditions, and with resident plants and other beings.[61] As Harold Massingham puts it, the Celtic churches of Britain took up 'a sanctification of the entire world of nature', which provided as true an echo of the rural Christ of the gospels as could be found anywhere in Christendom.[62]

The influence of the Celtic saints established monastic dwellings and chapels across Ireland and much of North and West Britain through the fourth to the seventh centuries. And their authority gradually spread throughout the islands so that the influential monastic rule that Columba promulgated on the 'mother house' of Iona, and that was adopted in Northumbria, was reflected in legislation governing monasteries as far south as Hertford in the eighth century.[63] Celtic influence, over agriculture, household governance and political community, sustained the care of dwellings, communities and beings in *place*.

The crucial source of this influence was the shared engagement by monks and peasants in place-making *practices*, including most especially food growing and eating, the gathering of fuel and the sharing and protection of water sources.[64] Over the centuries of Celtic governance, and subsequently of Benedictine and Cistercian governance until their corruption by wealth, such spiritually oriented but practical care for being in place evolved into place-governed institutions. In particular there emerged in England and Scotland under monastic rule social arrangements for the careful use and sharing of environmental commons, including crop lands, grazing areas, rivers, uplands, and woodlands, while craft guilds evolved to govern non-agricultural forms of creative work and exchange.[65] These institutions and practices were formed around parochial polities in which monastic communities and parish churches played central roles, while royal courts were remote and relatively weak in their influence over land and people as compared with the modern era. These institutions underwrote the gradual evolution of European farming from a slave or serf economy to a peasant economy in which individual smallholders held and could pass on their land use rights to succeeding generations. Analogously in the towns, medieval guilds were institutions that trained craftsmen, enabling them to become free citizens, and ensured fair prices for their products. But these evolved forms of governance in place were gradually undermined by the centralisation of land and governance by early modern nation-states, of which the first was Tudor and Stuart Britain.

The Dissolution of the Monasteries, begun in England by Henry VIII and his chancellor Lord Wolsey between 1536 and 1541, was the seminal event in the breaks between nature and religion, food growing and urban living, town and countryside, that are implicated in the modern ecological crisis.

The background to the Dissolution events reaches back centuries to the contest between Celtic, and more indigenous, monasticism of Britain and the Latinate monastic practices of the French Benedictines, and later the Cistercians. In the sixth and seventh centuries the Church in the more populous south of Britain was prone to corruption and in-fighting between rival bishops, and Benedictine monasticism spread from France to Britain as a needed reforming influence. However, the two variant forms of monastic practice and doctrine did not sit well together on a small island and eventually, at the Synod of Whitby, as famously recorded by Bede in his *Ecclesiastical History*, it was agreed that Celtic monastic customs would be suppressed in favour of Latin and Benedictine practices, and Benedictinism became the dominant ecclesiastical shaping force in Britain until the Reformation.[66] We shall never know how things would have turned out if Celtic Christian practices and customs had not been suppressed. But while Britain became one of the most heavily monasticised of all countries in Latin Europe under Benedictine, and later Cistercian, influence, the wealth that ultimately accrued to the monasteries by the fourteenth century turned monastic influence from a benign to a corrupting force in British church and society.

The origin of the wealth of the monasteries, which ultimately led to abbots and monks becoming rentier property owners rather than co-workers with peasants on the land, was in particular the considerable successes the Cistercian monks had in the breeding of sheep. The Cistercian order originated as an attempt to live the Benedictine rule more rigorously than had become customary in France by the eleventh century. The first monastery was built on 'desert' or waste land 'overgrown with Woods and Brambles' at Chalon sur Soane in Northern France.[67] The order spread through Northern France and thence to England, where the first Cistercian Abbeys were established at Waverley in Surrey and Furness in Lancashire with the Isle of Man. Subsequent famous Cistercian monasteries included Fountains Abbey in Yorkshire and Tintern Abbey in Gloucestershire. Seeking to escape the wealth and property of the corrupted Benedictine order, the Cistercians set out to plant monasteries on desert or waste ground and hence their expertise grew in draining marshes, clearing scrub, building roads, planting woodlands and quarrying stone, all of which the monks engaged in as they built their abbeys and churches with their own hands. As Massingham puts it:

> In their able and diligent charge craftsmanship assumed its proper planetary position in the solar system of agriculture. The Cistercian idea of wholeness as inseparable from holiness faithfully translated into action the recognition of Christ both as transcendental Godhead and the Peasant Craftsman on earth who expressed a cosmic wisdom in the terms of peasant speech.[68]

Cistercian influence was greatest on agriculture because their interest in productive farming on marginal lands led them to become experts in the rearing of sheep. In the thirteenth century they reared the Lion breed of Cotswold sheep, which they reared throughout their lands and it produced so much wool that they made 'the fortune of England' in the fourteenth century. Hence monks who had learned to produce 'plenty out of barren places became traders and dealers in wool'.[69] And this wealth rapidly led to the same corruption by wealth and leisure that had formerly overtaken the Benedictine monasteries. In his sixth-century monastic *Rule*, Benedict said of monks who worked on the land by necessity to meet their needs that they are 'monks in truth, if they live by the work of their hands, as did also our Fathers and the Apostles'.[70] Rembert Sorg describes how, as monks became unintentionally wealthy through their success in crafts and agriculture, they became increasingly religious professionals, scholars and economic stewards.[71] As they spent increasing amounts of time in prayer, study and book-keeping, the monks ceased to participate in the holy work of manual labour that had been prescribed in the original rules of Benedict and Columba, and taken up again with alacrity in the Cistercian reform. Sorg notes that many Benedictines no longer read the *Rule* as mandating manual labour, but he argues that it was the decline of such labour among the monks that led to the corruption of the monasteries and ultimately to their dissolution in England, Scotland and elsewhere at the Reformation. Sorg also suspects another part of the problem came from the endurance of the institution of slavery in the West, whereas it disappeared early in Byzantium. This produced a social hierarchy, which Western monasteries were weak in resisting and which ultimately they replicated; from the seventh century the Benedictines began ordaining monks as priests and eventually introduced 'lay brothers' who did the manual tasks the priests no longer performed.[72] Benedict himself opposed slavery, and his rule therefore mandated manual labour within monastic enclosures be performed by monks, since it would have been contrary to the Gospel of Christ to permit a labouring class to divide the monastic community.

The rise of wealth, particularly from wool, and the demise of good work in the monasteries turned them into economic corporations and large-scale landowners. There is good evidence the monks were gentler owners of serfs than manorial lords and princes, but that monks came to own people as well as land and sheep, indicates the depth of the loss of the message of Christ. Their power and wealth, in a country as dominated by monasteries as was Britain, eventually came to be seen as an alien imposition and an unhealthy and unproductive monopoly that required breaking up by the Crown. But nonetheless the Dissolution that the Crown imposed on the villages and towns of England, and then Scotland, had considerable and mostly malign consequences for the peasant households and communities of place that the monks had governed. The Dissolution moreover ushered in a succession of further changes in rural Britain, under the successive Acts of Enclosure of the English Parliament, that in the seventeenth and eighteenth centuries saw the gradual theft of the smallholdings of peasants, and their shared common grazing grounds, river banks and woodlands by landowning families who had initially been offered by the Crown or forcibly taken over the lands of the monks into their own estates. Only as the effects of the Dissolution became clear over time is it possible with hindsight to see how this attack on the religious shaping of communities of place throughout Britain marked the seminal break between nature and culture, food growing and urban living, countryside and town. This break is for sure one of the 'unintended' consequences of the Reformation.[73] But, combined with the subsequent Acts of Enclosure, it led to the dispossession of a rural peasantry, and the loss of the glory of Britain, which its free self-sufficient yeoman farmers and clansmen and women had represented south and north of the Scots border until the Enclosures and the Scots Clearances.

The Dissolution of the Monasteries set in train the first nation-state making process in modern history as the powers and wealth of the land of England and Wales were concentrated in the Palaces of Westminster and Whitehall. As the nascent nation-state drew the power and wealth of the land to itself, and to aristocratic courtiers who, with the Crown, were the principal beneficiaries of the State-driven monopolisation of the land, the vestiges of place-based governance – customary use rights to commons including grazing land and woodland, regulations about the shared use of waterways, and craft guilds – provided an important cultural bulwark *against* the evisceration of place by the statist forces of centralisation. But as the English Enclosures proceeded in the seventeenth and eighteenth centuries this bulwark gradually unravelled, although it has never entirely disappeared. Hence when the historian or the anthropologist drills down into the narratives of particular places – as I do above in the Introduction – it is possible to discern that through the built environment, community memory, land forms and resident species, a sense of place, and of care for beings (nature) in place, has endured. But the remaining forms of this endurance are fragile and weak when set against the place-indifferent governmentality of States and economic corporations, which continue to extract wealth and power from communities of place, and so degrade their beauty, diversity and distinctive stories.

The key point from this brief historical survey is that it was precisely an assault on *sacred* place, and the secularisation of nature, as lands once held in trust by the Church were taken over for the principal purpose of wealth accumulation, which is the root of the modern ecological crisis, and the break between nature and culture, whose consequences I chart in the essays that follow. But the early modern and modern history of place is not only a history of material transformations driven by statism and mercantilism. The gradual evisceration of place in modernity also reflects significant change in the cultural and intellectual concept of place and space in the history of ideas that is traceable in theology and philosophy as well as in the natural and social sciences. This change is well characterised by Juliet du Boulay in her late twentieth-century study of a Greek hill village where residents were growing old and young people were moving away. What was drawing people out of the village was the change from a 'traditional and symbolic way of thinking to modern and secular thinking' and the 'fundamental social and metaphysical presuppositions' on which the values and social actions of people in such villages had formerly been based.[74] But if it leaves an ethnographic trace, the origins of this move from place to space are deep in the transition from the medieval to the modern worldview that began at the Renaissance and the Reformation, as the growing scholarly literature on the genealogy of place and space evidences.

Investigation of the historic roots of the assault on place, and governance in place, in modernity is closely related to investigation of the historic roots of ecological crisis. This is because the same processes that destroy the distinctive features of diverse human communities – such as language or building and farming vernaculars – also destroy the diversity and resilience of species communities.[75] But whereas Lynn White locates the roots of the crisis in Christianity, it is clear from the brief description of its historic roots just undertaken that its roots are not Christianity *per se*.[76] Instead they are in the transformation of practices, and a related transformation of beliefs about place, space and cosmos, which promoted a changed attitude to nature characterised by an increasingly mechanistic and domineering relationship with the earth and her creatures, in the centuries after the Dissolution of the Monasteries and the Reformation. Furthermore, the ideational changes that accompanied these historical events originated not in Christian theology but in the influence of repristinated Greek ideas about physical space in the European Renaissance.

Edward Casey argues that the key move originated with Bruno Giordano and Nicolas of Cusa in the fourteenth century. Both took up the view of an obscure twelfth-century hermetic text that the universe has no centre; not even the sun, as their contemporary Copernicus claimed. On their account no place is different from any other and space is boundless. It is just the presence of bodies at particular places in space that sustains the illusion of place as bordered or contained. Hence Aristotle's classic account of place as contained, and his related account of a limited or bounded universe, were both resisted. In the new post-Aristotelian account the perception of bodies resting in contained places masks the existence of something that is more universal and unbounded, which is infinite space.[77] It did not occur to medieval thinkers that this infinite space was empty of God; instead God was coterminous with space. But the new sense of infinite space opened up European consciousness on the cusp of the Renaissance to a new mode of exploration of space that underwrote the great world explorations of the fourteenth to sixteenth centuries in which the colonial, mercantilist and scientific control of earthly space – or *other peoples'* places – began.[78]

If the growing primacy of space over place encouraged a new European expansionism, it also paved the way for the emergence of the scientific conception of space as absolute, and hence as self-subsistent, independent of, and non-relational to, other beings, whether divine or human. The most influential account of space as absolute and non-relational to divine or human being is Isaac Newton's *Principia Mathematica*. In this breakthrough work Newton adumbrated new universal laws of time and motion that underwrote a new cultural attitude to space, which is the key genus of the placeless trajectory of European colonial and capitalist cultures since the Renaissance and the Reformation. The mechanistic metaphor favoured by Newton and his heirs to describe space privileges extension and mobility over emplacement and stability.[79] The mathematisation of space as extension and of the movement of atoms and bodies in space in early modern physics interacted with the nominalist account of univocal being, and produced what Alfred North Whitehead calls 'simple location'.[80] As a consequence, modern science and philosophy are shaped by what Whitehead insightfully calls the 'fallacy of misplaced concreteness', in which the abstract position of a being or thing in space – its 'site' – is privileged over its concrete, or embodied, location in a particular place, and hence over its relations to other beings or things in that place.

The late medieval doctrine of God, again under the influence of Greek philosophy, also paved the way for the collapse of place into space. Duns Scotus and William of Ockham ascribed abstract properties such as infinitude and ubiquity to the being of God. If God is greater than any category that can be conceived then all being, all space, are potentially empty unless filled by the divine presence.[81] Space on this account is passive and penetrable by the presence of God, and thence by all created beings. As Casey argues, the result of the new primacy of space over place, and the loss of a sense of place as mediated by relations between beings, is that:

> the inherent dynamism of place, its power to act or simply to resist, has given way to the supineness regarded as an indefinitely passible, even a passive, medium. What Plato and Aristotle (and even more markedly Iamblichus) had considered to be the capacity of place to influence direction and movement, generation and corruption – to effect physical change in general – yields to a conception of place as a merely quantified portion of an equiform and empty space: place has become a residuum with no inherent ability to alter the course of things in the natural world. All that remains of place is its very name – and an empty name, a mere *flatus vocis*, at that.[82]

All that is left for 'place' to identify by this nominalisation of place and space is the small part of the extensiveness of space that is taken up at any particular moment by a body in motion or stasis.[83] For Newton and his heirs, 'places are conceived as the mere parts of space', while space is geometrically governed by the laws of mechanics and motion.[84] Newton's God, whose sensorium is the universe, is so much the possessor of all particular places 'as to be equivalent to the endless space that God shares with the universe at large'. Consequently, it makes sense for Newton to identify God with what he calls 'absolute space'.[85] God in other words is equivalent to space not only because God is infinite and so universally present in or to all space, but because God is also infinitely extended. Hence for Henry More it makes sense to call the universe itself an extended physical being, which is the being of God. With this move More, and then Spinoza, completed the absolutisation of space and further underwrote the subjection of all particular beings, and places, to nominal status within an order of absolute being that extends into infinite space.[86]

While Renaissance and early modern scientific philosophers, including Newton, sought to combine the new cosmology of mechanism combined with a metaphysics of divine infinitude coterminous with the universe, nonetheless the rise of a concept of absolute space and divine infinity (and limitlessness) produced the paradoxical result of evacuating agency and being from place, and thence the divine from space. Hence for the deists and atheists who are the heirs of the new cosmology, the earth as humans encounter it is no longer 'filled with the knowledge of the glory of God', as it was for their predecessors, since the divine is as much in Pluto or the distant stars as in the earth. Consequently the earth – land, forests, water and the places they constitute – are more available to the heirs of Newton for reordering and re-engineering by human beings after human purposes than they had been in predecessor European cultures.

The rising primacy of space emptied places of relational power and provided ideational superstructure to the growing claims to control over space of merchants and monarchs in and after the Renaissance. Hence the theological changes in the relation of space to place underwrote the revolutionary moves of the early modern Tudor State to take to itself power over place throughout the island of Britain, as most seminally in the Dissolution of the Monasteries, and subsequently in the acts of Enclosure. The theologian who, more than any other, understood the political implications of the new theory of place and space for the human relationship to land, and for money and politics, was John Locke. When Locke observed the actions of colonists in taking over the places of natives in Virginia in the seventeenth century, he argued that they had acquired the right to the land that had formerly belonged to the natives because they were using it more productively and were also turning land into money; by storing up the wealth of nature as money, Locke argued, they were in effect redeeming the earth from its infertility and unproductiveness when not subject to land title.[87]

But this new phenomenon of claims of sovereignty over land and place by sovereign power of moneyed owners and invading State representatives – such as colonial companies like the Virginia Company, chartered by James I to colonise Virginia – is not confined to the colonies. It also became the central determining reality of political economy in Europe. Carl Schmitt argued that the political and economic crises of the twentieth century, and which led to two world wars, were a consequence of the unbound and unlimited nature of modern political economy. As economic corporations and imperial nations neglected the borders between places, and procured resources without regard to the ecological or social integrity of these places, they corroded the conditions for political governance. For Schmitt central to the 'concept of the political' is recognition of who and what belongs in a place, and politically negotiated arrangements for the non-coercive sharing of the earth's goods in each place.[88]

The dissolution of place in the face of capital power is famously described by Marx as the translation of distributed land use rights, such as persist in pre-capitalist societies, into land as capital whose benefit is taken up by its new owners as rental value. But this analysis misses the extent to which prior arrangements of ownership and use in place constituted a set of exchange and production relationships. Hence Karl Polanyi suggests that there is a more complex set of social relationships involved in the 'great transformation' from what Marcel Mauss called the 'gift economy' to an economy of rental space and labour time.[89] But the frontier between the gift economy and the rental economy is not only a historic frontier. It still exists as a spatial boundary in a number of domains, as the capture of place by economic and political sovereign power and its transformation into rental space continues to spread through regions of the earth where land is still 'under-capitalised' because still not subject to legal title and instead still used under customary systems of land use and economic production that Ostrom calls 'commons governance'.[90] The nation with the largest land area still governed by customary use arrangements is Indonesia. But the pressures from State governments and corporations to transfer this land into a 'development' economy where it becomes available for corporate wealth accumulation – for example as oil palm plantations – give rise to political and social conflict that threatens the monopoly of violence, which is the subliminal but enduring essential monopoly for a State to remain a viable source of political order.[91]

The competing claims of nation-states and empires in the early and mid-twentieth century over borders and spaces led a small number of philosophers in continental Europe to investigate the possibility of the cultural recovery of place, and the stability in place, as ways back to modes of human dwelling in and making sense of the life world. Central to this recovery was the recognition that what had been potentially lost in the secularisation of the European occupation of space was a memory of the sacred origins of Western Christian civilisation in the hierophanies and sacred dwelling places of the ancient Israelites and of Christians before modernity. Hence Martin Heidegger, like Eliade, argued throughout his oeuvre that there is an ontological depth to being in place that premodern religious cosmologies, myths, practices and rituals mediated, and which is dissolved by the modern valorisation of space over place, and of sovereign power over indigenous communities and their inherited place-based myths and rituals.

For Heidegger, the concept of 'being in a place' invokes four root meanings. First, to dwell in a place – *bauen* in German – has a root in Old

English in the word *nachgebauer*, which means near-dweller or neighbour, so to dwell in place is to be near others. Second, to dwell involves cultivating things and constructing a *bauen* or building. Third, dwelling means to *remain*, to *stay* in a place, and in the Gothic *wunian* this has the quality of *peace*, which is made possible by freedom from harm and danger. Fourth, the place of dwelling is 'on the earth' and 'under the sky', hence to dwell there is to remain 'before the divinities'. So a safe place is a dwelling where divinities and mortals and nonhuman creatures, including rock and water, plant and animal, 'belong together in one'.[92]

In a related *political* account of the twentieth-century pathology of placelessness, Simone Weil, in *The Need for Roots*, argued that Germany and France both gave in to the rising evil of Nazi dictatorship because of alienation from the proletarianisation of the urban populations of these countries.[93] As we have seen, the European process of depeasantisation Weil criticises began in Tudor England as accompaniment to the Reformation attack on the dominance of the Catholic Church over local governance and economy in communities of parish and place. The Dissolution of the Monasteries was the first act in the emergence of modern centralising states of Tudor England and Stuart Scotland. The Dissolution had radically deracinating effects on local communities, unsettling arrangements for the longstanding governance of people in place that had endured, despite infractions from Romans, Saxons and Normans, in the lands of the Celts and the Angles for many centuries. Dissolution led to the collapse of many peasant economies that were deeply intertwined with the large landowning monastic communities.[94]

Weil's critique of the de-moralised working proletariat who colluded with the Nazis now reads as a nostalgic throwback to an era when Europe was the industrial production centre of the world. With the displacement of production from Europe and North America to the developing world the majority of modern European citizens no longer participate in industrial making, except as consumers. Being a 'consumer' but not a producer represents another kind of alienation than that of the landless proletarian machine minder, and one that is heightened for those millions of children and grandchildren of former workers who can no longer find secure gainful employment, in Europe and North America as well as in the developing world. Consumers, as Michel De Certeau argues, deploy tactics to 'turn to their own ends forces alien to them' that now influence and provision from the corporate proprietorship of the means of production and the land.[95] Such tactics as growing vegetables, baking and cooking from raw ingredients, or installing solar panels for domestic energy, represent the tactics of the weak. They are modes of action of consumers who in order to produce, and so not merely consume, must reassert ownership and agency against the powers of the State and economic corporations that have promoted the centralisation and cartelisation of the ownership of land and accumulated wealth, and hence advanced the breakdown of local exchange economies and the order and stability of communities of place.[96]

The loss of stability in place affects both rural and urban areas. As global sourcing has driven down the price supermarkets are willing to pay for locally produced foods, farmers turn to ever larger machines, and imported fuels and fertilisers, to turn a profit on what in Southwest Scotland remain principally tenant farms. At the same time in the town of Dumfries, that Robert Burns called home, jobs involving growing or making in the formal economy are far below those in public administration, and unemployment or 'economic inactivity' among working age men in the region is over 17 per cent.[97]

The global mobility of the factors of production that has seen the jobs of workers exported beyond the shores of Europe has its roots in another form of monarchic expropriation of land in early modern Europe. The kings of Catholic Spain and Portugal were the first to sponsor explorers to the 'New World'. As the colonists that followed claimed for European monarchs land that had once been the place of American, and then African and Asian natives, it became necessary to conceive of land not as belonging to its ancestral users and their heirs, but to those who are most industrious and productive in the use of land. For John Locke and Adam Smith, private land titles and rent – the measure of the productivity of land – lie at the heart of the civilising forces of capitalism that would overtake the world. In this way the mathematisation of space and place precedes, and then legitimates, the mathematisation of creation – increasingly called 'nature' – as usable space. In the process, use rights to land that had once been conceived as deriving from the enduring dwelling of peoples, and their customary laws of inheritance, in particular places are also mathematised and commodified.[98] This enables and legitimates the exclusion of people from their ancestral environments and the natural benefits they confer, including their role in the production of wealth.[99]

Environmental exclusion continues to characterise the impact of modern spatialised political economy – and its mobile agents – on the communities of people who had previously been sustained by the customary sharing of places, and their natural values, among themselves. The places of such peoples are penetrated first by the ships, and much later by the trucks and planes, of European colonisers in the New World and then in other continents. Now it becomes harder to find any place – within or beyond Europe – that does not display the marks of the homogenising influence of modern culture, so that all places begin to be more alike. This homogenisation is underwritten by the mathematical logic of cosmological mechanism, which legitimates the takeover by mobile money power of the local politics of place. It also stimulates the mathematisation of human affairs with the invention of double-entry book-keeping, which provides an essential device without which the quantification of land and labour as rent and wages would not have been possible on their now global scale.[100] Hence the mathematical logics of profit and loss, or 'efficiency', accompany the near ubiquitous mobility of the factors of production in modernity that the invention of the oceangoing tall ship, the steam engine, and then the combustion and jet engines, have made possible.

Efficiency is another word for cost-benefit analysis and there are few places where the logic of efficiency has been applied with more blindness to place than the continental United States.[101] Barring the national parks, it is rare to find any habitable place on that continent that is not filled with the sound of automobiles and the ugliness of freeways and neon signs, marred by concrete office blocks, strip malls or monotonous suburban housing, or marked by the circular arm of myriad mechanical irrigators. The same infection increasingly visits modern Britain with the development of what some call 'cloned towns', so that from Devizes to Dumfries and from Perth to Plymouth main streets take on a similar appearance and are filled with largely the same stores and goods. Such 'cloned' towns are made possible by the ubiquity of the motor vehicle and the reach of metal containers and delivery logistics with the aid of which goods made on the other side of the planet by rural-urban migrants on low wages cost less than those made locally.

The built environment is similarly infected by mobility-enabled homogenisation, so that offices, factories, schools, hospitals and houses are increasingly built to designs and with materials that have no reference to the region or place where they are situated. This is why it is notable to find a place like Durisdeer that still feels like a place. If it had been more economic to build the modern road through the village than to metal a more recent mountain pass, then the local government would have built it. The flows of material goods, people and species that are sustained by the near ubiquity of road, rail, ship and air travel over the earth's surface have a deracinating effect on ecosystems as well as an alienating effect on the identity and wellbeing of people in place. The effects of constant movement are felt not only by humans, but by other species, and increasingly, since modern movement is fossil-fuelled and emissions from burned fossil fuels are changing the climate, by the earth system as a whole.

Modern technologies of surveillance and movement including the camera, other cartographic instruments, the car and the computer have given an imperial reach to contemporary humans that is a modern analogy to the imperial roads that the Romans put down across the lands of Europe from the first century of the Christian Era, as witness the straight track that runs through and out of Durisdeer. Tim Ingold argues that the construction of networks of rails and roads – and the drawing of the maps that record them – promotes a new kind of dwelling in the world, which is characterised less by habitation than occupation. 'Wayfaring' he suggests is the 'funda-mental mode' through which 'living beings, both human and non-human, inhabit the earth'.[102] The lines on modern maps that mark the passageways of cars and trains indicate an 'appropriation of the space surrounding the points that the lines connect or – if they are frontier lines – that they enclose'.[103] The drawing of lines on maps connects places into routes along which progress is made and where the emphasis is not on the way or the journey but on the speed of passage to the intended destination. Lines, maps and roads make possible, and often accompany, an imperial intent 'to occupy the inhabited world' by 'throwing a network of connections across what appears, in their (imperial powers) eyes, to be not a tissue of trails but a blank surface'.[104] Surveys, lines and roads subject a landscape to a mode of dwelling that is non-participative and invasive. They connect near and distant places, and typically they are all joined to the nodal points of empire, which are its ports and principal cities. Lines and roads enable the insertion of peoples, species and goods – to say nothing of embryos – into places near and far whose end is imperial occupation.

Against this imperial mode of line drawing Ingold suggests that the wayfarer – who might be a hunter gatherer, a shepherd or a fox – travels in place in such a way as to 'participate from within in the very process of the world's continual coming into being'. In so doing she lays 'a trail of life', which 'contributes to its weave and texture'.[105] This conception of wayfaring as participation in being, in contrast to the mode of technological control, is reminiscent of Heidegger's account of *dasein* – which roughly translates as 'being in' – in his *Being and Time*. An analogous contrast is to be found in an essay of Thoreau on *Walking*. The true practitioner of the Art of Walking is one 'who has a genius for sauntering' and prefers the open air to the close air of the study or workshop. Thoreau contrasts the walker, who enjoys freedom to walk in the wild wood, with the surveyor, who stands with 'some worldly miser':

> looking after his bounds, while heaven had taken place around him, and he did not see the angels going to and fro, but was looking for an old post-hole in the midst of paradise. I looked again and saw him standing in the middle of a boggy Stygian fen surrounded by devils, and he had found his bounds without a doubt, three little stones where a stake had been driven, and looking nearer I saw that the Prince of Darkness was his surveyor.[106]

For Thoreau walking in trackless swamps and forests – rather than surveying fields and journeying rapidly on highways and city streets – enables a truer life, a depth of character and a reforming spirit that cannot arise from urban occupations alone:

> A town is saved, not more by the righteous men in it, than by the woods and swamps that surround it. A township where one primitive forest waves above, while another primitive forest rots below, such a town is fitted to raise not only corn and potatoes, but poets and philosophers for the coming ages. In such a soil grew Homer and Confucius and the rest, and out of such a wilderness comes the reformer eating locusts and wild honey.[107]

Before Ingold, Heidegger and Thoreau, the ur-text in Western civilisation for these contrasts between wayfaring and occupation, dwelling and control, wilderness and city, was the story of the settlement of a nomadic tribe in a land whose ancestor Jacob is fondly remembered as 'a wandering Aramean' (Deuteronomy 26: 6). In the perspective of the seminal exile of the mythological ancestors Adam and Eve from the habitable and peaceable Garden of Eden, the journey from Eden to the plains of Moab through Egypt and Wilderness to the Promised Land becomes the founding saga of the small but seminal nation of the Hebrews, from whose patriarchs Christians and Muslims as well as Jews claim descent. At the heart of the saga is the divine intention to redeem the Hebrews from nomadism, slavery and landlessness as they struggle for a place of their own in the midst of the great empires of Egypt, Babylon, Persia and Assyria.

In the era of peak oil and melting ice, movements of resistance to the economic corporations who eviscerate the powers of people in their own places have emerged on the Celtic fringe region of Britain. The Transition Town movement, which began in Totnes, Devon, has the purpose of identifying ways of relocating the sources and exchange of food, fuel and fibre in each locale rather than relying on the import of these things from distant locations with unsustainable impacts on the health of ecosystems and on the earth's climate.[108] This quest for new resilient local economies has spread to every region of the earth and is impacting the design of cities, and the relation of cities to ecological regions and nation-states as discussed below. This quest represents a new citizen movement from below to unwind the centralising and centrifugal tendencies of modern nation-states, landowners, and corporations, which have had such deleterious impacts on communities of persons and species in place. Transition Towns represents a genuine and hopeful attempt to relocalise political economy in order to bring human consumption and exchange activities back into sustainable scale to the capacities of local ecosystems to support them. Recalling as it does the time in Britain and Northern Europe when powers were located in parishes, abbeys and city guilds, it is indicative of a new ecological civics of place, which finds significant analogy in the ecclesial politics of space that I describe below. It is also suggestive of the form of civilisation that those who come after us will likely be forced to develop as the present unsustainable emissions of greenhouse gases unsettle the earth's climate to such an extent as to make nonviable the present highly complex global production and supply chains on which so many now depend for food, fuel and fibre.

For the second-century neoplatonist Iamblichus place was both the dwelling-place of embodied beings and the potential meeting place of embodied life with God. For if the Creator made all places, and does not dwell in any one place in particular, 'real being – that which truly is and which is in itself incorporeal – is everywhere'.[109] Christians believe that the Creator God chose to dwell in the body of Jesus Christ at one particular time and place on earth. After Christ's Ascension the bodily presence of the

Incarnate God is no longer experienced. Instead Christians experience this presence in sacramental worship and in meeting together. But Christians from the first century to the twenty-first have also experienced particular and revelatory meetings of God in places beyond worship gatherings in the human and more than human environment, from Paul's conversion on the Road to Damascus to Saint Antony's desert dwelling to John Muir's religious experiences in the Californian Sierra. The experience of the holy – the sacred – is a form of experience that exceeds Christian culture, though Christians claim it reaches a perfection in those who encounter the Christ that it does nowhere else. And even Christ, when he seeks encounter with the one he calls Father, goes to wild and desert places, far from the city and the crowd. Uncreated material place is the means through which embodied minds find and experience reality, both physical and spiritual.

Despite the modern allure of mobility and speed, humans are still born, nourished and nurtured in particular places, built and unbuilt. And even the built places are only habitable because of the services rendered to them by the ecosystems that surround and sustain them. For all of the post-Copernican decentring of earth that the Newtonian exaltation of space over place achieves in Western science, the earth remains the only home planet for human beings: it is still *our* central and determining place, and one we share with the only community of species that exist in the known universe. For the three score years and more that we humans live as corporeal souls, this earth is our place, and no one knows this experientially better than those who have for a brief time dwelled in fragile pressurised suits and spacecraft beyond the habitable atmosphere of mother earth.

The growing psychological and spiritual alienation of modern urbanised humans is related to the loss of direct, embodied relations to ecological place. This loss underlies the growing tension between the practices of industrial civilisation and the biodiversity, beauty and fertility of the home planet. In this book I argue that consciousness of the ecological encircling of embodied humans in biologically rich and fertile places is a vital source of resistance to the destruction of biologically rich places and socially rich communities. I also argue that religious communities should attend more closely to the sensory character of their rituals, and their enduring role as focal places for the *moral* geography of human and more than human life. I argue that it is only possible to understand the human moral life, and the role of religious communities in sustaining that life, through a phenomeno-logical account of the emplaced character of communities, and of the small scale in which such communities necessarily find their most optimal form.

In *Small is Beautiful*, E. F. Schumacher wrote one of the classic texts of the modern environmental movement.[110] In so doing he recognised what the biblical historians long ago observed, which is that empire and large scale and remote organisation are inimical to peace and to the resilience and sufficiency of local communities. Agriculture and long-distance transportation first made possible in the Ancient Near East the large-scale societies – or empires – which throughout subsequent history have invaded and disrupted the places of local communities. Large-scale, remote decision making, concentrations of material power and wealth have always promoted the emptying out of the powers of place into the cities where such concentrations are gathered. The biblical critique of this tendency, which has analogies in modern anarchist literature as well as bioregionalism, indicates that the spacialisation of place is accompanied ultimately by moral and spiritual destruction. This is in part because it makes it possible for chains of decision-making to cause great suffering in particular places while not troubling overmuch the consciences of those agents who cause it: out of sight, and preferably in another county or country, often is out of mind. Hence I argue in what follows that although many Europeans and North Americans have lost the sense that their places of dwelling, and the gathering of those places into boundaried nations, have a sacred genealogy, the recovery of that genealogy using the dominant religion of these nations, which is Christianity, is a powerful source of redemption and repair to the pathologies of extreme mobility, placelessness and ecological destruction that characterise contemporary life.

2

Lament for a silent summer

In a scientific survey with the evocative title *Silent Summer,* fifty-seven British ecologists charted Britain's wildlife and biodiversity in the first decade of the third millennium and found them in significant decline, despite the conservation efforts of English Nature, numerous wildlife charities, scientific conservationists and conservation volunteers.[1] Among the most visible declines were those in numbers of individuals of particular bird species, including turtle doves, wood warblers and dotterels, while the range of many other bird species had declined particularly on arable land and hedgerows.[2] The authors identified the main cause of bird decline as synthetic pesticides and herbicides, which reduce numbers of small insects on which birds feed, and eradicate bird habitat. Hence three quarters of Britain's butterflies are in decline because the plants on which they live as caterpillars are being eradicated with more powerful herbicides. Moth numbers were down one third from 1968, with 20 species down 90 per cent. Pesticides also impacted significantly on rivers with cadis fly, mayfly and stonefly all in serious decline. But despite their crucial place in the food chain, both of humans and other animals, the decline of small creatures, such as butterflies or worms, attracts less public attention than the demise of eagles or otters. As David Attenborough states:

> We tend to focus on the bigger animals and ignore the smaller ones – but small creatures like these are the basis of our entire ecosystems and they are disappearing faster than ever. That loss is transforming our wildlife and countryside.[3]

Millions of people in Britain are supporters of conservation and wildlife charities, and in particular the Royal Society for the Protection of Birds, which, with over one million members, has the largest membership base of any charitable organisation in Britain.[4] Given the number of supporters of conservation charities in Britain, the continued destruction of the nation's wildlife by industrial farming might be said to require some explanation. Its roots go back to agricultural policy since the Second World War when food supplies from Europe, on which the nation had been dependent for more than a hundred years, dwindled because of attacks on shipping. After the War, the British State set about increasing indigenous food production, and growth in yields – in particular of cereal crops, milk and meat – became a national strategic priority. Growth in yield was achieved by new breeding techniques, by the use of new agrochemicals, and by the increasing substitution of farm machines for manual labour. This has had the effect of reducing the number of people who work on the land, decimating jobs in rural communities.[5] At the same time the use of larger tractors and harvesting machines, together with rising use of agricultural chemicals, saw a growth in field size, and the removal of hedgerows and 'wastes' or patches of land between and on the edges of fields. Paradoxically, while crop yields have increased, and the weight of meat and milk from farm animals has grown similarly, this has not significantly changed the dependence of Britain on imported foods. What it has done, however, is reduced the price of food significantly, albeit at a great cost in terms of ecological destruction. As consumers pay less for food relative to their incomes than all previous generations, they unwittingly contribute to the toll of destruction of rural communities and wildlife of mechanical and chemical farming.

The onslaught on British wildlife in the nation's farms, while the people of Britain still see themselves as 'nature lovers' who enjoy a still remarkably diverse rural landscape, recalls what Wendell Berry identifies as the central paradox of the modern conservation effort.[6] Conservation charities and State conservation agencies set aside parts of the landscape from industrial farming. But the onslaught on mother nature elsewhere continues, and it is not confined to the British Isles. It is estimated that the land area of the UK is sufficient to feed its annual consumption of goods and services until April each year. After that the forests, mines, oceans, rivers, soils and wetlands on which Britons rely for their 'ecological footprint' – a term first coined in a study of the footprint of the city of Vancouver – are provided by the willingness of other nations to subject their patrimony to industrial production methods to meet British consumption.[7] And this substitution carries a high price for humans as well as nonhumans in the developing world, where environmental regulations and legal protection of land use and fishing rights are weak; when shrimp farms replace paddy fields in South India, pelagic fishers trawl the seas off Senegal, and coffee and cotton plantations displace peasant farms, farmers and fishers are forced to migrate to more marginal lands, to urban shanty towns or to other countries.[8]

Wendell Berry comments on the conservation paradox when he notes that the Sierra Club – America's largest and oldest conservation charity – while it devotes its resources to the conservation of wilderness areas from industrial development had at one time invested its funds in stocks and bonds of some of the most destructive industrial enterprises, including Exxon and an open cast coal mining company. As Berry observes, wilderness conservation is 'specialized conservation', memorialised in the Sierra Club's aim 'to explore, enjoy, and protect the nation's scenic resources':

> while conservationists are exploring, enjoying and protecting the nation's resources, they are also *using* them. They are drawing their lives from the

nation's resources, scenic and unscenic. If the resolve to explore, enjoy, and protect does not create a moral energy that will define and enforce responsible use, then organized conservation will prove ultimately futile. And this, again, will be a failure of character.[9]

The Sierra Club has its origins in the Romantic aesthetic of John Muir, who campaigned to preserve the Sierra Nevada of the American West from hydrological, mining and other industrial developments. Romantic protest against the modern domination of nature produced the modern wilderness and conservation movements. But while these movements set aside picturesque, scenic parts of nature from the destructive interventions of the engineer they do not challenge the underlying trend of industrialism towards control and extraction without replenishment or enhancement. The authors of *Silent Summer* do not speak of the ecological crisis as a moral crisis, but for Berry 'the use of the world is finally a personal matter' and it can only be conserved 'by the forbearance and care of a multitude of persons' whose character is formed by habits, practices and virtues that sustain rather than destroy the world.[10] This multitude cannot be replaced with the work of a number of conservation organisations, whether charitable or governmental. Hence neither English Nature nor the RSPB are conserving the wildlife of Britain. Only the people of Britain can do that if they turn from the irresponsible relation to nature sustained by a consumer economy, which reaps where it does not sow.

The title *Silent Summer* recalls Rachel Carson's *Silent Spring,* the single most influential text in the modern environmental movement, which awoke a generation to the assault of chemical farming on wildlife in North America and beyond. Her ground-breaking and beautifully written essay showed that synthetic pesticides, the most poisonous of which – organophosphates developed as nerve toxins for use in warfare in the 1930s – were being put to use in croplands, forests and pastures. Widespread use of these new chemicals was exacting a devastating toll on birds and other creatures, while also representing significant health threats to humans.[11] When Carson's book was being considered for publication one of the chemical companies that manufactured pesticides suggested that her ideas represented a 'communistic' assault on American capitalism, and the publishers delayed publication while they sought to establish the truth of the allegation.[12] But the chemical companies need not have worried. Though her book led to the banning of one type of pesticide – DDT – in Europe and North America, and to a decline in its use in the developing world, pesticides and herbicides are now produced in greater quantity than ever, they pollute the air, freshwaters and soils, and their residue is detectable in the fatty tissues of mammals, including humans, on every continent.

As Carson and others show, numerous illnesses – including cancers, nervous system disorders, heart, liver, lung and stomach disorders – are associated with these chemicals. They are also the cause of significant illness, and death, among farmers worldwide. But despite widespread evidence, and a significant growth in cancers and immune and nervous system disorders in the human population in the last forty years, direct causal linkages are still resisted by crop and chemistry scientists, and by government regulatory bodies, which are mostly staffed by such scientists. The European Union has taken a more precautionary approach in recent years, but many pesticides banned in Europe are still permitted by the UK pesticide regulatory regime, which conducts no independent tests but relies instead on testing by the manufacturers.

The title of Carson's influential book recalls a line from Keats, which she quotes in the opening pages: 'the sedge is wither'd from the lake and no birds sing'. In the middle of *Silent Spring* is a chapter entitled 'And No Birds Sing' which commences:

> Over increasingly large areas of the United States, spring now comes unheralded by the return of the birds, and the early mornings are strangely silent where once they were filled with the beauty of bird song. This sudden silencing of the song of birds, this obliteration of the colour and beauty and interest they lend to our world have come about swiftly, insidiously, and unnoticed by those whose communities are as yet unaffected.[13]

The chapter ends:

> Who has decided – who has the *right* to decide – for the countless legions of people who were not consulted that the supreme value is a world without insects, even though it is also a sterile world ungraced by the curving wing of a bird in flight? The decision is that of the authoritarian temporarily entrusted with power; he has made it during a moment of inattention by millions to whom beauty and the ordered world of nature still have a meaning that is deep and imperative.[14]

Carson draws powerfully on Romantic imaginary in *Silent Spring* and it is the combination of evidence-based science with this quality in her writing that helps to explain its great cultural influence. *Silent Spring* awoke the baby boomer generation of the 1950s and 1960s to the toll being exacted by chemical agriculture on wildlife, and the threat it also posed to human health. The book was a key origin of the contemporary environmental movement in the United States, and ensuing democratic pressures led to the formation of the Environmental Protection Agency under the Republican administration of Richard Nixon in 1970, and to Congressional Clean Air and Clean Water Acts.

Far more than a scientific description of the dangers and destruction wrought by modern agrochemicals, Carson combines in *Silent Spring* four central ideas that feature in most versions of modern environmentalism. The first is a critique of the Baconian quest to dominate nature to the extent of eradicating her own internal ends and order, and those of other creatures, as inferior to those that rational science-informed humans impose on her by will and whimsy.[15] The second is a challenge to the dualism between nature and culture, mind and body, originated by René Descartes. As Carson indicates, it trains people to forget they are embodied animals raised and sustained by plants and photosynthesis, weeds and water, and that the human economy is set within, and limited by, the greater economy of an embodied earth. The third is a recollection of the intrinsic beauty of nature that gives richness, meaning, lustre and grace to all life, as is most fully appreciated by human beings. The fourth is a recollection of the aggrandising power of the modern nation-state, in partnership with economic corporations, as they unite economic organisation and scientific instruments in the subjugation of nature to the imperative of growth without at least considering the question of whether further subjugation will necessarily advance flourishing.

The environmental imaginary on which Carson draws originates in large part with the Romantics. Romantic philosophers, poets and artists resisted the Enlightenment valorisation of the scientific control of nature as manifest in the spread of industrialisation.[16] John Muir, William Wordsworth and John Ruskin wrote lyrically of the beauty and fecundity of the forests, lakes and mountains they inhabited, and described them as sources of moral guidance and spiritual transcendence. Through their writing they sought to persuade the public – and politicians – of the importance of setting aside areas of particular scenic beauty from industrial development for city water storage, forestry and mining.[17] In bringing into existence the world's first national parks – first the Californian Sierra and then the English Lake District – they established a form of nature conservation that is now present in almost every country in the world and remains a core strategy of the conservation movement.[18] But as *Silent Summer* illustrates, such parks do not protect wildlife from the insidious spread of industrial chemicals through ecosystems any more than they will provide protection from a climate changed by greenhouse gas emissions into the atmosphere later in the present century.

Romantic philosophers and poets criticised the effects of industrialism on the environment as the infection of rational and scientistic dominion. But a potential implication of their critique is that it is the *presence* of humanity that is the heart of the problem. Hence the landscapes and picturesque characteristics the Romantics valorise are features such as ruined monastic buildings, tumbledown and empty peasant cottages, beggars and gypsies, and high mountains, moorlands and forests emptied of people.[19] In their aesthetic celebration of an emptied out land, the Romantics elevated art over nature, and nature over culture. In so doing they valorised the very things that were the historic root of nature's subduing – the Dissolution of the Monasteries, the Enclosures, the monopolistic capture of nature as rent by the British aristocracy, and the criminalisation of evicted peasants and smallholders as vagrants destined for the workhouse and coercive wage labour. Romanticism of the picturesque or the scenic does not redeem nature from the dread destruction of the industrial nation-state. Instead, the turn to nature as aesthetics replicates the commodification of the world that drives its destruction.[20] From Thomas Gray's first *Guide to the Lakes* it is a short step to the modern touristic industry that sells visits to nature, ruins and remains as the picturesque for urban consumers. And hence the modern conservation movement engages city dwellers in the struggle to save nature from industrialism at one remove from its fundamental cause in the spread of the extractive economy of industrial cities, large corporations and international trade. The conservation movement attracts funds to save 'beautiful' and charismatic creatures and places that are 'valued' as scenic. But the conservation of especially valued places does not halt the assault on creatures great and small that are displaced or extinguished by the systemic reduction of fields and forests to locations for the production of monocrops or meat on an industrial scale, and using agrochemicals that destroy all life apart from fertilised crops or domesticated animals.

In defence of the Romantics, Jonathan Bates argues that they correctly and prophetically identified the root of the industrial destruction of nature in the modern nature–culture split, and that they used poetry, prose and art in a sustained attempt to resist it. In a comparison of two poems – Byron's *Darkness* and Keats' *To Autumn* – Bates finds in the first a prophetic sense for what we would now call ecocide, and in the other an elegiac account of the interconnectedness of nature and culture, and of climate and what it means to be human. Byron wrote *Darkness* in the summer of 1816, a summer that in the Northern hemisphere had been exceptionally cool and wet because of the climatic effects of volcanic ash from the Tambora Volcano in Indonesia.[21] But Byron does not only blame nature, but the long weary decades of the Napoleonic wars:

> And War, which for a moment was no more,
> Did glut himself again; a meal was bought
> With blood, and each sate sullenly apart
> Gorging himself in gloom: no love was left;
> All earth was but one thought – and that was death,
> Immediate and inglorious; and the pang
> Of famine fed upon all entrails – men
> Died, and their bones were tombless as their flesh.

And just as the bad weather brings a conflict to an end, so Byron imagines famines to follow that presage the extinction of humanity:

> Unknowing who he was upon whose brow
> Famine had written Fiend. The world was void,
> The populous and the powerful – was a lump,
> Seasonless, herbless, treeless, manless, lifeless –
> A lump of death – a chaos of hard clay.

As Bates comments 'bad weather was a scandal to the modern Constitution' because the Enlightenment was one long attempt to erase meteorology from the human condition.[22] Reason, science and demystified politics are said to have revealed humanity at last as the master of nature. And hence the modern social contract is not only a contract to bind human beings to the monopoly power of the nation-state. It is also a contract that binds them to the Newtonian idea that the earth is a predictable law-governed machine over which the nation-state has finally achieved mastery through knowledge on behalf of its citizens. But *Darkness* indicates that weather remains 'the primary sign of the inextricability of culture and nature'.[23]

Keats' *To Autumn* also celebrates this inextricability, written as it was in 1819 towards the end of the first really good summer Keats, or anyone, had had since the Tambora Volcano.

> Season of mists and mellow fruitfulness,
> Close bosom-friend of the maturing sun;
> Conspiring with him how to load and bless
> With fruit the vines that round the thatch-eves run;
> To bend with apples the moss'd cottage-trees,
> And fill all fruit with ripeness to the core;
> To swell the gourd, and plump the hazel shells
> With a sweet kernel; to set budding more,
> And still more, later flowers for the bees,
> Until they think warm days will never cease,
> For Summer has o'er-brimm'd their clammy cells.

Keats celebrates the rich ecology of species of a cottage garden warmed by the late sun, and of a corn field where poppies – mentioned in the second stanza – have grown along with the corn. The poem suggests that Keats had an understanding of:

> the underlying law of community ecology, namely that biodiversity depends on a principle which we might call illusory excess. In order to withstand the onslaught of weather an ecosystem needs a sufficient diversity of species to regenerate itself; species which serve no obvious purpose in one homeostasis may play a vital role in a change environment.[24]

For Bates, *To Autumn* refuses the Cartesian separation between inner and outer states, mind and body, nature and culture, humans and nonhumans, emotions and ecology, time and weather.[25]

This poetic and Romantic sense for the close interpenetration of human civilisation and the fate of the earth reflects the emergence of a new reading of Hebrew poetry by Robert Lowth, an Anglican clergyman who was appointed Professor of Poetry at Oxford University in 1741. In his

influential *Lectures on the Sacred Poetry of the Hebrews* Lowth argued
that vernacular and rabbinic translations of Hebrew literature had missed
its parallel form, and hence missed the symbolic power of the free-flowing
parallel verse of the Hebrew poets and prophets. Lowth argued that
vernacular and oral texts not only revealed the parallel character of the
Hebrew original, they also highlighted the earthy and sensual character of
Hebrew poetry, and the animistic tendency of Hebrew historians, poets
and prophets to see the hand and heart of the Creator in the behaviours of
cloud and ocean, wind and rain. In his lectures Lowth praised the directness
and simplicity of biblical language and metaphor that the Romantic poets
began to emulate, and he contrasted it with the fashion in England at
the time for Classical nature imagery, which was more human-centred and
less earthy.

Lowth encouraged a generation of poets to turn from the fashionable
neoclassical versifying of Dryden or Pope and take up the freer, more
emotive, style of Hebrew poetry and the animism of the Hebraic description
of nature. In so doing he also encouraged a moral seriousness among the
Romantics who wrote not only poetic praise of pastoral beauty, love
and lambs but prophetic condemnations of the darkened skies and dread
desires that greed and avarice had spawned in the new industrial cities.
This combination is manifest in Wordsworth's description of his environmental awakening in *The Prelude*. Alone in the hills while stealing eggs from
a raven's nest, Wordsworth sensed the wind coming after him:

> While on the perilous ridge I hung alone
> With what strange utterance did the loud dry wind
> Blow through my ear? The sky seemed not a sky
> Of earth – and with what motion moved the clouds!

The fearful presence he felt he recognised as the creator Spirit:

> Wisdom and Spirit of the Universe!
> Thou Soul that art the eternity of thought,
> That givest to forms and images a breath
> And everlasting motion, not in vain
> By day or star-light thus from my first dawn
> Of childhood didst thou intertwine for me
> The passions that build up our human soul;
> Not with the mean and vulgar works of man,
> But with high objects, with enduring things –
> With life and nature – purifying thus
> The elements of feeling and thought,
> And sanctifying, by such discipline,
> Both pain and fear, until we recognize
> A grandeur in the beating of the heart.

As Gordon Strachan notes, the wind in *The Prelude* is the spiritual agent of moral change that enlivens Wordsworth's conscience, and stimulates his desires towards environmental virtue:

For I, methought, while the sweet breath of heaven
Was blowing on my body, felt within
A correspondent breeze, that gently moved
With quickening virtue.

In *England 1802* Wordsworth sets against this quickening virtue the new culture of the industrial city, whose greed and idolatry drove young men to abandon nature and 'the student's bower for gold':

The wealthiest man among us is the best:
No grandeur now in nature or in book
Delights us. Rapine, avarice, expense
This is idolatry; and these we adore:
Plain living and high thinking are no more:
The homely beauty of the good old cause
Is gone; our peace, our fearful innocence,
And pure religion breathing household laws.

The 'ledger' is the book of nature's grandeur, which is captured by the clerk's accounting rule. Against this quantitative mindset, and its collectivising grasp on the cities, citizens and fields of industrial England, Wordsworth sets the heroic individualism of poetic feeling for beauty, nature and the sublime. There is a prophetic tenor to the poetry of Byron and Wordsworth, but it is subordinate to their assertion of the power of individual feeling, and passionate identity with nature, as means to resist the rationalism of the age. For both writers, while they may have taken inspiration from Hebrew poetry, the religion they exalt is neither that of Yahweh nor of Christ but of *aesthetics*, and hence of the human spirit in response to nature.

While we may agree with Bates that the Romantics challenge the nature–culture divide, nonetheless the aesthetic turn to 'wilderness' and the sublime fails to challenge the source of the infection of the rural landscapes that continue until today to destroy Britain's biodiversity. This source is not *persons*, and their traditional rural dwellings, gardens and small farms, but the agency of landowners, parliamentarians and civil servants. From the Dissolution of the Monasteries in sixteenth-century England and Scotland, the State organised or legislated for the takeover and enclosure of smallholder farms, and common lands, including strip-farmed fields, woodlands, grazing and marshland commons. The land was parcelled up into large estates and in the process self-sufficient rural communities were gradually destroyed, and the customary owners and users of the land were evicted from their ancestral homes and, in most cases, forced into parish workhouses or urban slums, or into exile in the colonies.

The English Enclosures were the first attempt by a modern nation-state to evict the people from the land on a large scale. They inaugurated a pattern of State-driven concentration of land ownership into fewer hands that is repeated since in every nation that takes up the path of industrial development, and is now called depeasantisation. This process, while justified by agricultural improvement, also led to dramatic reductions in biodiversity. This is because the new and larger ploughed fields and animal grazing lands replaced a much more diverse landscape, which included strip-farmed fields, commons, heathlands, 'wastes' and woodlands where peasants had formerly found fuel, game, grazing and household materials.

Because the Romantics frequently neglect this historical process and its seminal role in destroying both the biological and social integrity of communities of place, they inaugurate a strain of environmental discourse that is misanthropic. There is, however, no misanthropy in the biblical account of the reasons for environmental declension in ancient Israel, nor in the biblical vision of ecological restoration. For the Hebrew poets and prophets the decline of the integrity and stability of place, both for human dwelling and for other creatures, is human greed and injustice – and in particular the quest of rural and urban elites to sequester for themselves too much of creation's bounty. Jeremiah is the most explicit on this when he describes an ecological, as well as a political calamity, in the land of Israel during the Babylonian Exile. The Israelites were no longer living according to the just commands of God, and instead had followed idols, wealth and war. Their neglect of the Creator also led to their disruption of created order:

> But this people has a rebellious and defiant heart,
> they have rebelled and gone their own way.
> They did not say to themselves,
> "Let us fear the Lord our God,
> who gives us the rains of autumn
> and spring showers in their turn,
> who brings us unfailingly
> fixed seasons of harvest."
> But your wrongdoing has upset nature's order,
> and your sins have kept from you her kindly gifts.
>
> JEREMIAH 5: 23–25

But while the fertile land turns infertile and so punishes the wicked, covetous and idolaters, the Psalmist has it that the wild land will give life and succour to those whom the wicked had evicted from their ancestral inheritance:

> He turns rivers into a desert, springs of water into thirsty ground,
> a fruitful land into a salty waste, because of the wickedness of its inhabitants.

He turns a desert into pools of water, a parched land into springs of water. And there he lets the hungry live, and they establish a town to live in; they sow fields, and plant vineyards, and get a fruitful yield.

PSALMS 107: 33–37

The contrast with the Romantic valorisation of the scenic – and the related conservation project to save biodiversity from destruction by setting apart 'wild' nature from human work – could not be greater. The Hebrew Bible suggests that true ecological restoration will only be found when the introduced divisions of city and countryside, wealthy and peasant, human and nonhuman are overcome, and the poor and the wild animals again both have their place in the land, while the power of the rich who took it from them is restrained, and their palaces and high towers are in ruins. Just as the land loses its fertility and diversity when some humans use violence to 'join house to house, that lay field to field, till there be no place' (Isaiah 5: 8), so the original plenitude and rich diversity of creation is restored when rich no longer exclude the poor from the land, and when the people again 'build houses and inhabit them' and 'plant vineyards, and eat the fruit of them' (Isaiah 65: 22) on land in which they again have use rights.

Old Testament insight into the relatedness of concentrations in land ownership and the destruction of emplaced human and species communities, though absent from mainstream Romantic writing, nonetheless was an important theme in the poetry of John Clare and Robert Burns. Unlike Wordsworth, Ruskin, Keats and Shelley, Clare and Burns were born of peasant stock, and were consequently more sensitive to the venal nature of the theft of land in the name of agricultural improvement launched by the English Enclosures and the Scottish Clearances.[26] Clare and Burns saw at first hand the extent of human immiseration wrought by the wealthy capture of the land and the enforced mass movement from smallholdings to slums. They were also sensitive to the large-scale assaults on *place* launched by the takeover of fields, glens, marshes and woodlands for the spatially oriented project of agricultural 'improvement'. In *The Lament of Swordy Well* John Clare, whose parents were landless labourers, writes of the piteous state of vagrancy to which the landless were reduced by the Enclosures:

I hold no hat to beg a mite
Nor pick it up when thrown
Nor limping leg I hold in sight
But pray to keep my own
Where profit gets his clutches in
There's little he will leave
Gain stooping for a single pin
Will stick it on his sleeve

For passers bye I never pin
No troubles to my breast

Nor carry round some names
More money from the rest
I'm swordy well a piece of land
That's fell upon the town
Who worked me till I couldn't stand
And crush me now I'm down

In parish bonds I well may wail
Reduced to every shift
Pity may grieve at troubles tale
But cunning shares the gift
Harvests with plenty on his brow
Leaves losses taunt with me
Yet gain comes yearly with the plough
And will not let me be

Alas dependance thou'rt a brute
Want only understands
His feelings wither branch and root
That falls in parish hands
The much that clouts the ploughman's shoe
The moss that hides the stone
Now I'm become the parish due
Is more then I can own.

To be on the parish, reliant on poor relief and shifts in the workhouse, was indeed a piteous condition, far inferior to the life such persons knew when they had a place to call their own, even if they had to work others' lands to put bread on the table. Clare is in no doubt that it is the rule of commerce and the surplus harvests enjoyed by the new landowners that are the source of this unjust suffering. In *The Cotter's Saturday Night* Robert Burns lauds the life of the cotter (cottager or smallholder), which was increasingly threatened in the Scottish Borders by the Clearances that had spread south from the Highlands:

November chill blaws loud wi angry sugh;
The short'ning winter-day is near a close;
The miry beasts retreating frae the pleugh;
The black'ning trains o craws to their repose:
The toil-worn Cotter frae his labor goes,
This night his weekly moil is at an end,
Collects his spades, his mattocks, and his hoes,
Hoping the morn in ease and rest to spend,
And weary, o'er the moor, his course does hameward bend.

At length his lonely cot appears in view,
Beneath the shelter of an aged tree;
Th' expectant wee-things, toddlin, stacher through
To meet their dad, wi flichterin noise and glee.
His wee bit ingle, blinkin bonilie,
His clean hearth-stane, his thrifty wifie's smile,
The lisping infant, prattling on his knee,
Does a' his weary kiaugh and care beguile,
An makes him quite forget his labor and his toil.

Belyve, the elder bairns come drapping in,
At service out, amang the farmers roun;
Some ca' the pleugh, some herd, some tentie rin
A cannie errand to a neebor town:
Their eldest hope, their Jenny, woman grown,
In youthfu bloom, love sparkling in her e'e,
Comes hame; perhaps, to show a braw new gown,
Or deposits her sair-won penny-fee,
To help her parents dear, if they in hardship be.

With joy unfeign'd, brothers and sisters meet,
And each for other's welfare kindly spiers:
The social hours, swift-wing'd, unnotic'd fleet;
Each tells the uncos that he sees or hears.
The parents partial eye their hopeful years;
Anticipation forward points the view;
The mother, wi her needle and her sheers
Gars auld claes look amaist as weel's the new;
The father mixes a' wi admonition due.

Towards the end of the poem Burns contrasts the dignified and homely simplicity of the cotter with the luxury and indolence of princes and lords:

From scenes like these, old Scotia's grandeur springs
That makes her lov'd at home, rever'd abroad:
Princes and lords are but the breath of kings,
"An honest man's the noblest work of God";
And certes, in fair Virtue's heavenly road,
The cottage leaves the palace far behind;
What is a lordling's pomp? a cumbrous load,
Disguising oft the wretch of human kind,
Studied in arts of Hell, in wickedness refin'd!

O Scotia! my dear, my native soil!
For whom my warmest wish to Heaven is sent!

Long may thy hardy sons of rustic toil
Be blest with health, and peace, and sweet content!
And O! may Heaven their simple lives prevent
From Luxury's contagion, weak and vile!
Then, howe'er crowns and coronets be rent,
A virtuous populace may rise the while,
And stand a wall of fire around their much-lov'd Isle.

For Scotland's favourite bard and one time smallholder, princes and lords risked infecting the Virtue of Scotia with the contagion of luxury, and the corrupt rents of the aristocracy risked destroying the self-sufficiency of a godly people.[27]

The association between princely and statist efforts to capture the product of the land and increase agricultural production with the eradication of species has deeper historical roots in the British Isles than the Enclosures and the Clearances. Caledonian bears were likely eradicated before the Anglo-Saxons arrived, although wolves endured much longer; Mary Queen of Scots hunted wolves at Blair Athol in 1563. However, in 1532, in the reign of Henry VIII, the newly centralised government in Whitehall passed an edict mandating the slaughter of 'vermin' throughout England and Wales. The principal aim of the act was the extermination of crows but the first Vermin Act was followed by more wide-ranging acts, the most draconian of which was Elizabeth I's Vermin Act of 1566, which mandated the killing of an extraordinary array of species. The goal of the Tudor Vermin Acts – which had their precursors in Scotland – was crop protection. The period in the sixteenth and seventeenth centuries during which the acts were passed was a bad time for harvests because of what is known as the Little Ice Age, which produced more than a hundred years of excessive rain and cold, and signally depressed harvests. The result was that even as the Tudor court was growing in luxury and power the lot of the majority was a struggle for survival.[28]

The Vermin Acts were not, however, only about crop protection, since they mandated the killing of kingfishers, cormorants, wild cats and shags, which are no threat to crops or gardens. Hence these Acts initiated a scale of slaughter in the British countryside that is almost unimaginable given the relative paucity of wildlife in contemporary Britain. They were organised through the English and Welsh parish system. Under Tudor legislation parish churches became centres of local government as the emergent unitary nation-state expanded its legislative, economic and military power across the island of Britain. Each parish vestry – and in particular the churchwardens – was therefore responsible for making payments mandated under the Vermin Acts for the heads of crows, foxes, hares, hedgehogs, kingfishers and the rest. These payments were often quite large, and oddly disproportionate. A peasant could claim four pence for the head of a hedgehog while a returning soldier from a king's foreign war could receive six pence in compensation for having had his tongue cut out by Turks.[29] It was also parishes – the real cradles of English democracy – that decided how to implement the Vermin Acts, and which species to render payment for. Consequently, in some parishes there was much enthusiasm: for example 6,600 bullfinches were killed in one parish in Cheshire in just six years, and 700 kites in eight years. But in other parishes – such as Worfield in Shropshire – so few vermin were killed that county commissioners at Bridgnorth upbraided its vestry for failing in its duties under the Act.[30]

The Vermin Acts manifested a larger cultural turn against nature, and towards vicious and violent hunting, which is not explained by the quest for agrarian improvement alone.[31] The Tudors and Stuarts saw hunting deer and other animals as the recreational sport of kings and courtiers: it provided a leisurely approach to killing when they were not raiding their respective state treasuries to fund wars against each other, or the French, the Spanish or the Dutch. In the process they purloined large areas of what had previously been common-use forests and grazing lands for their own use. The large-scale takeover of the land of England for king and courtiers was the key element in the emergence of a centrally governed English State under Henry Tudor, and began in earnest with the Dissolution of the Monasteries which owned around one third of agricultural and forest land. Dissolution, which occurred on a large and rapid scale between 1536 and 1540, enabled the Crown to acquire vast swathes of England and Wales, which included peasant-run farms, heaths, forests and shorelines and which had been managed relatively benignly by monasteries and abbeys for centuries. Many of these lands were then gifted to courtiers and aristocrats in return for their financial support for Henry's wars and other lavish projects. The result was a revolution in rural areas as peasant farmers found their use rights undermined by newly ennobled aristocrats who wanted to extract more of the value of the land as rent.[32]

Britain six centuries after the Dissolution is not only a land in which biodiversity is seriously threatened, but it is also more economically divided than it has ever been in its history. Compared to the gargantuan wealth – and capacity for ecological destruction – of the banks and investment houses of London and Edinburgh, Henry Tudor was a dwarf, as well as rather shorter in stature than any who have played him in recent times. At the time of the Vermin Acts, the power was still in the hands of the people whether to carry out the killing the Acts mandated. In contemporary Britain nine-tenths of the land belongs to a small number of very rich individuals and powerful corporations.[33] The majority of British people are effectively landless, since even among the 60 per cent of households who are owner occupiers, the majority owe much of the value of their homes to banks or building societies, who retain rights to the property title until the mortgage is redeemed, which is often not before retirement. Hence they can only express their feelings about the effects of corporate ecocide by supporting wildlife charities, buying organic food, or writing to their MPs.

One of the first acts of the Edinburgh parliament of a newly devolved Scotland was a Land Reform Bill, which, in 2003, put back in the hands of rural tenants and the propertyless the capacity to buy back land from the lairds and investment bankers who own more than 90 per cent of the forests and moorlands of England and Scotland, and where so much culling of Britain's wildlife has occurred since Tudor times.[34] Land reformers who have organised local community purchases of Scottish Western Isles such as Eigg and Gigha, and sporting estates, are literally reversing the Clearances.[35] And in so doing they are making it possible for the land to be repeopled, for empty and broken buildings to be repaired, for hills to be reforested and for new employment and local wealth creation where before there was the tyranny of the absentee ownership and corrupt city money. In so doing they are not only repairing an ancient human wrong. They are also restoring biodiversity, as evidence from Eigg of increases in bird and mammal numbers and species diversity, since the community buy out of the island ten years ago already indicates.[36]

Fredric Jameson argues that in the midst of ecocide and the idolatry of mass consumption there is a need for a renewed utopianism in which it becomes possible again to dream of a lived future towards which we might move from the present.[37] The Scottish land reform movement represents just such a vision, inspired as it was in part by the utopian claim of the Hebrew Bible that the earth belongs to the Lord, and not the laird, a claim that remained in Scots law long after it was forgotten in England. Land reform represents a genuine move to put the parish back at the heart of British political life where the recovery of property by the people produces a moral vision of a community of species and of real work on the land where energy, food, fibre and furniture are again locally and sustainably produced rather than extracted and mined – locally and globally – without regard for the lives of future generations or species.

Given the role of the parish in the extinguishing of Britain's wildlife as charted in the parochial records of England, it may seem counterintuitive to suggest that the parish might play a central role in its recovery. And yet if present and future generations are to live sustainably without coal and oil, and without diminishing biodiversity, then local care of species and of soils, and local generation of energy and growing of food, will need to become biopolitical priorities in a way they have not been for generations. Just as the Tudor State mandated the parish to undertake what was then understood as agrarian improvement, so a successor State in response to growing extreme weather events, and other challenges to the long and fragile supply chains that currently characterise the global economy, will need to find ways to divest itself of its centrist powers – and corporations and landed estates of accumulated land and wealth – and enable local communities again to dwell in and care for land and ecosystems in ways that will enable a more localised, just and sustainable economy.[38]

Some suggest that farming without corporately managed and chemically drenched fields will not produce enough food, let alone energy and fibre and construction materials, for the nine billion people who will likely be alive in

2050.[39] But the cause of hunger in the present – without considering the need to centrally plan for an imagined future that just extends out from the present without change – in developing and developed countries alike is still either lack of access to land, or cash, or some combination of the two. In the UK and the United States, as much as in India or Tanzania, the reason people are driven to seek access to charitable food supplies, such as food banks, is not lack of food in their nations' silos, supermarkets and warehouses but the absence of the means to purchase or grow food for themselves. Some claim that organic farming will not produce as much food as chemical farming. But scientific studies of organic farming demonstrate that while it produces lower crop outputs – by around 10 per cent in the case of cereal crops – these lower outputs are achieved without fossil fuels and agrochemicals, and hence without imposing on society the social and ecological costs of climate change and ecocide.[40] And because organically managed land involves more human work – and less dependence on imported machines, fertilisers and chemicals – this traditional form of farming provides more rural workers with remuneration from which to purchase food. Organic farming also restores community, not only to the species with whom the organic farmer works in a symbiotic relationship, but to rural communities, since organic farming and horticulture require more manual, human, work.

Of course not everyone can leave the city and go and work on an organic farm. But in the city too there is a need for a more utopian and ecologically benign conception of human dwelling than that promoted by the corporate consumer economy. And there are already hints of a move away from dependence on distant and imported foods and consumer goods with the return of farmers' markets, and the movement towards urban farming that is gaining strength as I discuss below. But again national and local government could do much to increase the parochial character of the food economy if they looked again at the relationship between the city and the countryside.

Around every British city is a greenbelt that is often a mix of chemically farmed fields, herbicide-laced golf courses, and recreation areas with a smattering of allotments. Around German cities and towns there are similar green areas, but a far greater proportion of them are constituted by what in Britain are called allotments where families have for generations grown food at weekends, and where they often camp out overnight in tents or temporary dwellings in summer. I invite the reader to imagine a future in which every British city is surrounded by a band of land twenty or thirty miles in extent which – in between the existing villages – has been turned over to allotments for city dwellers to go to at weekends and on holidays, and for some to work in full time, growing food and flowers and fibre for consumption in the city. Currently around 30 per cent of food eaten in Britain is imported in oil-fuelled trucks, planes and ships. Even without climate change, conventional oil – oil that does not come from vastly polluting production methods such as athabasca sands and deep-sea oil – is going to run out. Absent a movement of people back to the land in much greater numbers in the next fifty years, it is doubtful that the food supply as currently arranged will continue to bring food to Britain at prices future inhabitants will be able to afford. It is also unlikely that large multinational corporations, like Tesco and Asda/Walmart, will be permitted to continue to extract water from subterranean aquifers to grow air-flown flowers in Kenya and asparagus in Peru, and so spread hunger and ecocide beyond Britain's shores in a world in which climate change will make food and water increasingly harder to obtain.

In a well known critique of the Enlightenment, the British moral philosopher Alasdair MacIntyre suggests that the contemporary West is like Rome before its collapse, the barbarians are already at the gates of the cities, and the collapse of empire will soon follow. He called for 'another Benedict' to point the way through and beyond the end of empire, and the dark ages that will presumably follow.[41] If a sudden collapse in Britain's food supply later in the present century is to be avoided, it would seem prudent to begin to recover more holistic and sustainable approaches to agricultural *and* industrial and craft production *within* Britain. Such a recovered food and craft economy will need to be resituated in the carrying capacities of local ecosystems, and to engage more of the population in the growing of food and in the making, maintenance and repair of artefacts and building materials. If a collapse in the global food economy does occur later in the present century, the crucial difference with the end of the Roman Empire is that whereas Rome's collapse was primarily political in its effects, and confined to the Mediterranean region and Northern Europe, the collapse of the present global empire will reach into every ecosystem on the planet because of the global and remotely organised economic corporations who increasingly dominate the world food and industrial economies and which I discuss in the next chapter.

3

Artificial persons and the political economy of place

The failure of the Copenhagen Climate Conference in December 2009 to produce a draft treaty governing international greenhouse gas emissions cast a pall over the prospects for the mitigation of anthropogenic climate change. Climate change represents the most significant global-scale threat to biodiversity. Research indicating that global climate change is producing growing droughts and heavier rainfall in shorter time periods was published in 2010. Together these resulted in an unexpected net decline of plant productivity of 1 per cent in the exceptionally warm decade of 2000 to 2009.[1] This contrasts with the previous decade in which the same scientists recorded a net global gain of 6 per cent. Climate change above 2°C on preindustrial levels threatens the survival of tropical forests, which contain approximately 80 per cent of global biodiversity.[2] Raised temperatures, and drought, also threaten arable and arboreal food crops, such as wheat and olives, in temperate regions. Rising global emissions of carbon dioxide are also causing increased ocean acidification, which is reducing marine fertility and biodiversity.[3]

The global treaty designed to protect the planet's biodiversity is known as the Convention on Biological Diversity, and it was signed into international law in 2000. But a global audit of biodiversity after the first decade of the signing of the Convention found that one in five of the plants studied in the sample were at risk of extinction, while ongoing threats to amphibians and mammals were even higher.[4] Hence the goal of the CBD 'to achieve by 2010 a significant reduction of the current rate of biodiversity loss at the global, regional and national level as a contribution to poverty alleviation and to the benefit of all life on Earth' had not been realised.[5]

The biggest global cause of biodiversity loss is continuing destruction of moist tropical forest prior to land use change towards commercial-scale monocrop plantations such as soya and oil palm. This destruction is driven in large part by economic corporations rather than by local populations whose traditional harvesting practices depend on natural biodiversity, not on single cultivated species.[6] If maximising the income of indigenous forest dwellers were the priority in the use of tropical forests, then community-based harvesting of timber and non-timber forest products would always win over forest burning, and their replacement with mono-crops. Community-based timber projects in Costa Rica give considerable economic benefit to local people, while the small-scale and labour-intensive nature of this approach results in much less damage to the forest than large-scale commercial logging.[7] Conservationists are also exploring the potential of local community forest harvesting of Non-timber Forest Products such as nuts, fruits, resins, bamboo and herbs for medicine and cooking. One case study of Areca nut palm harvesting in Southeast Asia shows that this approach retains 90 per cent of local bird species, which is far better than the outcomes for conversion from tropical forest to oil palm monocrop.[8] Markets in these products need to be balanced with conservation concerns if they are not to unsustainably diminish supplies.[9] Moreover, *local* harvesting of these products by communities that inhabit tropical forests has the potential to sustain Common Property Regimes in forest management, while also sustaining local supply chains and hence further maximising regional employment and income potential from the forests.[10] On the other hand the principal markets for tropical monocrop products are in North America, Europe, Japan and Australasia where human populations are relatively stable but consumption continues to grow. Soya is utilised primarily as animal feed, and palm oil in processed foods, cosmetics and detergents, and increasingly as biofuel. Action in developed countries to limit imports of products sourced unsustainably from tropical regions is insufficient though the European Union made a start with a ban on illegally sourced Indonesian timber in 2011.[11] Without such action the CBD will not drive reduced degradation of biodiversity hotspots in tropical regions.

The second biggest cause of habitat destruction is pelagic ocean fishing.[12] Again the principal agents are not peasant fishers but large technologically sophisticated fishing fleets owned and managed by commercial corporations. The global catch capacity of commercial fishing fleets far exceeds the capacity of the oceans to supply them.[13] Over-harvesting threatens to turn large areas of the marine environment into marine deserts by mid-century at present rates of destruction.[14] It also undermines the ability of traditional fisher communities to fish locally and sustainably. Here the principal markets are in both rich developed nations in North America, Europe and Japan, and increasingly in China, and other developing nations as they emulate excessive and unsustainable consumption patterns in developed countries. While consumer awareness of the unsustainable sourcing of fish is growing, voluntary action – without legislation – is insufficient to stem the scale of destruction of biodiversity from unsustainable fishing.

Industrial corporations, often licensed or subsidised by national governments, are presiding over what a growing number of scientists are calling the 'sixth extinction'. Though it will be the sixth major wave of species loss in earth history it is the first caused by one species, and the rate of species loss is already faster than any previous event.[15] The failure of the first global treaty on biodiversity to stem the tide of extinction reflects an enduring conflict between the political influence and power of the primary agents of economic development – economic agencies and corporations owned by governments and private shareholders – and the aspirations and projects of conservationists in government, in non-governmental organisations and in the scientific community.[16]

Aspirations to conserve the environment are not confined to conservation experts. A 2008 survey found that 95 per cent of individual citizens in Europe believe that environmental protection is very important, though most think action is more important at the governmental level and through global agreements rather than at the level of the individual consumer and householder.[17] Cross-national studies, which include data from North America, also indicate that there is a sustained level of concern for a healthy environment in all developed countries.[18] However, there are few occasions on which an environmental issue has played a major role in voting patterns in either Europe or North America, although the election of the Rudd government in Australia in 2007 was partly due to its stance on climate change.[19]

Conflicts between citizen aspirations and conservation strategies and the commercial interests of private corporations are evident in the failure of global scale treaties to address ecological problems such as biodiversity decline. Such conflict is also clearly implicated in national-scale failures. These conflicts reflect an enduring and structural problem of power in relation to conservation. Conservation biologists seek to restrain the ecological impact of economic development on wildlife by strategies that involve a focus on particular endangered species or habitats. Thus a range of national laws, international treaties and scientific conservation projects involve the identification, conservation and, where possible, reintroduction of individual endangered species, which are often also 'charismatic species' such as orang utans or polar bears.[20] Another array of legal, scientific and nongovernmental activities involve attending to and saving 'biodiversity hotspots', 'sites of special scientific interest', or 'scenic' places.

The construction of conservationist spaces involves the reconfiguring of human–nature relations in these spaces, which often privileges external actors over indigenous ones. Consequently, indigenous people – residents, tribal peoples, local communities, traditional users of lands appropriated for conservation – find themselves drawn into a new mode of 'environmental governmentality'.[21] In many cases this new governmentality is added to existing disciplining and restraining invasions by government and corporate agents, which are often the principal cause of biodiversity losses. This is evident, for example, in the contrast between indigenous management of tropical forests in the Amazon, Borneo and the Congo with the effects of governmental and corporate uses of these forests. Traditional users – whose uses may have endured for thousands of years without significant biodiversity reductions – lose their agential power to manage environments in ways that enable them to feed and house themselves while not diminishing ecosystemic richness.[22] As access to their traditional lands is denied them, and in most cases land use rights conferred instead on corporations, they find themselves turned into poachers, or even refugees. The same thing happened in the British Enclosures. Until today poaching is one form of modest resistance to the capture of so much of the land by landowners from its traditional owners. The outcome of such ecological governmentality is that local populations are subject to increased surveillance and control by the State, while their use rights to local forest and land-derived produce are taken from them and handed to private corporations and private landowners, whose historic record of environmental destruction is infinitely greater than that of indigenous communities.

Ecological governmentality manifests the contradiction at the heart of the modern conservation movement, modern environmentalism and ecological science, which we identified above. Economic growth sustains growth in conservation and ecology journals, conferences, books, organisations, projects, scientists and volunteers. But this activity depends upon the same growth engine that is the root of the problem, which is growth in corporately driven and sustained consumption and production in the developed and, increasingly, in the developing world. As we have seen, Wendell Berry argues that the problem is ultimately one of a failure of moral character.[23] But while Berry is surely correct that the ecological crisis is a failure of character the question is: whose character? In the developed world many citizens are no longer actively engaged in food growing or manufacturing as corporations have out-sourced production to other countries. But citizens have to eat, and to find clothing and housing. Social scientific studies reveal that citizens of post-industrial societies increasingly value non-material goods, including environmental quality.[24] But the condition of being a consumer without land and without the tools of a trade is one of extreme dependence on an economy increasingly dominated by corporate actors, in which preferences for goods those corporations do not value are hard to express through the thin medium of consumer choice. To blame the moral character of citizens for the ecological crisis leaves out of the picture the most influential agents of this crisis, which are not citizens but economic corporations, which have the rights of citizens, and far greater powers than citizens, but lack citizens' capabilities for moral discernment.

Gus Speth is also critical of environmentalists, but not because they lack good intentions. Instead he suggests environmentalists are guilty of incrementalism; they have focused too much on the effects of ecological destruction and not enough on the underlying causes. For Speth the causes are the governmental quest for unrestrained economic growth, and the quest of large private corporations to maximise shareholder value regardless of ecological or social costs to the communities and habitats in which corporations operate.[25] Focusing as Berry does on the moral failings of citizens – as though they are the principal agents of environmental destruction – runs the risk of colluding with the disempowering effects of ecological governmentality on citizens and local communities, while leaving the main agents and promoters of ecologically destructive production and consumption – large economic corporations – free to continue with business as usual. Furthermore, it neglects the way in which the political powers of citizens and local communities have been transferred by the State to economic corporations in the last two hundred years.

The rights of corporations emanate from the chartering and licensing of corporations by the nation-state. This process began in the fifteenth century when the monarchs and emergent nation-states of modern Europe began to derogate their own powers of incorporation to other corporate entities, and so granted to corporations a share of the sovereign powers that the nation-state drew to itself in the post-Reformation period over land and natural resources contained within the boundaried spaces claimed by the State.[26] In post-revolutionary America the status of joint stockholding corporations was ambiguous. Some argued that since they were chartered by the King of England they should, after the Revolution, be made subject to the will of the people in the towns in which they were situated. This claim was soon tested in the courts in a conflict between the Trustees of Dartmouth College and the governor of New Hampshire that went all the way to the Supreme Court. The governor had declared the College a public body, removed its charter and seal of office, and countermanded decisions of the College Trustees in an effort to turn it into a public university. The Trustees and their lawyers argued that the Royal Charter of George II, which had established the College, was a contract that remained in force even after the Revolution. In a precedent-setting case the Supreme Court found for the corporation of Dartmouth College over the State of New Hampshire.[27] A subsequent judgement in the UK – Salomon versus Salomon – had a similar effect in British company law.[28] The result was the creation of a fictive legal personality – or artificial person – to which are ascribed the same legal rights as existing persons.

The modern economic corporation has its roots in the charters that monarchs and governments conferred on corporate entities such as the East India Company and the Hudson's Bay Company in the exploration and exploitation of territories beyond national jurisdictions. Over generations, this device to extend the agency of the State beyond the places within its own sovereign territory became a means to affirm the independent sovereign power of such royally chartered companies in the post-revolutionary and republican space of the United States, and thence in the British homeland as well. Thus was born the modern Anglo-Saxon business corporation, largely independent of the sovereign power of government and answerable only to its stockholders. Today economic corporations possess more wealth than most of the national jurisdictions that birthed them. Through this wealth they are able to lobby parliaments, fund political parties friendly to their interests, and underwrite the election and office expenses of politicians who claim to represent the will of really existing people, not artificial people. Similarly corporations, such as News Corporation, can purchase media across different formats and nations, and create outlets whose purpose is not to inform the public in a balanced way over environmental and other public concerns, nor to seek the truth, but to advocate a 'corporate-friendly' worldview that focuses on the sexual and other misdemeanours of celebrities or politicians, while neglecting corporate crime and distorting public perceptions of major issues that might otherwise provoke more corporate regulation – and most notably climate change.[29]

In all three domains where News Corporation holds a major share of print and broadcast media – the United States, Australia and Britain – scepticism about the scientific 'theory' of climate change is widespread. Content analysis of four media outlets in these domains in the three months April to June 2011 reveals that *Fox News*, *The Wall Street Journal*, *The Times* (London) and *The Australian* – all Murdoch-owned outlets – carried a disproportionate number of stories suggesting that the theory is based on bad science, or suggesting that there is considerable disagreement among scientists as to the causes of climate change, or that the climate is not changing. News Corporation does not act alone. The corporate management of public perceptions of climate change science was first proposed in 1998 by the American Petroleum Institute, which aimed 'to inform the American public that science does not support the precipitous actions [the Kyoto climate treaty] would dictate, thereby providing a climate for the right policy decisions to be made'.[30] It would seem that News International have taken up this project with considerable success in the English-speaking world.

If they were real human beings, corporate artificial persons would be regarded as sociopaths, because the dominant interest of the corporation is the bottom-line of profit, and hence the value of its stock to its owners, and not the real suffering of persons and species which they underwrite when they neglect the environmental or human health costs of their activities.[31] If stock values rise by burning other peoples' forests, fishing out oceans beyond national jurisdictions, or polluting the atmosphere with climate changing quantities of CO_2, this is of no concern to the company since these burdens do not show up on company accounts.

It would, however, be an oversimplification to say that such activities happen without the consent or collusion of governments. In many cases of corporate environmental destruction governments are also involved: through tax-funded corporate subsidies or corporate tax breaks, or through the issue of government licences for forest conversion, fossil fuel or fishing extraction within national jurisdictions.[32] Governments also subsidise or underwrite – as most notably in the 2008 financial crash – the activities of large commercial banks that are the source of investment funds for fossil fuel exploration and monoculture conversion of forests. The largest failed bank by monetary value in history – the Royal Bank of Scotland – was rescued from bankruptcy by an 85 per cent British government buyout in 2008. RBS is also the largest single global funder of highly polluting or ecologically risky oil and gas projects, including oil exploration in the Arctic Ocean and tar sands oil extraction in Canada, and has remained so since it was taken into public ownership despite the climate change commitments of the UK and Scottish governments.[33]

Governments fund conservation agencies, and issue legislation designed to control the worst harms arising from the activities of private corporations and citizens. But public funds devoted to conservation activities and to the policing of environmental regulation represent a fraction of funds devoted to State subsidies and tax breaks to private corporations. US Federal subsidies to the coal, oil and gas industries in the period 2002–2008 amounted to just over $12 billion annually. Federal government spending on support of Wall Street banks and on wars in oil rich regions in the same period was more than $5 trillion.[34] By contrast the annual budget for the Environmental Protection Agency in the same period averaged $7.5 billion.[35]

The principal approaches to environmental ethics developed by philosophers in the United States and Europe neglect corporate behaviours and the role of governments in authorising and subsidising them. The most influential approach to environmental ethics involves the ascription of moral value to ecosystems, land and species. For Aldo Leopold ecological science reveals the interconnections that sustain the life community on which human life depends. Ecological and evolutionary science indicates that humans are members of the 'land community', and that instead of its conquerors they must act as its citizens. Ecology generates a new sense of right and wrong in the earth community, which Leopold called the 'land ethic': 'a thing is right' he argued 'when it tends to preserve the integrity, stability, and beauty of the biotic community. It is wrong when it tends otherwise'.[36] In a similar vein Holmes Rolston proposed that species and communities of life have 'intrinsic value' to the extent that they display goal-directed behaviours. Species rely on other species – and on natural processes such as photosynthesis – for the pursuit of their own purposes in enduring and reproducing. In this way, Rolston argues, values in nature have a prior or given existence independent of human culture.[37] The land ethic and intrinsic value provide an extra-cultural referent for human value, a measure of right and wrong that is more ecologically sensitive than culturally originated value systems such as pricing mechanisms or aesthetic judgements. This approach is also said to overcome the mind–body, subject–object and nature–culture divides that environmental philosophers argue have distorted human perceptions of the natural world since the Enlightenment, and hence challenge the ideational roots of modern environmental destruction.[38]

The concept of intrinsic value is reflected in the United States' Endangered Species Act (1973). The purpose of the Act states that certain species have been rendered extinct because of economic growth and development 'untempered by concern and conservation', and others have been depleted in numbers and are therefore 'threatened with extinction'. The Act therefore commits the United States as a sovereign state to 'conserve to the extent practicable' other threatened species of fish, wildlife and plants that 'are of esthetic, ecological, educational, historical, recreational, and scientific value to the Nation and its people'.[39] New Zealand's more recent Resource Management Act uses the phrase 'intrinsic value' not only with respect to endangered species but also to ecosystems. It states that the act is designed to promote the conservation of 'aspects of ecosystems and their constituent parts which have value in their own right, including – (a) their biological and genetic diversity; and (b) the essential characteristics that determine an ecosystem's integrity, form, functioning, and resilience'.[40] However, in both domains the rise of the anti-statist and growth-at-any-cost rhetoric of neoliberalism is diminishing democratic preparedness to challenge industrial developments that threaten biodiversity. Thus while the preamble of the New Zealand RMA recognises the intrinsic value of ecosystems, the 788 pages of the RMA contain many clauses that diminish the legal capacities of citizens or local authorities to appeal or halt corporate behaviours or practices that threaten ecosystem integrity in particular places.[41]

In the United States the annual budget of the EPA diminished during the Bush-Cheney administrations of 2000–2008, and again since 2011 under the Obama administration. So too did the ability of the EPA to act prudentially on well-established but, in the United States, politically controversial scientific judgements, such as the link between climate change and fossil fuels, or climate threats to endangered species within US territory. Changes in federal law during the Bush-Cheney administrations also reduced the ability of citizens democratically to resist corporate environmental pollution at county or state level.[42] The Bush-Cheney administration also strengthened efforts to curb the ability of citizens to mount Tort actions to seek damages against corporate environmental harms in state and federal courts and hence to promote environmental care through civil action.[43]

Intrinsic value is an important philosophical idea and in the United States' Endangered Species Act and New Zealand's Resource Management Act it has signally entered political and legal discourse, providing a new cultural warrant for the executive powers of government to restrain corporate environmental destruction. In practice, however, corporations continue to use their great wealth, and their lobbying and monetary influence over parliamentary and governmental executive processes, to pursue environmentally destructive developments in terrains that have formally recognised the intrinsic value of species and ecosystems. There is also an unintended consequence in the adoption of intrinsic value as a political value by the State. In the absence of a formal mechanism internal to the accounts and practices of private corporate entities, and citizens, attempts to enforce interpretations of intrinsic or natural value increase the powers of the State relative to citizens as well as corporations. In libertarian discourse this increase in environmental governmentality is represented as growth in the powers of the State over the individual. Hence Cass Sunstein represents precautionary environmental regulation in relation to air and water pollution as founded on a climate of fear, and as over-reaction to 'worst case scenarios'.[44]

Attempts to legislate for the recognition of intrinsic value have another disadvantage for they suggest that the nation-state is the principal agency responsible for protecting or redeeming nature from ecological destruction. This is an ambiguous claim when in many cases corporate activities are licensed, and subsidised, by the same governments that claim to 'protect' nature.[45] The promotion of the nation-state as guardian of the environment is also problematic because, in the great majority of cases, environmental destruction is place specific, and hence local in character. But the nation-state in its history has had a tendency to gather to itself and its executive agencies the local powers of people and communities that reside in particular places, and therefore to prevent local communities from exercising ecological care over their own habitats.

The second main approach to environmental ethics may be best described as 'wilderness ethics', as first enunciated in John Muir's account of the wilderness of the Californian Sierra as a landscape that ought to be set apart from economic development because of its divine beauty. Campaigning against what he saw as the growing humanisation of the American West, Muir argued that there is more wonder, beauty, strength and gracefulness in animals 'cared for by Nature alone' in mountain pastures and ancient forests than in domestic animals in cities and plains.[46] Similarly Thoreau argued that humans have a cultural and spiritual need to experience natural beauty in relatively unmodified natural areas, and that 'wildness is the preservation of the world'.[47] As we have seen, Wordsworth, Ruskin and Muir argued that industrial civilisation must place limits on its use of wild lands, and set apart a proportion of wild lands for conservation. The choice of which lands to set aside was determined principally by aesthetics: certain kinds of landscape – mountains, waterfalls, lakes and wide rivers running through lowland hills – were identified with the Romantic ideal of the natural sublime.[48] For conservation scientists the choice of land to be set aside is determined more by ecological values such as species richness, or the presence of endangered and endemic species in particular areas.[49]

While the wilderness ethic has played a valuable role in the setting aside of certain species' rich or aesthetically pleasing areas of land from industrial development, it has not proved sufficient to global-scale problems such as ozone depletion, pelagic ocean fishing or anthropogenic climate change. Further, the wilderness ethic may even have the perverse effect of giving an ecological gloss to industrial civilisation while permitting citizens and corporations to continue destructive behaviours in all those parts of the earth that are not specifically designated as wildlife reserves or national parks. Creating wilderness areas will have little ultimate ecological effect if corporate extraction of fossil fuels, or corporate pollution of watersheds, destroy the climatic conditions or fresh water on which species in these areas depend for their survival. The wilderness approach also has an analogous effect to the intrinsic value approach when it valorises the nation-state as the 'owner' and maintainer of wilderness areas, while excluding or restraining local residents from traditional use rights to areas set aside from normal uses. The unintended consequence of the wilderness or set-aside approach, as noted above, is often to alienate local communities from government-led or corporately managed conservation projects.

Given the failures of earlier approaches to ecological ethics to stem global and local reductions in biodiversity and destruction of habitats, a third approach has emerged in the last twenty years with the aim being to measure the monetary value of the services ecosystems and species render to human beings, and inscribe them in corporate and national accounts as 'natural capital'. This involves a significant intervention in the evolution of financial accounting. The origins of modern accounting may be traced to the invention of double entry bookkeeping by the Franciscan friar Luca Paciolli in the fourteenth century.[50] The great advantage of Paciolli's approach over previous accounting methods was its simplicity. Paciolli in effect changed the nature of accounting practice from a set of narratives to a set of numbers. With the requirement to keep two columns of numbers it becomes possible to arrive at a reliable representation of the activities of a friary or monastery, and later of business and public corporations, without reference to detailed and context-specific narratives about the factors of production, which traditionally were land and labour. The practice also involved a shift in accounting practice from a broad focus on what economists sometimes call 'use values' to a narrower focus on exchange values, either realised in corporate activities or remaining as potential in the assets of the corporation. This shift meant that descriptions of the lives of workers or domestic animals, or the conditions of plants, rocks, soils or water sources used during the accounting year, could be left out from the accounts.[51]

Double entry bookkeeping is the historical root of modern economics. Under its aegis modern economists hold that measures of exchange value are the appropriate means for determining the monetary value of a corporation's annual activities or the annual product of the natural and human resources of a nation-state. Where scarcity causes the market price of a non-renewable resource such as copper to rise, classical economists argue that alternative substitutable resources will be found or developed through human ingenuity and technical innovation.[52] But there are a range of cultural and natural goods – endangered species, a stable climate, potable water, clean air, human dignity and quality of life – which are not easily reducible to market mechanisms or measures of exchange value. Many of these goods are not conventionally bought or sold in markets, and they therefore do not show up on corporate or national accounting mechanisms. Ecological or environmental economists have thus begun to develop measures of the economic value of the benefits or services that ecosystems and species confer upon humans. They propose that such measures should be factored into the profit and loss or cost and benefit accounting procedures that guide economic planning and development, and hence corporate behaviours, in modern nation-states. In a global study, in which a range of studies of the value of particular ecosystem services were synthesised, it was estimated that the annual value contributed to economic activities by the ecosystem services provided by the planet was $33 trillion. The total value of the human trading economy, at the time of the study was estimated at $18 trillion.[53] In this light the human economy is clearly less valuable than the economy of the earth in which it is set, and furthermore is depleting natural wealth at a rate faster than it is being replaced by human wealth.

Ecological economists propose that Aristotle's classic distinction between exchange and use values – encapsulated in his distinction between *oikonomia* and *chrematistics* – remains valid. Hence citizens and parliaments ought to be capable of deliberating on environmental use values in such a way as to resist the modern default subjugation of use values to exchange values. They propose that such deliberation ought to inform environmental policy-making and hence require market actors to value use and not only exchange values.[54]

In practice, however, efforts to require market actors to recognise and account for use values lack cultural or political purchase. To give just one recent example, in the United States and Europe growing numbers of bees are suffering from the recent phenomenon of Colony Collapse Disorder (CCD). Bees pollinate two-thirds of the plants eaten by humans. Entomologists identified a link between CCD and the introduction in the last ten years of systemic pesticides – and in particular neonicotinoids – which are expressed through plants coated in such substances as seeds instead of being topically applied during growth.[55] This discovery, combined with protests by beekeepers, led to the banning of neonicotinoid pesticides in France and Germany. However in the United States, where such seeds were first introduced, and where CCD was first identified, the use of neonicotinoids continues. The UK government has similarly refused to ban neonicotinoids. The annual contribution of domesticated bee pollination services to US agriculture is estimated at $20 billion, and the value of wild insect services to US agriculture is estimated at $57 billion.[56] The combined annual profit of Monsanto and Cargill – the two largest global seed companies – were just $2.9 billion in 2009. But in a contest between exchange and use values, exchange values win in the economically neoliberal domains of the United States and the United Kingdom.

Key to the problem with attempts to render the intrinsic value of nature as 'natural capital' is that these carry the assumption that monetary value is a good way to promote environmental ethics and sustainable behaviours. However monetary appeals for 'valuing' nature do not have the intended effect. This is because appeals to money values affirm materialistic values and such values are precisely those that motivate corporations and individual citizens towards environmentally destructive practices to facilitate wealth accumulation at the cost of enduring and diverse ecosystems. Those who are most inclined to materialistic values tend to value relational sources of wellbeing *less* than others, including relations with nonhuman creatures and places, and hence to put a higher value on material consumption and wealth accumulation as intrinsic goods regardless of their effects on ecosystems or other species.[57] Appeals by governments, corporations and NGOs to respect the environment in order to save money, or to promote economic margins for corporations or households, tend to underwrite rather than challenge materialistic accounts of the human good, and hence undermine broader cultural recognition of the *intrinsic* value of behaviours and practices that promote care for ecological habitats.

Biodiversity and a stable climate are goods of inestimable value when their use to future generations is taken into account. But the materialistic ethos sustained by the dominance in economically liberal domains of the interests of private corporations, and the related marketing and promotion of consumer behaviours, gives priority to exchange over use values, and to the values realised by present over future persons. Artificial persons, though treated as equivalent to human beings in law, lack the capacity to become the kinds of people who express the moral character of those who love nature, and who use nature carefully and with forethought for future generations and other users both human and nonhuman. This is because the exclusive guiding goal of the Anglo-Saxon economic corporation is the maximisation of shareholder value, or profit. Efforts by conservation-minded citizens, NGOs and conservation scientists to restrain corporate economic activities therefore require resort to the nation-state and the law courts as the original source of the sovereign power of corporations. But there is a political, and hence a legal, reluctance to put environmental goods, and their use values to present and future generations, above corporate interests. This reluctance does not just reflect the political influence, and legal status and powers, of corporations. It is also informed by the preference of modern economists and a growing number of politicians for market allocation of the social and environmental costs of natural resource use since markets are said to be more 'efficient' than more deliberative forms of cost allocation by rational choice theorists.[58]

The refusal of corporate actors, and classical economists, properly to account for the inestimable gifts that the earth and the sun confer on humankind is a deep moral and philosophical conundrum, which is not resolvable by conservation projects that sequester parts of the environment – diversity hotspots, scenic places, endangered species – from the ravaging effects of an economy devoted to exchange over use values. Moral and legal appeals to intrinsic values have proven similarly insufficient. The 'conservation contradiction' identified above is thus revealed to be interconnected with the rising influence of artificial persons as corporations over the political and economic organisation of contemporary societies: the power and wealth of modern economic corporations, and their control over ever larger areas of the planet's surface, including subterranean minerals and fuels, grows apace. Neither scientific conservation, nor environmental ethics, are capable of preventing the resultant and persistent depletion of the health of ecosystems and destabilisation of the earth's atmosphere. This points to a deeper contradiction between the guiding logic of Western – and now global – civilisation and the health of ecosystems and the creatures that constitute and inhabit them.

On the face of it the project to measure the monetary value of ecosystem services, and incorporate these as 'natural capital' into corporate and national accounting procedures, presents the best device for reforming the advancing pace of ecological destruction. Unlike intrinsic value or wilderness ethics it presents the ecological problem in a numerical and monetary form that ought to be capable of incorporation into the accounting procedures and decision-making processes of economic corporations and government agencies. However, as we have seen, this approach tends merely to underwrite the cultural treatment of 'nature' purely in terms of her use value for economic activity and material accumulation. It is therefore unsurprising that efforts to incorporate natural capital into corporate and government accounts have proven ineffective in stemming ecological destruction. The best known of these efforts concerns the creation of markets in carbon emissions. But these markets are expensive to create, they encourage fraud, and they have proven ineffective.[59] In essence carbon credits are financial derivatives. As with other derivatives markets, trading in them has provided lucrative business for banks and investment houses but it has made no impact on the global rate of fossil fuel extraction.[60] In Europe carbon trading was introduced in response to the Kyoto Protocol but it has proven ineffective in persuading corporations, government agencies and private citizens to reduce their carbon-emitting activities. Trading in pollution permits began in the United States power industry as a way to reduce sulphur pollutants from coal-fired generators. Trade in pollution is designed to change the economic status of pollution from a social cost external to the market to an external good analogous to profit and loss measured on company accounts. Advocates argue that this approach is more efficient than government regulation. But this claim only holds true where corporate compliance with environmental regulation is weak, as it is in the United States.

There is a fourth major approach to environmental ethics that I have not yet touched on and this arises from the Aristotelian-influenced style of moral reasoning known as virtue ethics. In this approach the focus moves from commands, duties and values regarding nature to the virtues that characterise those individuals and communities who act rightly towards nature and their fellow inhabitants. After the Second World War, the prominent English philosopher Elizabeth Anscombe argued that the duties and values that philosophers since the Enlightenment have made the principal language of ethics are reductive because they fail to describe what makes some individuals behave well, and others badly, in similar circumstances.[61] Aristotle's emphasis on virtue requires attention to those institutions, practices, relationships and roles that shape the character of good people and direct their lives towards the good.[62]

Aristotle wrote in a society constituted by households as the fundamental unit. In his account the key spatial condition for the acquisition of virtue was the dwelling of people together in communities of place in which they were formed and nurtured over time. Modern societies, dominated as they are in many ways by the activities of national governments and multinational corporations, are organised on a much larger scale and this creates unique problems for moral formation. But even in the modern world, as Alasdair MacIntyre argues, small-scale communities – in the form of family, church, neighbourhood, school and workplace groups – are still the places in which individuals are formed as children either to live well or badly as adults.[63] Living well indicates an ability to realise the classical and Christian moral excellences, which include justice, humility, love and care. But such living well is threatened by the large scale of modern social structures in which people behave differently from how they do in small communities of place where they are known, and they and others can see the moral choices they make and their impacts on others whether for good or ill. In geographically dispersed social structures, the remoteness of procurement decisions obscures the burdens or costs they may impose upon others. A board member of a palm oil company may not intend to burn down a common use forest that is used by local people as a source of food and water for a new plantation. And a consumer of the product in which the palm oil grown there subsequently ended up may not wish that it had been made at such cost. But the scale and remote decision making of the multinational palm oil corporation make it possible for both to hold that they did not intend to cause the homelessness of an indigenous family when its forest home was burned for the growth of palm oil.

The virtues approach, as adapted by MacIntyre and other communitarian philosophers, underwrites the importance of small place-based communities in the formation of morally sensitive individuals. The virtues tradition has also been taken up by a number of environmental philosophers. Elsewhere I describe the ecological potential of the traditional virtues as follows: love for nonhuman beings and wild places, temperance in balancing human needs and the carrying capacities of ecosystems, justice in the use of the environments of other people and other animals, prudence in attending to the needs of future generations for a habitable planet that remains aesthetically enjoyable, courage in preparedness to challenge ecologically destructive behaviours and make the case for radical reform of industrial and corporate practices.[64] Exemplary practices that inculcate such virtues include learning to identify species by name and spotting them in trees or undergrowth, walking, cycling or canoeing in wild places, clearing trash or invasive species from foreshores, lakes, rivers or woodlands, recycling used materials and reducing waste and energy and material consumption in households and the workplace. Institutions where individuals might learn such skills include the family, schools, churches, clubs, higher education and conservation organisations devoted to such activities, and workplaces where sustainability is encouraged. Ecosystem communities in the natural world also play a crucial role. The biographies of environmental and ecological pioneers, such as Rachel Carson and E. O. Wilson, reveal that they were shaped in their love of nature by childhood encounters with wild places such as ponds and woodland.[65]

How though might a corporation be shaped and formed virtuously, and so as to love nature? For Aristotle, business is devoted to exchange values, or chrematistics, and this promotes the vices of avarice and usury, or lending money at interest. Only households can properly be said to be virtuous in their pursuit of *oeconomics* since in the household economic activity has the purpose of sustaining family and community and in this personal context is more likely to be characterised by the virtues of justice and temperance.[66] However, modern economists since Adam Smith argue that the business enterprise is capable of promoting the good of others regardless of whether it is a family business or a large-scale multinational economic corporation operating in many places at once, provided those who work in it devote themselves to making well the products they purvey and exchanging them according to the laws of the market economy. On this account individuals who work in business learn the virtues from the internal goods and practices that business promotes, such as accountability to others, skill in manufacture or personal service, and diligence, and from participation in economic markets.

For Robert Solomon, Aristotle's claim that businesses cannot be ethical neglects that they, and the individuals who work in business, are part of the *polis* or the wider community, which sustains citizens and forms them towards the good. Citizens work in businesses and, if they are rightly formed by the wider community, and participate honestly in market exchanges, they will behave responsibly in business. Businesses also foster many of the practices through which other moral communities – such as families or schools – foster virtuous individuals. Businesses are communities that foster loyalty, and inspire or require teamwork and cooperation. Businesses inculcate excellence in relevant skills such as bargaining and negotiating. Businesses foster interpersonal roles between seniors and juniors. All of these features make businesses analogous to other moral communities. There is therefore no ultimate antagonism between business and the common good.[67]

In Solomon's account businesses are no different to other communities of persons. They may love or hate nature no more or less. But there is a crucial problem that Solomon does not admit and this is that the guiding profit motive requires that businesses devote themselves to that good above other goods. The history of modern business has therefore required the elaboration of a great body of corporate law designed to restrain businesses from exploiting their workers unjustly, or unduly polluting the air and water around their premises or further afield. Geoff Moore also argues that businesses may still be virtuous if they exercise a balancing judgement between the bottom line – or external good – of profit and other internal goods such as care for their employees, and diligence in maintaining the quality of their products, though he neglects ecological concerns in his account.[68] But in the absence of regulatory changes in accounting rules, and changes in corporate law, corporations will not voluntarily include the full social or environmental costs of their activities for species and for present and future generations on their balance sheets.

Against the claim that businesses are no different morally from other human communities of practitioners, it cannot be said of a music teacher that she instils the good of excellence in performance or appreciation of great music in her pupils without exploiting them only because the law restrains her. A music teacher who needed such legal restraint would not be considered a good or a virtuous teacher. But a corporation that is not restrained by law will coerce its workers, as for example did the Chinese company Foxconn, which drove its workers so hard that they began to commit suicide.[69] Foxconn makes Ipads and Iphones for Apple Corporation – the world's second richest company. What of Apple Corporation's duties to the 'global community' (Solomon's term) from which it derives mammoth shareholder value? It designs its products in California, but exploits workers to make them in places thousands of miles from California. This is because to employ Californians to make the products in the places they are designed, manufacturing processes would need to be designed according to North American environmental and labour laws. Apple would therefore not be permitted to pollute the environment with cheap sulphurous coal to smelt aluminium for its computers, to deplete precious water supplies and pollute rivers to manufacture silicon chips, or to pay workers wages that do not permit them to live decent lives as householders instead of being coercively housed in factory dormitories on subsistence wages.

Virtue ethics has the considerable advantage over other approaches to environmental ethics of highlighting the importance of face to face relationships of education and nurture, and of small-scale communities of place, in the formation of moral agents. From this perspective multinational corporations are always at risk of creating a vicious character in their behaviour, that outweighs the virtues of the individuals that work for them, because of their large size, and the remoteness of their decision making chains. But like the other approaches to ecological ethics reviewed here virtue ethics still leaves us with a problem. How might citizens and communities teach environmentally vicious corporations environmental virtues? The conventional answer to this question is government regulation. But this is still prone to the libertarian critique of the growth of what Sunstein calls 'laws of fear'.[70] Government regulation is also prone to money politics and corporate lobbying. Where corporations buy political influence it is unlikely that politicians will promote effective environmental regulation of their activities. Is there another way?

Some argue that the answer is shareholder democracy. In this approach individual environmentally aware consumers buy shares in corporations and use their votes at shareholder meetings to persuade the companies to adopt more ecologically sustainable practices.[71] However, the votes of individual shareholders rarely change corporate policies, since the majority of shares are owned by other large corporations. Another approach is consumer pressure. Corporate environmental campaigns – such as the 'Green my Apple' campaign – have shown some success.[72] Before the campaign began in 2006, Apple computers were loaded with fire retardants, PVC, lead, mercury and other toxic elements, while Apple's 2011 products are actively promoted by Apple as free of such elements and hence 'environmentally friendly'. But against such gains it must still be acknowledged that if Apple made its products in the United States, its factories would have to meet much higher environmental and social criteria than they do in China.

To sum up, the conservation contradiction reveals a mismatch between the growth of environmental governmentality and the continuing devotion of private corporations to growth in shareholder value regardless of environmental destruction. On this account the devolution by the nation-state to economic corporations of its monopoly powers over the ecosystems and environmental spaces of its citizens and local communities is an important but largely unacknowledged root cause of the ecological crisis. Major legal reform of accounting practices designed to identify and bring into company balance sheets the full social and ecological costs of business practices is therefore essential if the guiding principle of shareholder value is not to continue the advancing pace of species and habitat destruction.

If, however, special interests and short-sighted law makers continue to resist social and ecological accounting reform and regulation, there is one other possible approach that might be pursued. Companies are controlled by executive directors, Board chairs and directors. Ecological education of this group of people – and many directors and chairs serve on more than one board – might offer another way forward. A major funded programme of environmental education for business leaders in the United States, Europe, Japan, China, India and Brazil – the locations of the majority of the world's largest company headquarters – might for example offer significant rewards. This programme would involve funded visits to wild and endangered habitats during which scientific information about threats to natural capital represented by declining species and habitats would be explained by leading scientists. The programme would also involve in-company education in the business and social benefits, as well as the ecological advantages, of corporations adopting the ecological virtues as enumerated above. Perhaps major donors, such as large philanthropic foundations in the United States, might be approached by the AAAS and NAS to fund such an educational programme. Ecologically virtuous corporations will ultimately only be shaped by changes in legal regulation of their responsibilities and of their accounting practices. But such corporations will also need to be led and managed by business leaders who have a fuller understanding of the mid and long term threats to human, as well as species, flourishing from continuing with 'business as usual'.

This proposal does not, however, address the problem of the large scale and remote operations of extra-national corporations. The more we learn about the character of ecosystems, and the complex symbioses that constitute relations between species and individuals within them, the more we discover that ecosystems are place and scale specific. They include within them a fund of animal and plant based local knowledge, which enables them to continue as support systems to their residents. And they do this in ways that are within scale to the geographic setting of ecosystems. Ecologists recognise the role of 'niches' in small-scale ecosystems in providing 'homes' for a variety of species. Biodiversity in ecosystems such as alpine meadow, freshwater ponds or tropical rainforest is therefore a function of the extent to which species interact in these settings to create niches for other species in what ecologists call species communities.[73] As Anthony Paul Smith argues, the niche is a model of the immanent habitat of plants and other animals that departs radically from pre-ecological conceptions of nature, such as the Darwinian metaphor of nature 'red in tooth and claw'.[74] Recognition of the niche valorises the capacity of species unwittingly to foster conditions in their own small-scale emplaced 'neighbourhood' for other species in mutual co-dependence upon them and hence to foster life in the midst of the 'dog eat dog' violence that also exists in every food chain.

Ecological science, more than Darwinian biology or genetics, has valorised small-scale communities of species as essential life vessels that have fostered the evolution of species that otherwise would not have lived.[75] These myriad small-scale communities of species together constitute the large-scale community of biodiverse species that make up 'spaceship earth', and which 'maintain' an equable climate for mammalian life. The recognition of the essential contribution of the small scale to the large is a guiding principle in E. F. Schumacher's *Small is Beautiful,* which was one of the most influential of environmental texts of the late twentieth century. A mining engineer by profession, Schumacher argued that giantism was central to many of the inconsistencies between modern social structures and institutions and the health of the small-scale communities of life which have evolved together to support life on earth in tens of thousands of places. Against the modern adulation of giantism, Schumacher argues for the virtue of smallness.[76] The closest analogy to smallness in the traditional canon of philosophical and theological virtues is humility, a virtue favoured as it happens by Christian rather than classical philosophers. Schumacher argues that if politics and economics are to be modified to reduce ecological destruction, and so to sustain biodiversity and a habitable planet for future generations, then they will need to be more humble, and hence smaller, and this means they should be organised more locally, in small communities of place characterised by face to face rather than anonymous, remote relationships. This is a radical proposal and it is easy to see why Schumacher's advice is largely neglected in a modern world increasingly dominated by large corporations.

Schumacher's attention to scale not only finds analogy in scientific ecology, but it has consequences for environmental philosophy and theology. Two important measures of the functioning of individuals and species within ecosystems are spatial size and temporal longevity: an elephant contrasts on both counts with a beetle. Consequently, an elephant can be a keystone species to the functioning of many other individuals and species within an ecosystem. Take out the elephant, or take out sufficient habitat for the elephant to roam, and you create a range of ecological problems. But ignore the beetles and you also create a range of problems, since they provide many ecosystem functions on which even elephants ultimately depend.[77]

The multi-scalar character of ecosystems is different from the hierarchical modes of organisation in which giant corporations and bureaucracies tend to function. This is a crucial, though often missed, reason why giantism tends to be ecologically as well as humanly destructive. Ecological accounts of the multi-scalar and intra-temporal character of the creation by species of apparently spontaneous order in ecosystems contrast significantly with reductionist economic accounts of the self-organising character of human societies conceived as large-scale 'markets' in capital, labour and commodities. As William Connolly argues there is a fragility to the character of ecosystems that is poorly captured by economic 'laws' of supply and demand and the efforts of economists and politicians to fashion institutions and organisational processes, which, they imagine, are analogous to the self-organising properties of ecosystems.[78]

Giantism is humanly, and not only ecologically, destructive. Persons depend for their flourishing on cognitive, embodied and moral capacities, which are uniquely complex and easily impaired in ways that give rise to mental or physical suffering. The larger the scale, and layers of hierarchy, involved in the social structuring of life, the greater the potential for stress and psychological and physical dysfunction to enter into human life experience. Epidemiological studies of large-scale organisations, such as a longitudinal study of the British civil service, reveal that low control over working circumstances among those at the bottom of large hierarchical organisations occasions raised levels of stress hormones, which promote high blood pressure, cardiovascular disease and mental illness.[79] This suggests that human beings are not well designed physically to live and work in hierarchies in which they have little agency or power. The research of Richard Wilkinson and Kate Pickett clearly evidences that significant levels of inequality of power and wealth, of the kind that are promoted by extensively layered hierarchies, and large remotely organised agencies, are a significant source of ill health both mental and physical. And the same research reveals that ill health occasioned by inequalities is not confined to those lower down the social scale but contributes to higher mortality rates, including infant mortality, among both rich and poor in highly unequal, and hence more socially stressed, societies.[80]

In the Hebrew Bible scale is also seen as a problem, as is indicated by the story of the Tower of Babel, and by the critique of kingship and the suspicion of empires in the history and prophetic books. Ara Norenzayan argues that monotheism of the kind first practised by the Hebrews was a response to the novel problems of scale that emerged in agrarian societies. In small-scale societies of the household and tribe, individuals are surveyed by other known individuals and this acts as a moral constraint on their actions. But in large-scale societies, of the kind that agriculture, food storage and the division of labour made possible, such moral constraints are absent. In this new cultural context an all-seeing God, who can observe a person's behaviour even when other persons do not, is therefore a device for limiting the power of individuals, and the potential for the misuse of power.[81] In the light of this proposal, it is notable how frequently in the Hebrew Bible reference is made to the all-seeing powers of Yahweh. In the Book of Job, Yahweh sees through clouds (Job 22: 14) and his eyes 'are upon the ways of man, and he sees all his goings' (Job 34: 21) and in Deuteronomy keeping the law is linked with the eyes of Yahweh: 'When you shall listen to the voice of the LORD your God, to keep all his commandments which I command you this day, to do that which is right in the eyes of the LORD thy God'. (Deuteronomy 13: 18).

But despite divine surveillance, the Hebrews inhabited the land of Israel in ways that increasingly saw land accumulating in the hands of an elite. The Hebrew prophetic critique of the amassing of land and political power by merchants and monarchs, and their alternative vision of self-sufficient small communities, is an ancient source of anarchist political ideals, and influenced Tolstoy, Gandhi and Ellul in their opposition to empires, large landed estates, and nation-states, and their advocacy of bottom-up, household and land-based forms of social order.[82] If giantism, and especially corporate and bureaucratic giantism, are at the heart of the modern ecological crisis, then breaking up large-scale organisations, reducing the tendency of corporations to spread their influence from one political territory to another, and increasing the capacity of small-scale communities of place to morally and ecologically govern their own places, will be crucial to its resolution. It is no wonder then that one of the most popular new myths of the twentieth century – J. R. R. Tolkien's *Lord of the Rings* – has at its heart just such a vision of a polity ordered by small face-to-face communities of the 'Shire' and not large-scale extractive enterprises of the kind described in Mordor. But in the real world the tentacles of corporate extraction continue to grow, and the chains of production and decision making become ever longer and more remote from the metropolitan centres of corporate power in New York, Tokyo, London and Beijing, encouraged as they are by the neoliberal philosophy that holds that territorially based governmental regulation of economic corporations is at odds with an economically productive social order.[83] Hence governments at the present time are becoming more reluctant to restrain the giantism of corporations that visit their rent-seeking behaviours on places far distant from their headquarters. And indeed governments in the United States, Europe and Asia are promoting new multilateral trade treaties that are clearly designed to promote the rights and interests of transnational corporations over local and national regulation of human and ecological goods and services. In this context, groups of citizens and communities in place have the primary moral responsibility to guard their local places and to try to find ways, legal or extra-legal, to restrain corporations from ecologically destructive developments. In the next chapter I show that religious communities situated in place can play just such a role.

4

Place, religion and resistance to corporate power

The largely treeless Hebridean island of Harris, off the west coast of Scotland, was the occasion of a major environmental controversy in the 1990s because of the submission of a plan by Redland Aggregates to locate a large quarry at Rodel on the coast of Harris. Like other parts of the Western Isles, Harris has a distinctive religious and linguistic culture, elements of which, and in particular Sabbath observance, were mobilised in significant ways in local and national debates about the proposed quarry. This distinctive religious culture was also the occasion for the presentation of theological arguments by expert witnesses, including a Hebridean Quaker ecologist, a Free Church Professor of Theology and a Canadian Native Indian Chief, at the public inquiry held in 1995 to adjudicate the planning application. Local evidence presented in opposition to the quarry focused on the potential damage the quarry would offer to local and traditional modes of production, including crofting and fishing, and to tourism. Local support for the quarry, because of the potential benefit of local employment it offered, gradually turned into opposition as the community realised through the lengthy process of the public inquiry that industrial development on the scale of the superquarry would mean the end of forms of religious and community life that people have enjoyed on Harris for many hundreds of years.

The public inquiry ultimately found against the proposed quarry. The proceedings of the inquiry and its eventual outcome demonstrate how local knowledge, traditions and ritual practices in a pre-industrial community of place present resources for resistance to corporate and bureaucratic sponsors of the capitalistic transformation of natural goods into units of industrial production. It also illustrates how religious discourses and practices, particularly as these occur in traditional religious communities of place, challenge the differentiation of social life into distinct realms, a differentiation that legitimates the priority of economic considerations, such as the prospect of employment, over the maintenance and preservation of cultural and environmental resources. The case also illustrates the importance of local communities recovering power from the State in pursuance of the related projects of nature conservation and the quest for more sustainable life-styles than those sponsored by the modern partnership between states and capitalist corporations.

The proposed superquarry was dubbed 'the final clearance' by a letter writer to *The Scotsman*, Scotland's Edinburgh-based newspaper of record.[1] The Clearances were a paradigmatic event in the history of the Scottish Highlands and Islands and appeals to their contested significance were to play an important role among resistors to the quarry. Mackenzie sees this appropriation of the symbol of the Clearances as part of the contested terrain of discourse and symbolism in the controversy surrounding the quarry. On the one hand advocates of the quarry proposed that it would provide jobs for the local community, thus stemming continuing migration of people from Harris, and other Hebridean islands, in search of economic opportunities. Opponents of the quarry, on the other hand, argued that the quarry was itself another, if not the final, clearance.[2] First the people and their crops and domestic animals had been cleared from the land, and now even those rocks that they left behind were to be cleared also.

The first ground of controversy over the quarry, and the occasion of much of the evidence at the public inquiry, concerned the claim that the quarry would offer a major economic opportunity to the local community, whose very existence was threatened by the spiral of depopulation and economic decline that the Clearances are said to have begun. Since the Clearances of the eighteenth and nineteenth centuries the remaining indigenous people of the Scottish Highlands and Islands have endured poor economic and environmental conditions and high unemployment. The Clearances involved the conversion of local subsistence economies, many of which were viable, some of which were thriving, and some very poor, into a new commercial system of land ownership and control designed to maximise rents and income from animal grazing. In the process thousands of people were driven from their homes, the timbers of which were frequently burnt as they left to ensure that they could not return to rebuild in a land with few trees. Some were put onto ships to Canada and Australia, or forced into local exile in the burgeoning industrial slums of Glasgow and Edinburgh. Lands that had supported traditional strip farming and cattle grazing, interleaved with broadleaf woodland to protect crops from the elements, were denuded of crops and trees and given over to sheep farming and to the raising of animals for sport, including grouse and deer.

The breaking up of self-subsistent Highland communities in the Clearances is represented variously by historians and in folk culture as internal coloni-sation, or even genocide, by the emergent British state, or as the inevitable outcome of poor farming practices combined with a growing population which the over-worked land could no longer sustain. The Clearances were preceded by the last Highland Rising, which was put down by the English at Culloden in 1746. Defeated chieftains had their lands confiscated and the 1747 Act of Proscription banned the carrying of arms, the wearing of

Highland dress, the playing of pipes and many other distinctive cultural practices throughout the Highlands of Scotland.[3] Resistance to the Clearances was very limited because in the main the 'reforms' were prosecuted by Highland chiefs, rather than by English landowners as they had been in Ireland. Highland chieftains and landlords saw the rich potential of these lands for sheep grazing and as sheep displaced people income from land increased dramatically.

The depopulation of the Highlands and Islands has continued throughout the twentieth century as employment opportunities have shrunk further with the continuing demise of the traditional subsistence and barter economy, and as the land itself has become more sparse as a consequence of over-grazing and of deforestation. Fraser Darling characterises the Scottish Highlands and Islands as 'wet desert' because of the extreme decline of biodiversity that the introduction of grazing animals and the demise of mixed forests and horticulture since the Clearances has brought about.[4] Economic conditions on the Hebridean Islands have been particularly difficult and in the last fifty years the islands have been subject to a continuing process of depopulation wherein the children of islanders have migrated to the mainland of Scotland, and further afield, in search of economic opportunities. However, this migration is also characterised by a pattern of return in later life, and is offset to a certain extent also by the phenomenon of incomers who move to Harris, and other Hebridean Islands, from Scottish cities, and from further afield, precisely because of their remoteness from metropolitan life and their distinctive cultural and communal traditions.

The response to the economic problems of the Highlands and Islands, which has been fostered by lowland planners and economists, despite the Land Reform legislation of the Scottish Parliament, has not challenged the concentrated pattern of land ownership established since the Clearances. In Scotland in 2010, 88 per cent of the land that is classed as rural was owned by approximately 2,000 individuals, or 0.04 per cent of the population.[5] Neither has it challenged the predominant use of rural land for sheep, deer and grouse rearing, with their dire impacts both on the land and on the human ecology and economy of Scotland: this use of land is both ecologically destructive and generates very little employment compared with alternative uses such as forestry and horticulture.[6] Instead government agencies, working in partnership with industrial corporations, have supported the establishment of large development projects such as hydroelectric generation, aluminium smelting, monocrop forestry and paper production. Large-scale quarrying is the most recent form of such industrial development in the Highlands and Islands and finds sponsorship by a combination of official government agencies, including the Scottish Office and the Department of the Environment, as well as quarrying companies.[7]

In response to a claimed rising demand for aggregate and a growing resistance to land-based quarrying in heavily populated England and Wales, because of its deleterious environmental effects, super-quarries are intended to capitalise on the increasingly exposed rocks of Scotland's eroded and under-populated coastal regions, whose minerals are shipped and traded as aggregate for highway construction in England and for large engineering projects such as the construction of new rail links and airport runways. Coastal quarries allow a large scale of aggregate production while they are said to minimise disutilities to nearby communities as much of the detrimental impact of quarrying is defrayed by remote coastal locations, which limit sight and sound of quarrying activity to sparse local populations, reduce the impact of blasting, and enable the use of ships, rather than lorries on local roads, for transportation. The ocean also provides a ready route for the importation of landfill, in the form of domestic, industrial and construction waste, which is typically used to refill quarrying sites.

Partly in recognition of government proposals on the provision of aggregate from coastal quarries in Scotland for construction projects in other parts of the United Kingdom, Ian Wilson, a businessman from Dunblane, purchased the mineral rights to a number of sites around Scotland, including Lingerabay on the Isle of Harris, and in 1991 his company, Redland Aggregates, submitted a planning application for the removal of 600 million tonnes of rock from Lingerabay over 60 years at an annual rate of extraction of 10 million tonnes.[8] Daily blasting would involve the use of 3.5 tonnes of explosive and the blasting of 30,000 tonnes of rock. The application also sought permission to expand an existing jetty, used for a small existing quarry, to permit the docking of bulk carriers of up to 120,000 tonnes capacity, for the hugely expanded scale of quarrying proposed. The proposed extraction would slice into the hillside of Roineabhal from 180 metres below sea level to 350 metres above, and would leave a giant hole in the ground some 2 kilometres long and 1 kilometre wide. The rocks at Lingerabay are pink anorthosite and of particularly high suitability for use as building and road aggregate, and the application rested on the case for increased demand for such aggregate outlined above.

The planning application was submitted to the Western Isles Island Council and was given a mixed reception by the people of Harris. Initially, the prospect of a large number of locally available jobs meant that it attracted a good deal of support from local people. The company claimed that the quarry would initially provide up to 30 local jobs, and that up to 140 jobs would eventually be created for local people.[9] Against this would be set the despoliation of the side of a mountain, which faces the sea, is more than ten miles from the nearest substantial community on Harris, and whose current inhabitants are sheep and sea birds. This setting of jobs against environmental degradation is a common tactic in development discourse, and in the case of Harris, as elsewhere, was designed to split the community. In particular it was intended to split locally born families from so-called 'white settlers', the pejorative language sometimes used to characterise Harris inhabitants who originate in the Scottish lowlands or England and move to Harris for its distinctive culture and landscape.[10]

A referendum to gauge island opinion on the proposed quarry was organised by the Harris Council for Social Service in 1993 and revealed precisely the kind of split that the developers might have hoped for, with 62 per cent of those voting in support of the quarry while 38 per cent opposed it. However, in 1995, towards the end of the public inquiry, a second referendum was held and this time the position was the reverse, with only 32 per cent favouring the quarry and 68 per cent against. The turnout for the second referendum was also much higher than the first, with 83 per cent of eligible islanders voting, 22 per cent more than on the previous occasion.[11] As a local councillor put it, this considerable turn around in island opinion was clear evidence that 'the quarry is not wanted by the community, who have delivered a decisive "no" to the developer'. Another councillor saw it as a 'triumph for local democracy over municipal high-handedness, secrecy and manipulation'.[12] Shortly after the referendum, and before the final summative submissions at the public inquiry, the Western Isles Council debated the superquarry and resolved by 21 votes to 8 that 'the nature and scale of the proposed quarry is prejudicial to the integrity of the area and compromises other developments which depend on clean air and water'.[13] The vote caused considerable controversy as the Council had until this point strongly supported the proposed quarry, and spent £375,000 on making the case for the quarry, including instructing a barrister to put the Council's case for it, alongside Redland Aggregates, at the eight month long public inquiry.

This dramatic change in opinion on the island was connected with the presentation and public airing of evidence submitted to the public inquiry, and with efforts by Redland Aggregates to suppress at the public inquiry the full scale of the potential impacts.[14] Districts involved with fishing expressed strongest opposition to the quarry after much evidence had been presented of the possible adverse effects on local fishing, for shell fish and other in-shore fish, as a consequence of the de-ballasting of large super-tankers before taking on the quarried aggregate. Environmentalists and marine pollution experts argued that ballast water from the tanks would contain contaminants from the aggregate and would also introduce foreign organisms into the seawater as it would have been taken on board from sea areas distant from Harris. Harris-originated shellfish fetch a market price premium because of their exceptional quality, which in turn rests upon the crystal clear and unpolluted waters of the seas around Harris. The threat to this industry became a major concern as the inquiry proceeded. The possibility that jobs in the fishing industry might be threatened by the quarry became even more controversial when it emerged that of the employment opportunities that the quarry would create, less than one quarter of these, around 30, would eventuate as long-term job opportunities for the inhabitants of Harris, the majority of jobs going to people elsewhere in the Hebrides and further afield. The other threat to jobs that the quarry was said to represent concerned the local tourist industry, which is currently the largest single source of employment on Harris. The gigantic scale of this industrial activity, with its associated noise and water pollution, would present a threat to the attraction of the unique environment of Harris to visitors. This threat would have a significant economic impact on local employment in tourism. Taken together these material threats to employment in fishing and tourism were significant factors in undermining the purely economic case for the quarry.

The underlying material significance of the discourse of the Clearances also asserted itself in the response of the local community to the evidence presented to the public inquiry. Witnesses argued that far from the quarry bringing extensive economic benefits *into* the community, it would instead be an extractive development, whose material outcome would involve not only the extraction of a very large quantity of rock from the island, but the loss of alternative economic and production opportunities, which are intricately tied up with the cultural distinctiveness and the unique natural heritage of Harris. The superquarry, its opponents argued, would have added to the depopulation pressures that the Highlands and Islands have continued to experience since the Clearances.[15] Advocates of the quarry had claimed, ironically, that it offered an opportunity for 'sustainable development', a language that was 'summoned as part of a modernist project of progress and growth: employment and economic prosperity would accompany the super-quarry and ward off the spectre of a community portrayed on the verge of extinction'.[16] The use of the language of sustainability was intended to subvert local environmental opposition by pointing to the prospect of new local jobs that would *sustain* the local economy. This polarisation between economic and environmental sustainability is a common feature of the deployment of the term 'sustainable development' in bureaucratic and corporate circles.

Despite their deployment of the language of sustainability, the urban-based corporate and bureaucratic elite lost the argument about the material outcomes of the proposed quarry in this remote and culturally distinctive rural and island community. The argument over outcomes of the quarry was not confined to economic criteria among the islanders, nor lost on these grounds alone. Suspicion about the underlying presuppositions, and even the framing of the evidence, by advocates of the quarry, began to emerge as the inquiry proceeded. This suspicion appears to have been related to the deeper cultural issues that are at stake in the controversy over the superquarry. During the long eight-month saga of the public inquiry, the islanders came to perceive the superquarry not just as a cost-benefit calculation of jobs lost and jobs gained, but as a threat to the distinctive character of their island community, and not just to the integrity of its natural environment, but to the integrity of its unique cultural and religious identity.[17]

When Hebridean ecologist Alastair McIntosh declared in his oral and written theological testimony to the public inquiry that he opposed the quarry 'because it was not part of the movement of love', a Scottish journalist observed that Redland Aggregate's inquiry team found it difficult to keep a straight face.[18] McIntosh's testimony was part of a half day of presentations by himself, drawing on a distinctive combination of Celtic shamanism, biblical exegesis and liberation theology, and by his two supporting witnesses, Professor Donald MacLeod, a Free Church Professor of Theology, also hailing from Harris, and Chief Sulian Stone Eagle of the Mi'kmaq Nation in Nova Scotia, Canada. The occasion for this unique day of theological or spiritual testimony was McIntosh's argument before the Chief Reporter of the inquiry in her precognitions in Edinburgh that the distinctive religious culture and community of Harris, under which the issue of Sunday working would be considered at the inquiry, legitimated the presentation of related theological arguments on the matter of the quarry.

The people of Harris, like all those of the Outer Hebrides, are devoted to a particular style of Scottish Presbyterianism whose adherents hold to a very strict moral code based upon close adherence to the Ten Commandments. Their ritual life is also patterned on the Commandments and on interpretations of elements of ancient Israelite culture in which the Commandments were first promulgated. Worship in Presbyterian churches on Harris is a unique cultural experience, involving a good deal of plain talk and long sermons, very infrequent celebrations of the Lord's Supper, and instead of modern hymn singing, rhythmic and harmonic recitation of the Hebrew Psalter in Gaelic. The rituals of the Free Church resonate very strongly with two of the Old Testament Commandments, the first being the prohibition of idolatry – hence the plainness of the rituals and ritual spaces of Harris churches – and the second being the commandment to observe the Sabbath. Life on Harris comes to a virtual standstill on Sundays. No work is to be performed on Sunday in Harris. All hotels and shops are closed and no newspapers are sold. Ferries run up to midnight on Saturday and from midnight on Sunday, but not at all in between. Harris householders save their washing up from the Sunday meal for Monday morning, or else time their dishwashers to come on at midnight. Anyone who hangs out washing or cuts peat for the fire on a Sunday is at risk of being ostracised by their neighbours.

Unlike the rest of Scotland, where an average of 11 per cent of Scots attend church once every Sunday, approximately 54 per cent of people on Harris and the other large Hebridean islands attend church at least once on a Sunday, many twice, and many a mid-week service as well.[19] This distinctive religious culture is strongly at variance with mainland Scotland, where Sabbath observance is mostly a distant memory and shops open seven days a week. And it was the preservation of this culture that was of most concern to the islanders when they first encountered the quarry proposal from Redland Aggregates. The islanders were much less concerned about threats to the unique environment of Harris than they were about threats to the ritual time by which the Sabbath observance confers sacred significance on their lives.

Until the public inquiry, religious and cultural concerns about the superquarry had been primarily articulated on Harris in relation to the distinctive ritual and temporal concerns arising from the Sabbatarian traditions of the people. In response Redland Aggregates had drawn up a Sunday Agreement with the Island Council, under which the company undertook that there would be no work on Sunday at the quarry barring emergency, such as flood or storm, and 'essential maintenance' needed to enable the first shift to start work on time on Monday morning.[20] There would also be no regular loading or unloading of ships on Sunday, though again if they were delayed by bad weather they would be allowed to berth on a Sunday. However, the Sunday Agreement did not resolve the issue and there were concerns among the islanders both about the partial nature of these conditions and about the extent to which they actually bound the future operators of the quarry to abide by them.

Sabbath observance was the principal religious issue raised at the inquiry. John Reed, Queen's Counsel for the Western Isles Island Council, raised the concern that the Sunday Agreement was not legally enforceable by the Council on the quarry operators, and that it would be even harder for the Council to enforce it against third parties such as shipping companies. The Reverend Kenneth MacLeod, a local minister, argued in his oral testimony that the Sabbath was a crucial local amenity the keeping of which was a moral issue that was fundamental to the ordered life of the people of Harris, who are law-abiding and among whom there is no crime. He and other church witnesses were concerned that, ultimately, reverence for profits would take priority over reverence for the Lord's Day, and that in a part of the world given to violent extremes of weather, the quarry operators would seek to make up for lost time by working on the Sabbath. MacLeod and other church witnesses testified that they saw the quarry as a threat to the ordered and religiously-rooted life of the community of Harris and expressed the view that its putative social and economic benefits might not be realised, while it could do lasting harm to the culture of the Western Isles if Sabbath observance were undermined. Another church witness quoted Psalm 121 – 'I to the hills will lift up mine eyes, from whence doth come mine aid' – and observed that 'I will lift up mine eyes to the quarry' did not have the same ring.[21] A further concern raised was about the impact of the quarry on the 'cultural asset' of an ancient place of worship. St Clement's Church in Rodel stands only yards from the proposed borders of the superquarry and its foundations would be shaken by the constant passage of heavy machinery and the use of heavy explosives to blast the rock.[22] The church is of the same ancient Lewisian gneiss rock as the planned superquarry, and is of cruciform shape with a substantial tower, built around 1520 by the Chiefs of the MacLeods of Harris. Its location reflects the presence of an Augustinian monastic community at Rodel in the pre-Reformation era and hence the quarry would also disturb a place that has long spiritual associations.[23]

Having argued that the Sabbath issue permitted a broader consideration of theological concerns, McIntosh led a half day of theological testimony before the inquiry, which, while it did not figure in the Reporter's final judgements, nonetheless attracted much publicity on Harris, in the rest of Scotland and further afield. McIntosh's opening argument referred to the anthropological premise of the Calvinist Westminster Confession that the chief aim of man is 'the glorification and enjoyment of God'.[24] McIntosh argued that God is glorified or reverenced by humans and by nature, citing the Hebrew Prophet Isaiah as evidence: 'the mountains and hills will burst into song before you, and all the trees of the field will clap their hands' (Isaiah 55: 12). The providential and sustaining action of God is also revealed in the non-human creation and this is why wild places such as the Outer Hebrides are places where people have traditionally experienced a 'composure of soul'. Against advocates of the quarry who argue that Harris is like a moonscape, and that the quarry will not fundamentally alter an already desecrated landscape, McIntosh argued that the Lewisian Gneiss glaciated scenery of Harris, and other parts of 'the Celtic fringe on the Western edge of the continent of Europe' have inspired some of 'the greatest poetry, song and music of the European tradition'.[25]

McIntosh's argument, like MacLeod's, which followed, proposed a Calvinist theological aesthetic in which the conservation of wild space is both out of respect for the Creation as a 'theatre for the glory of God' and because in wild and magnificent places such as the Hebridean shore people experience evidence of the 'nature-conserving Creator who "sendeth forth his spirit" and "renewest the face of the earth ... who laid the foundations of the earth"'. Against the economic value of the aggregate, McIntosh argued that the 'undesecrated' land of Harris has a spiritual value, which requires that humans respect its 'integrity'. Reverence for nature is indicative of reverence for the Creator who sustains the creation and who gave Noah the sign of the rainbow as a sign that 'God will never again lay waste to the Earth', a symbol that is 'observed with frequency in the Western Isles'.[26]

Professor Donald MacLeod opened his testimony by drawing on Calvinist, and Highland, theology in the affirmation that 'God as creator has absolute sovereignty over the environment' and that 'we must use it only in accordance with his will'. Human use of nature will be part of God's judgement of the individual at the Day of Judgement when 'we shall answer collectively, as well as individually, for all our decisions in this area'.[27] Like McIntosh, MacLeod also argued that 'the primary function of creation is to serve as a revelation of God' and that despoliation of the kind the superquarry represents 'disables creation' from performing this function. The people of Harris are, like all created people, intimately linked to the soil and have a responsibility to till the soil and to keep it, since the bible 'designates man as the guardian and protector of the ground'.[28] MacLeod argued that the conflict over the quarry was ultimately a conflict between capitalism, and a promise of jobs to sustain the economic viability of the island community, and the deepest instincts of the people of Harris, which are to guard the land as their Christian calling.

MacLeod's testimony raised an issue that had begun to figure elsewhere in the debate over the quarry, and this is the extent to which the proposed development would challenge the cultural traditions of the people of Harris, including the connection between their religion and their traditional agrarian way of life, which derives livelihood from the keeping of the land. This potential threat to the community's cultural identity also came to the fore in the testimony of Sulian Stone Eagle Herney of Cape Breton Island, Nova Scotia, who argued that the people of Harris are an indigenous people, like his own people, whose land was also the subject of a superquarry planning proposal, and whose way of life was also threatened by 'the environmental destruction that is plaguing all of mankind'. He compared the threat from the quarry to the people of Harris with the longer term threats to the cultural identity of his own Mi'Kmaq people, threats that originate in 'the influence of non-natives to our territory', who 'became parasites of Mother Earth, thus destroying her natural bounty'.[29]

The articulation, by both a Free Church Professor of Theology and a Canadian First Nation Chief, of the potential threat that the superquarry represented to the religious and cultural identity of the community was a significant moment in the wider publicity surrounding the public inquiry and the history of the superquarry proposal. During the inquiry, the people of Harris began to see themselves as an indigenous people whose distinctive and religiously guarded way of life was threatened by a non-native development whose economic outcomes, which were presented as a device to preserve the community, were in fact more likely to destroy its unique integrity and way of life. In the end environmentalist discourse about threats to wildlife, or the destruction of a mountain, did not count for much for the indigenous people of Harris. What did count was the realisation of the fragility of their culture.[30] The presence of Stone Eagle was a powerful symbolic pointer, much imaged in the media, to the danger that the scale and intensity of the superquarry, by introducing the alien, non-native culture of industrialism, would disrupt the ordered temporality of a Sabbath-observing community, that this alien culture would destroy the integrity of one of the last indigenous communities of Northern Europe.

The interaction of culture, religion, nature and power in the Harris superquarry inquiry and its aftermath illuminates the cultural and political potential of local communities of place in at least two ways. It underwrites the importance of the micropolitics of local communities of place as they struggle with large corporate and governmental actors over the use of their own local places in the pursuit of industrial development in a global economy. It also has significance for the differentiation between human cultural identity and natural places, which modern capitalist culture increasingly sustains, and the related differentiation between communities of place and economic and political power. The resistance of the people of Harris to the proposed development of their island in the pursuit of the industrial transformation of the environment represents a place-based rejection of the global utilitarian discourse of cost and benefit, which sets the costs of ecological destruction to particular communities of place against benefits to the larger political community. In this discourse the people of Harris began to detect a hidden corporate strategy to incorporate the landscape of Harris into the global economy. Their suspicion was not, however, aroused primarily by the issue of ecological destruction, which was mostly raised by outside bodies, such as Scottish Natural Heritage, and by outside witnesses, such as McIntosh and McLeod, but by the perceived threat to what we may call the *human* ecology of the island, which was characterised by the different pace of life in which work is ordered by the practice of the Sabbath.

Redland Aggregates had sought to divide the community using a traditional anti-environmentalist strategy, setting nature conservers against people and community preservers. But ultimately the strategy backfired for, as McIntosh confesses in his testimony, the people of Harris do not have an 'environmental theology', but what they do have, and what they came to realise during the public inquiry, is a religiously and culturally distinctive way of life that is intimately connected with a particular *place* and landscape, and with the distance of its locale from the alien way of life of the metropolitan world.

Environmentalists and metropolitan capitalists both deployed discourses for their competing ends at the public inquiry, which differentially deploy a shared nature–culture distinction. Both environmentalist and capitalist discourses used at the inquiry assumed an opposition between the conservation of wild nature and the material needs of people. Both of these binary dualisms are the legacy of Cartesian mechanistic cosmology and of Enlightenment rationalism in Western culture.[31] Environmental philosophers argue that only when Western culture resolves this fundamental tension between conceptions of human selfhood and self-interest and conceptions of 'wild' nature, will modern societies begin to recover modes of economic and cultural production that do not rely on the further fragmentation of ecosystems.[32] But this distinction is not shared by indigenous groups whose places are threatened by development projects. Hence some environmentalists argue that Westerners still have something to learn from indigenous communities.

The defence of their community, and its place, by the people of Harris, was represented by advocates of the superquarry, and in some press comment, as an example of 'nimbyism' (not in my back yard-ism). The argument went that the aggregate was needed for the transport infrastructure of the United Kingdom and that if it could not be quarried in this remote region of Scotland, then it would be necessary to quarry it in Norway or in some other community. By taking a stand against the quarry the people of Harris could therefore be said to be displacing the environmental costs of development onto some other community in some other place. However, this accusation of nimbyism is another classic feature of global corporatist and developmental discourse. It relies on an underlying utilitarianism, which sets particular communities and particular places that may be harmed by a certain economic development against the benefits that the larger political community may be said to derive from these localised costs.[33] Thus, in the case of local pollution to fishing grounds as a consequence of quarrying on Harris, civil servants typically set the reduced journey times of English motorists on widened roads built with Hebridean aggregate, whose saved time is quantified in monetary terms, against the smaller monetary losses of a small number of fisherfolk, and reductions in biodiversity, in the place destroyed by the quarry.

In his fine ethnographic study of rice farming communities in the Northern states of Kedah and Perlis in West Malaysia, James Scott identifies a range of tactics of resistance that farmers and labourers used to defend themselves and their identity against the new urban landlords who have become the dominant power in the region as the costs of new hybridised seeds and expensive fertilisers have driven many subsistence and small farmers to bankruptcy.[34] Scott found that the tactics of the weak involved the use of irony and wit, petty theft and forms of subversion, which, while presenting no major threat to the economic power of the new landowners, nonetheless subverted their authority and enabled the local people to survive and to maintain some of their dignity. The amused reaction of the corporately hired lawyers to McIntosh's reference in his inquiry testimony to a 'movement of love'; the realisation that the people of Harris are an indigenous people and share the threat to their way of life experienced by indigenous peoples all over the world as modern industrial capitalism seeks new territory to transform into economic resources; the irony that observance of the Sabbath came to count for more than the promise of corporately sponsored jobs: these are all analogous to the tactics of resistance of which Scott speaks.

The universalising discourse of cost and benefit misconstrues the relationship between the flourishing of persons in particular communities and the *places* in which these communities are located; and this misconstruction arises, at least in part, from the atomistic and rationalistic account of human selfhood and the mechanistic account of 'nature', which are both features of Enlightenment philosophy. Plumwood argues instead for a conception of self-in-relation, which conceives of the identity of the self as constructed in relation to significant others, where others are not only persons but also the particular natural spaces in which a person first discovers their embodied identity in the material world of nature.[35] This has important implications for ethics because, instead of the exaltation of conceptions of impartiality and anonymity as guarantors of ethical propriety in utilitarian ethics, this approach finds being-in-relation, compassion and care to be core components of ethical experience and discernment.[36] Thus, efforts of resistance towards environmental depredation of the places that particular persons and communities actually inhabit are not to be understood as selfish nimbyism but rather as expressions of the relational character of ethical consciousness. Such an approach involves an ethical validation of the attachments to place that are most characteristic of the spatially stable lives of indigenous communities, and least characteristic of the lives of metropolitan persons, such as the author of this book who may have rediscovered an attachment to place in Durisdeer, but has no roots there and does not even live there all the time.

The attachment to place that finally triumphed in the attitude of the people of Harris toward the proposed superquarry is not primarily located in a distinctive attitude to 'nature' as distinct from persons. It is rather a feature of a larger constellation of symbols, pathways, life patterns and rituals that together constitute the distinctive religious and cultural identity of the Sabbath-observant people of Harris. In their experience of this constellation, indigenous communities such as the people of Harris reject, because they have never embraced it, the fundamental distinction between nature and culture, and the related distinction between religion and social power, which have become the reigning presuppositions of modern political and religious theory and practice.

Scotland, like most of the United Kingdom and Northern Europe, is a society characterised by a considerable degree of secularisation. The sociological theorisation of secularisation has laid emphasis upon three related processes, which characterise modern societies and accompany the process of secularisation, and these are rationalisation, differentiation and societalisation.[37] The public discussion of the Harris superquarry subjected elements of all three processes to critical scrutiny. As we have seen the rationalisation of a local pollution problem by reference to the larger benefits to society was rejected, as was the economic rationalisation of jobs versus cultural and ecological disruption. The people of Harris also rejected the modern differentiation of social life into different spheres, such as education, economic activity, entertainment, domestic life and religion. On Harris economic activity is controlled by religious time. Similarly, behaviour within the routines of domestic life is not a private affair but subject to public scrutiny and to the publicly affirmed moral codes of the dominant religious community. For the people of Harris religion plays a central role in political decision making, hence the inclusion of religious rituals, beliefs and value systems in the evidence admitted to the public inquiry. Like most indigenous communities, Harris recognises no separation of spheres of the kind obtaining in modern states between the religious and political, or between private (religious) life and public (political) life.

Resistance to the superquarry on Harris may be interpreted as a principled religious rejection by an *indigenous* community of key features of the secular culture of modern societies, and in particular the splitting apart of religious rituals and codes of behaviour – such as the Ten Commandments – and the power relations that characterise state governance and economic production. Like resurgent Muslims in Iran or Malaysia, the Hebridean islanders hold to a holistic approach to religion and culture, which sustains the authority and social power of religion at all levels of social life. Casanova observes that the

conventional sociological theorisation of secularisation has a hard time
with the public role of religion, of the kind evident on Harris, and increasingly evident in other parts of the world, not least in places where various
forms of fundamentalism have arisen. He argues that such resistance is
not necessarily to be read, however, as evidence of 'an antimodern funda-
mentalist reaction to inevitable processes of modern differentiation', but
may better be understood as 'counterfactual normative critiques of dominant
historical trends, in many respects similar to the classical, republican, and
feminist critiques'.[38]

Giddens calls this kind of resistance to dominant trends in modernity 'life
politics' and suggests that the role of religious traditions in this kind of
resistance is one of the possible consequences of the hegemonising tendencies
of the putatively progressive modern project.[39] Ecological life politics
involves the rejection of the universalising power procedures of modern
nation-states, which subvert the capacity of local communities to order their
own natural places in favour of a larger project of governance that hands
control over to bureaucrats and democratic representatives who are
predominantly representatives of a metropolitan culture in which corporate
capitalism is the dominant production and cultural force.

The impersonal procedures of modern production systems generate a
disarticulation between people and place, which is one of the principal features
of societalisation, the third social process that has contributed to secularisation.
Societalisation involves the transformation of human exchange relations from
ones that rely on face-to-face relationships between persons who are known
to one another into rational and impersonal systems in which most transactions
take place between persons who are unknown to each other, and that therefore
depend on varying degrees of trust and increasingly of risk and electronic or
legal surveillance. Once again in rejecting their incorporation into this larger
anonymous economy of risk and surveillance, the people of Harris are
effectively affirming a cornerstone of the distinctive religious culture of their
island – face-to-face community – while at the same time rejecting one of the
key social processes that generate secularisation.

The religio-cultural character of resistance to the superquarry on the Isle
of Harris points to a larger set of phenomena in the emergent life politics of
late modern societies, in which the progressive discourses of modern
development, even of 'sustainable' development, are sometimes countered
by the ironic articulation of seemingly weak and powerless symbols and
rituals, such as Sabbath observance, in small indigenous communities that
are on the frontiers of the territorial expansion of metropolitan capitalist
culture. As Mackenzie states, through these symbols opponents of the quarry
in the community created 'an alternative framework of meaning which
implicitly challenged the claims to truth of Redland Aggregate Lafarge's
discourse of sustainable development'.[40]

The entry of religious rituals and cultural symbols into the public world
of economic development and legal judgement at the superquarry public

inquiry may also be said to represent a challenge to the political arrangements under which nation-states partner and champion the corporate industrial assault on nature, for in indigenous communities there is no separation between place and community, persons and nature, religion and politics, or ultimately public and private. The prominent role of religious functionaries, rituals and symbols is an emergent feature of environmental resistance in places as diverse as Borneo, Rajasthan, Thailand and Zimbabwe.[41] Max Oelschlaeger argues that the secular discourses of scientistic progress and economic welfare lack the motive power to change the direction of modern civilisation, whereas, by contrast, religious traditions present a significant resource in the expression of ecological dissent to the utilitarian framing of human–nature relations.[42] Analogously, J. Baird Callicott argues that the different world religions present a shared discourse of responsibility for the earth which modern humans urgently need to recover as their sheer numbers as a species have enhanced so dramatically their physical dominance over, and hence responsibility for, the planet.[43]

The Harris superquarry story indicates the potential role that religious traditions can play as a vehicle for the expression of a human ecology, in which the welfare of place and of people are intricately connected. It is evidence of what I have elsewhere called 'parochial ecology', in which communities of place recover from the universalising hegemony of State and corporate actors a collective sense of responsibility for their own locale, including the birds, grasses, shrubs, trees, waterways and airways that delineate the pathways and rituals of local community life.[44] This parochial ecology does not, however, sustain, nor is it sustained by, a dualistic sense of the sacrality of nature, as opposed to ordinary (secular) human life. Instead, it expresses consciousness of the commonality of createdness that persons share with other creatures, and of the relationality of the human quest for transcendence to the emplaced habitats that the earth affords for that quest to find ritual and communal expression. In the next chapter I review a case study of the mainstream approach to conservation in Scotland, in which environmental *exclusion* of people from involvement in land use is viewed by landowners and nature conservation organisations as the preferred route to a 'sustainable' Scottish rural environment.

5

Wilderness, religion, and ecological restoration in the Scottish Highlands

The Lairig Ghru is one of the great wilderness walks of Scotland, approaching as it does the wild and rare mountain scenery of the Cairngorm plateau through some of the most beautiful landscape in the British Isles. The air is so pure that tree trunks and rocks are shrouded with a profusion of silver, green and blue lichens. A path through the dark mossy pine wood above the Linn of Dee car park reaches a track that follows the Luibeg Burn, a tributary of the Dee, which wends its way along the floor of a broad and gracious valley surrounded by striking rock formations and steep grassy slopes. The track runs over a bridge alongside the burn, and then above the meandering river, following the contours through a classic glaciated, heather-covered valley dotted with ancient Scots pine and the stone outlines of old crofting settlements, uninhabited since the Clearances. At the track's end is Derry Lodge, an old and now disused shooting lodge, around which the river meanders as it meets up with another Dee tributary, the Derry, and the mountain scenery begins to open up. An old wooden footbridge takes the walker across the Derry and up Glen Luibeg. This glen is one of the most delightful in Scotland. Far from any road or human habitation, it takes the walker into the heart of the Cairngorm plateau. As the valley walls get steeper, so the striking bronze red – the colour of sunset washed desert in Arizona or New Mexico – of the upper branches of old Scots pine becomes sharper to the eye, and the green glades of these rare indigenous trees present a soothing contrast with the harsh scree and bare rock faces of the encroaching mountain slopes. In this extraordinary landscape just one small patch of ground reveals a myriad diversity of alpine plant and insect life, a telling reminder of how biodiversity flourishes far from metalled roads and human habitation.

For all its apparent wildness, this landscape is still shaped by human beings, as witness the broad white sand tracks, the uninhabited shooting lodges, and the mountain huts on the floors of the glens. But a new force is at work in the Cairngorm. The National Trust for Scotland now owns the Mar

Lodge estate, which incorporates the Eastern side of the Cairngorm plateau and its approaches, and its vision is to return this beautiful area to pristine wilderness. This project was visible to this walker a few years ago. The first evidence was the destruction of the old vehicle bridge over the Luibeg at Derry Lodge. As I crossed the peat bog on the approach to the delightful Glen Luibeg, the noise of machinery came into earshot and a two-man team rose into view who, with the aid of a bulldozer and earth cutter, were reducing the unsightly white gash of the vehicle track, used for transporting shooting parties in Land Rovers, into a narrower sand and rock path through the trees and up the valley. They were therefore replanting heather across the old broad track, and repairing its cuts into the contours with repositioned peaty grasses. The human mark on the landscape was being systematically reduced, minimised, and the beauty of the wild 'restored'.

Other than *Homo sapiens*, the other species that has the capacity to shape this landscape for its own ends is the red *Roe deer*, which are now the principal beneficiaries of the peaty soils and rich water and air of these valleys. Roe deer have been managed for sport across Scotland since the nineteenth century, as the strip farms and byres of poor but self-sufficient crofting communities were destroyed to make way for the vast houses and sporting estates of the would-be aristocratic lairds of modern Scotland after the Clearances. The deer roam this wilderness in large and voracious herds, with the consequence that the groups of Scots pine that dot the landscape are unable to replenish themselves, as the deer eat anything that pokes its head above the height of the unappetising heather. Only in those areas fenced off from the deer is it possible for the forest naturally to regrow. In one such area, close to the Luibeg Burn, the resultant natural spread of seedlings and small trees among the heather forms a parkland of exquisite delicacy. Some suggest that the answer to the deer problem is to reintroduce wolves into the Scottish hills, after the example of some of the National Parks in the American West, which will provide a natural predator and help to keep the growing numbers of deer in check. In the meantime the culling of deer with the gun, and for sport, are the only ways to prevent the land from being eaten up by their growing numbers. And as the deer are reined in, the tracks and bridges removed, and the shooting huts and lodges, like the crofters' cottages, turn to uninhabited ruin, the Southern Cairngorms are reverting to a 'wilderness' the like of which has not been seen for generations.

The broken walls of the crofts are a reminder that not much more than a hundred years ago a different relationship obtained between humans and the land in this 'wilderness'. Until the mid-nineteenth century crofters dug peat for warmth, grew oats and barley, gathered wild honey, fished the rivers and lochs to feed themselves and their animals, and distilled whisky with the pure water of the glen to cheer themselves on cold winter nights. What the city-dwelling walker or stalker visits as wilderness, and into which he/she brings special clothing, rations, compass and map in order to survive, the Highlander saw as a bountiful, as well as beautiful, land where God had placed most that was needful for a good life. For the Gael, nature was not so much something to admire or to moralise about, as a great community of life of which they were also a natural, integral part.[1]

The idea of mountains as places of wild beauty, and in need of protection from human dwelling and shaping in order that they may be enjoyed in their pristine form, originates in the Romantic protest against the forces of industrialism and urbanisation that first drove the crofters from the Highlands. John Ruskin and John Muir were among the most influential English and Scottish advocates of the new idea of mountains as places of beauty. Ruskin, schooled in the Burkean idea of nature as sublime, viewed jagged mountain ranges and their surrounding regions as a ruin or dilapidation of an original form of creation, which would have been far more beautiful.[2] John Muir on the other hand, schooled only by his walks in the mountains and his Scottish Presbyterian upbringing, regarded the Sierra Nevada Mountains of the American West as a place that manifested the 'beauty of the lilies' as praised by Christ in the Gospels, and owned that 'man alone, and the animals he tames' were capable of destroying the reflection of divine glory in the mountains.[3] Whereas Ruskin viewed wilderness as a place marked by a primeval fall of the creation from some imagined state of greater perfection, Muir had no doubt that in the mountains he was closer than ever to the original beauty of the earth. These contrary judgements about the meaning of mountains are also in synergy with the descriptions of the strikingly different emotions that the mountains evoked for Ruskin and Muir. The Romantic adulation of the sublime advanced feelings of terror, which prefigured the adrenaline-filled rush of the modern mountaineer as he approaches the terrifying summit of a mountain like Ben MacDui on the Cairngorm Plateau when it is draped in snow and ice.[4] But instead of terror, Muir speaks of being exhilarated by the mountain air and of an 'excess of wild animal joy' as he walks in the high country of the Sierra with an Indian companion.[5]

The displaced Crofters who dwelt in many Highland regions that are now cleared of human habitation knew something of terror and something of joy as they actually lived in, rather than just visited, these harsh mountainous regions. No doubt life for the crofter in the Highlands was harsh and raw, a struggle for survival against the often hostile elements of wind and rain, and for sure some left in the nineteenth century of their own free will. But for many who were evicted from their ancestral homes and lands the life they lost was also one of joyful exaltation in the beauty and freedom of the high land. The combinations of gratitude and struggle, gaiety and suffering mark Highland culture and religion; their contrasting echoes may still be heard in the mellifluous singing of the Psalms in Gaelic in island communities in the Hebrides, which is one of the last living reminders of the Celtic religion of the Gael. These echoes may also be heard in the prayers collected by Alexander Carmichael in his *Carmina Gadelica*, many of which are indeed prayers of celebration for the present providence of God in the elements, while others are prayers for protection and survival:

> The Three Who are over me
> The Three Who are below me
> The Three Who are above me here
> The Three Who are above me yonder
> The Three Who are in the earth
> The Three Who are in the air
> The Three who are in the heaven
> The Three who are in the great pouring sea.
> Thou, my soul are in the great pouring
> Keep me at morning
> Keep me at noon
> On rough course faring
> Help and safeguard
> My means this night
> I am tired, astray, and stumbling
> Shield Thou me from snare and sin.[6]

If these prayers, transcribed and translated by Alexander Carmichael in his Highland wanderings in the late nineteenth century, are true echoes of the religion of the Gael, with its evocation of the Three's provision of a guiding moral frame in the bible, and dual recognition of the bounty and terror of nature, then it provided a very different approach to the meaning and the care of wilderness than do Ruskin or Muir, or even the National Trust for Scotland. Crofters dwelt on the land, but their dwelling did not create the biological devastation that the animals that displaced them have brought about. Whereas much of the Highland region today is classified by biologists as wet desert, it sustained much greater levels of biodiversity precisely at the time when it was managed by crofters. Under the management of the Lairds, who introduced new herds of sheep and deer, the heart has literally been eaten out of most Highland glens. Soil has been eroded as trees and shrubs have disappeared, virtually all mammals except grazing animals have been extinguished, bird song is rarely heard on the desolate open moor, and the rain runs off the hill so fast that rivulets turn to torrents that erode the very rock on which the soil sits. The removal of crofting communities by the Clearances and the cashing in of the Highlands as grazing for deer and sheep was a tragedy that parallels the tragedy of the destruction of many other native communities in Europe's colonies.[7] This removal was so intended by the English who wanted the independent communities of the Highlands not only subdued militarily but destroyed as a locus of self-sufficiency and hence of cultural and political resistance to the colonial economy after the Union with England.[8]

As sheep numbers are reduced, and deer fences are put up in some Highland areas to allow the forest to regrow, the Romantic idea of wilderness comes to the fore in opposition to the extractive cash economy of the nineteenth- and twentieth-century Highland estate. But as urban culture looks increasingly to wilderness as antidote to its inherent alienation from nature, wild land in effect is recommodified, only this time not as grazing land but as the locus for the summer houses of wealthy urbanites, and for restoration projects by ecological and conservation bodies based in Scotland's cities. With the advent of internet property sales, former crofts and agricultural workers' houses in the Highlands now sell for extraordinary premiums to buyers from the South of England and overseas in the latest version of the clearance as the children of contemporary Highlanders can no longer afford to purchase houses locally. The money economy into which Highland dwellings are now drawn speaks of the alienation between nature and lifestyle, which modern industrial culture has constructed. But for a Gael, a hearth and home literally hewn from a rocky terrain, and sustained by its fruits, spoke of the generous providence of God in providing means to human habitation in a commodious, if sometimes threatening, landscape, and not of the sublime of an alien wilderness.

This new clearance project should be no part of the restoration project of Highland management bodies such as the National Trust for Scotland or Scottish Natural Heritage. It ought to be possible for ecologically enlightened citizens and conservation agencies to support conservation projects to restore a richer flora and fauna in the Highlands for the enjoyment of present and future generations now that the trampling of too many deer and sheep is beginning to be recognised as a humanly introduced blot on a landscape that is a shared heritage. But the project of restoration of wilderness, and in particular the effort to evacuate evidence of human dwelling by active land management, has its own ambiguity as it reflects a conception of wilderness as parkland, which puts a block on the construction of new human dwellings, and connected copses and horticultural plots and so, together with a market in summer houses for the rich, helps to exclude humans, and especially Highlanders' children, from the land.

The National Trust in England was founded in 1895 to protect coastline, countryside and historic buildings and monuments from industrial and urban development. Its equivalent in Scotland was founded in 1935. Both organisations have the right to declare land 'inalienable', which means to say that it cannot be mortgaged, compulsorily purchased or sold without intervention by parliament. Both organisations take their rise from the larger Romantic project to protect and even to restore nature to its pristine state, limiting, or removing, the damaging marks of modern development. They reflect in their origins the Romantic protest at the restlessness of modern industrialism and of the social construction of nature as mechanism and resource bank that now dominates the Western psyche.[9] And in their restoration projects in highland, lowland and coastline they also display the Romantic and aesthetic appreciation of nature with its roots in moral and religious sentiments and ideas. For Wordsworth nature was the source of moral and spiritual instruction after the dethroning of the Protestant's failed God.[10] For John Muir the Book of Nature, rather than the Book of God, the Bible, was the source both of deep spiritual experience and of revelation of the sacred. For Muir, God was nearer, more real in the beauty of flowers and trees and mountains than in the bare stone churches of his Scottish Calvinist ancestry. God for Muir ceases to be a transcendent being known uniquely to the soul of man and seen through the mirror of nature. Instead, nature itself becomes divine; for him 'wild nature is ensouled'.[11]

The period of the rise of the Romantics was characterised by two contrasting trends. Nature was increasingly subject to instrumentalist exploitation under the demands of European population expansion, industrialisation, consumerism and imperialism. And yet at the same time, the changes which human society was visiting on nature evoked strong protest as philosophers, poets and ordinary people increasingly came to regard the natural world as a source of beauty, pleasure and moral and spiritual guidance. This quest for moral significance in, and emotional identity with, nature was also linked to the demise of traditional theism and the loss of a sacred cosmos. As God and creation were pushed apart further by the rise of modern science, so there was a correlative need to invest the cosmos with a new kind of meaning, not provided by God or Christian revelation, but by an account of the independent beauty and moral and spiritual significance of the natural order. The idea of nature as parkland, as a place for leisure and aesthetic recreation, involves then the setting apart of 'wild' nature from the normal exploitative use and abuse of nature that characterises modern industrialism.

This modern concept of wilderness as parkland is ambiguous because it excludes and seems to problematise human dwelling on the land, and because it introduces a new notion of wilderness as therapy for alienated city dwellers, which seems to necessitate government projects to bring them to the wilderness. In his *Desert Solitaire*, Edward Abbey, the founder of the radical environmental group Earth First!, recounts episodes from a period in his life when he worked as a seasonal park ranger in the Arches National Park near Moab in southeast Utah in the American West.[12] Like John Muir, whose writing he knows, he enjoys peak experiences in the wilderness, going off from his park service caravan for long walks with little more than a jacket and a knife to sustain him. But he also records his regret that the parks, established as a redoubt from industrialism, were being colonised by the United States Federal Government's National Park Service as commodified leisure spaces for car-addicted Americans:

> Now here comes another clown with a scheme for the utopian national park: Central Park, National Park, Disneyland National Park. Look here, he says, what's the matter with you fellows?—let's get cracking with this dump. Your road is bad; pave it. Better yet, build a paved road to every corner of the park; better yet, pave the whole damned place so any damn fool can drive anywhere—is this a democracy or ain't it?[13]

For Abbey the wilderness was in effect becoming an extension of the United States freeway network, a kind of glorified and aesthetically pleasing car park. Despite Abbey's no doubt well founded cynicism, the Federal Government's management of wild lands did much to promote this movement for, as that wonderful narrativist of the American West, Wallace Stegner, points out, it was only Federal management of public land that saved Western States from the kind of environmental nightmare that is Southern California.[14]

Against the commodification of modern urban life, and even of nature as parkland, a new 'wilderness movement', of which Abbey was a pioneer, emerged. Adherents of this movement view close encounters with the wild involving a minimum of technology – canoes or backpacks, maybe even bikes, are allowed but not cars or caravans – as vital pathways to healing and spiritual regeneration for driven, but increasingly distressed, urbanites. Wilderness therapy consultancies have sprung up across North America offering urban professionals seven or ten day experiences of the wild, from white water rafting and camping on the Colorado River in the Grand Canyon to off-trail hiking in the Sierra Nevada Mountains so beloved by Muir himself. Many of these consultants make both psychological and spiritual claims for their wilderness trips. Howard Clinebell, a pastoral theologian and long-time advocate of counselling as a core skill of religious professionals, commends encounters with nature as healing experiences.[15] The wilderness rather than the consulting room of the professional therapist is said to provide the opportunity for modern individuals to escape from the selfist narcissism of their consumer-dominated existence and recover a sense of connection to other beings, human and non-human, through an extended and relatively unmediated encounter with the wild. This turn towards nature as therapy indicates the return in contemporary America, and beyond, of what Catherine Albanese calls 'nature religion'.[16] But the claim that personal engagement with wilderness is central to the cultural turn that is called for by the ecological crisis needs to be treated with some scepticism. It may equally reflect a kind of schizoid split between the quest for wilderness as therapy for stressed-out affluent modern urbanites and the resource hungry global economy, which sustains their cities and lifestyles.[17] While fetishising the wild, wilderness as therapy fails to deal with the larger social, political and economic issues that lie at the root of the alienation between urban industrial civilisation and the earth.

The National Trust for Scotland, in their efforts to restore Glen Luibeg to a pristine condition, are attempting in one sense the impossible. They are in effect 'faking nature' as Robert Elliot puts it in a well known essay. Claims that we can restore nature after some environmentally damaging project, such as an oil field or a strip mine, can be problematic because they are so often, and successfully, used by governments and corporations to overcome environmental objections to major and destructive activities. Such claims may help advance a corporate and destructive agenda by making it seem that it is possible to repristinate nature after having first abused and raped and pillaged – as if the land has no memory. For Elliot, faking nature is like forging works of art and analogously because it fails to respect the provenance of ecosystems and the historical processes by which particular species communities have evolved to become natural to particular places, it results in representations of nature that are no more valuable than art forgeries.[18]

The value of a beautiful and well preserved landscape to an ecologist includes not just the view but the complex chains of being that that landscape represents. This value is represented in the clear linguistic differentiation, and the clearly different feel and reality, of 'old growth' and 'new growth' boreal forests, or 'primary rainforest' and 'secondary jungle'. Knowledge of the qualities inherent in the primary forest marks out the 'local knowledge' of the indigenous rainforest dweller or crofter from the universal knowledge of the commercial forester or sporting estate manager.[19] For the indigenous forest dweller or crofter, as for the visiting mountaineer or the jobbing forester, the values they find in the landscape of course reflect their own cultural constructions of the landscape. But there is a stronger relationship, a greater symbiosis, between the construction of a landscape by indigenous people whose culture has been shaped by the land over generations than there is in its construction by a forester who merely works there, or by a visiting mountaineer or tourist.

Eric Katz suggests that restoring nature is problematic because it is anthropogenic: it expresses an attitude of domination to nature, and hence 'nature is not permitted to be free, to pursue its own independent course'.[20] Katz's point may be illustrated with reference to the big hurricane that blew down so many trees in Southern England in 1987. In many places park managers and foresters sought to 'repair' the damage by removing fallen trees, but in those forests where the fallen trees were allowed to remain, better biological outcomes were actually achieved than where humans intervened. The fallen trees rotted and acted as home to fungi and insects, which in turn provided food to birds and small mammals while also providing a rich environment for new wind borne plants to find a niche, with the consequence that biodiversity was enhanced by nature's own response to the hurricane, whereas human intervention had no positive outcomes other than 'clearing up'. The problem, Katz suggests, is with the attitude of control. It is also the case, Katz suggests, that precisely when humans attempt to control and restore wild nature, they are in reality not redesigning nature but rather an artefact – a humanly created reality. Nature is not nature when it is restored by humans.

Katz and Elliot's criticism, while it rightly identifies problematic elements in the modern practice of restoration, nonetheless rests upon a dualism between nature and culture that is alien to indigenous cultures, and is not unproblematic in scientific and theological perspectives. Humans evolved in symbiotic interaction with other species and ecosystems. Their different cultures also evolved in ways which reflect their particular ecological niches or places. Local cultures, because they are place specific, therefore manifest customs, laws, rituals and traditions that enable human communities to live in particular places across generations without destroying their life-sustaining properties for future generations. This evolutionary account of the role of religion in local knowledge is first made in a study of a pig-keeping tribe in Papua New Guinea. Roy Rappaport found that religious sacrifice in the community played a finely honed role in matching the numbers of pigs the people kept with the carrying capacities of the forest ecosystem.[21] Hence local knowledges and practices may have scientific ecological values which, ironically, some kinds of 'universal' scientific knowledge – for example plantation forestry – may lack. [22]

Andrew Light argues that provided there is benevolence towards *nature* in efforts to restore nature, then these efforts may not in themselves be problematic, or express an excess of control. If the intent of these efforts is guided not by human design but by scientific knowledge of what 'nature' would have been like in the restored area before the relevant human intervention then, while the restored area may be a place that gives pleasure to visitors, it has not been restored purely to serve human desires. As Light puts it 'when we engage in acts of benevolent restoration, we are bound *by* nature in the sense that we are obligated to respect what it once was attempting to realize before we interfered with it'.[23] But this point still provides no answer to the situation of many Highland communities, where indigenous children can no longer afford to settle because of the high market value of homes with views of, or proximate to, wilderness areas such as the Cairngorm Plateau.

If wilderness restoration projects are designed to remove as many signs as possible of human dwelling, then the benevolence that such projects display involves the same nature–culture dualism that Elliot and Katz adopt. Benevolent acts of ecological restoration that do not perform this dualism would need, in the Scottish case, to be concerned not only with scientific knowledge of the state of Highland ecosystems before modern humans – with their introduced herds of cash animals, sporting estates, guns, and Land Rovers – interfered. They would also need to be guided by anthropological knowledge of the condition of the indigenous human populations in these areas before the advent of the modern post-Clearance sporting estate. True benevolence in Highland restoration projects would involve attempts to redress not only the injustices done to the many species that have been extinguished by these interventions, but the injustices done to Highland peoples and their descendants. But such justice considerations have been absent from the debates of environmental philosophers concerning ecological restoration. The principal objections of Elliot and Katz to ecological restoration projects are related to aesthetics, while Light, after Holmes Rolston III, is most interested in questions concerning the intrinsic values of wilderness, and with advancing the claim that restoration projects are capable of respecting and enhancing such values.[24]

The idea of ecological restoration participates in significant ways in the religious trope of redemption, both of humanity and of Paradise. However, biblical texts offer a different perspective on the redemption of place from humanity's destructive mark because they do not locate the value of wilderness solely in its aesthetic value, or in a conception of its intrinsic value apart from its relation to the Creator. Biblical images of ecological restoration, and in particular of the restoration of wilderness, are sharply distinguished from most modern approaches to ecological restoration precisely by their focus on human *and* ecological justice and shalom:

> He turns rivers into a desert,
> springs of water into thirsty ground,
> a fruitful land into a salty waste,
> because of the wickedness of its inhabitants.
> He turns a desert into pools of water,
> a parched land into springs of water.
> And there he lets the hungry live,
> and they establish a town to live in;
> they sow fields, and plant vineyards,
> and get a fruitful yield.
>
> PSALM 107: 33–37

For the Psalmist a desert that lacks water and where nothing grows because the soil is salinated is a place lacking fruitfulness, and the ecological restoration that Yahweh brings about makes of it again a fertile place. And this fertility has a particular purpose, for it is not just any who will enjoy its fruits but the poor, those whom corrupt princes have excluded from their rightful inheritance. The restoration of wilderness in this perspective is connected with the redemption of humans from landlessness and poverty, which are caused by human greed and sinfulness. Jeremiah reads the desertification and salination of wilderness, or the erosion of the treeless mountain, as a direct consequence of sin, and of the failure of the Israelites to live up to the standard of divine justice as elaborated in Torah:

> Take up weeping and wailing for the mountains,
> and a lamentation for the pastures of the wilderness,
> because they are laid waste so that no one passes through,
> and the lowing of the cattle is not heard;
> both the birds of the air and the animals have fled and are gone.
>
> JEREMIAH 9: 10–11

> Why is the land ruined and laid waste like a wilderness,
> so that no one passes through?

And the Lord says: Because they have forsaken my law that
   I set before them,
and have not obeyed my voice or walked in accordance with it.

JEREMIAH 9: 12b–13

Just as the land suffers from human wickedness according to Jeremiah, so for Isaiah ecological restoration involves judgement of the corrupt city where wicked princes oppress the poor while the wilderness becomes the fertile dwelling of the poor who there find justice and peace:

For the palace will be forsaken, the populous city deserted;
the hill and the watchtower will become dens forever,
the joy of wild asses,
a pasture for flocks;
until a spirit from on high is poured out on us,
and the wilderness becomes a fruitful field,
and the fruitful field is deemed a forest.
Then justice will dwell in the wilderness,
and justice abide in the fruitful field.
The effect of justice will be peace,
And the result of justice, quietness and trust forever.

ISAIAH 32:14–17

In this vision of ecological restoration the emphasis is not on the wilderness being returned to an original pristine state absent of human habitation. Instead, the wilderness becomes the place for a new harmony between human habitation and wild species, while the rapacious and oppressive city collapses. The desert becomes a place of refuge for threatened wild species and impoverished humans alike.

These biblical visions of divine ecological restoration are of particular significance when we consider the situation of indigenous communities, including crofting communities in the Highlands, who dwell close to, or in the midst of, habitats that city dwellers admire and designate as 'wilderness'. Efforts to preserve parcels of untouched nature have often led, and are still leading, to the exclusion of hunter gatherer cultures, which are a source of the kind of wisdom modern humans still need to recover if they are to learn how to dwell sustainably on the earth. While such efforts may be an example of a non-utilitarian attitude to nature, and in that sense preferable to utilitarian attitudes to nature as resource bank, nonetheless they serve more as a device for repristinating nature for the occasional visitor – whether for sport, therapy or tourism – than for recovering a more holistic and sustainable form of relationship between human dwelling and the wild. They are, therefore, in direct contrast to the biblical account of the centrality of justice to ecological restoration of wilderness: far from instantiating justice, they often interact with market forces and other social processes to advance even further the environmental exclusion of indigenous inhabitants.

Against the sequestering of Highland land, particularly since the Clearances, for the sporting and aesthetic pursuits of the few hundred landowners who own more than half of Scotland's land area, advocates of land reform seek to recover the traditional *human* ecology of the Highland landscape. Landowners attempt to legitimise their stewardship through articulation of symbolic and cultural systems including the reinvented traditions of tartan and chieftain, and the larger heritage industry.[25] However, the frequent failures of landowners in duties of care to the land itself, or to tenant crofters, have meant that a small number of crofting communities have begun to look for ways of removing the yoke of a class of landowner for whom the buying and selling of Highland estates has little to do with the welfare of resident communities.

The first attempt by an indigenous community to buy out a landlord was by a group of crofters on the Assynt Estate north of Lochinver in Sutherland. They raised a large sum of money and reduced the market value of the estate by vociferous campaigning, which suggested a private buyer would find it hard to enjoy the salmon, trout and deer that would be his principal interest. Already the new owners are making a difference to the land, applying for grants to develop native woodland of rowan, birch and Scots pine, which in turn will see the return of resident species, sustained by the ground and leaf cover, the insects, berries, fungi and other delicacies of a thriving native Scots woodland.[26] After Assynt, it was the turn of the islanders of Eigg to succeed in their protracted efforts to purchase their small Hebridean island from an unsympathetic foreign landlord who had presided over the gradual wreck of his estate.[27] As in Assynt, so on the Isle of Eigg there is already evidence that local ownership of the island is realising both ecological and human justice benefits. Whereas the majority of tenant housing was substandard, and the land largely denuded of trees, under new local management improvements to local housing are being made, while the land itself is being managed to enhance its ecological diversity and to provide employment for islanders. Since the buyout the island now has 100 per cent full employment, and this from a situation where in 1994 12 per cent of the islanders were facing eviction by the landlord, having neither security of tenure nor of employment. The purchase of Assynt, and then of Eigg, and later of the Isle of Gigha, has set a paradigm for land reform and reform of land law in Scotland, which was ultimately taken up by the new devolved Scottish Parliament as one of its first major pieces of legislation. The Land Reform Act, which achieved its third reading in the parliament in 2003, became law in May 2004 and sets in place a right to buy by tenants when landowners put up an estate, or portions of it, for sale. The Act also establishes a public land fund to assist in such purchases.

Wilderness is one of the principal preoccupations of the growing discipline of environmental ethics. But the failure of the proponents of this discipline to consider wilderness alongside questions of human justice seems to indicate that philosophers can be as prone to 'wilderness fetishism' as wilderness therapists and their clients. By contrast wilderness in the bible, and in the Christian tradition, is viewed as sites of aesthetic distinctiveness, ecological potential and human dwelling. This is not to say that there is no warrant in the bible, and more especially in the Christian tradition, for a love of wilderness for its own sake. On the contrary, it is quite clear from the life of Christ himself that he was drawn to wilderness precisely because the mountains and desert regions of Judea were places where people were scarce. It is possible – though the Gospels provide no direct evidence of this motivation – that Christ was attracted to wilderness because the hand of God was more in evidence, more real, in such places than in humanly managed landscapes. Christ's wilderness visits enabled him both to clarify his sense of mission, as in the temptations in the wilderness, and to commune with God. We might even say that Christ loved the mountains, for they were his most frequent retreat. A question remains over whether his spiritual experiences in the wild were inspired more by the absence of people – and hence the possibility of solitary communion with God – or by the spiritual power of wilderness. Whether it was one or other motivation, or some combination of the two, there is no doubt, however, that Christ's attraction to mountains and desert places – like that of John the Baptist or Elijah or Moses before him – is in many ways analogous to the modern fascination with these places. The wilderness is an environment that has not been manipulated by, and is not inhabited by, people. As such it offers a place where the human can commune with the divine creator Spirit in a more direct way for it is more directly formed by, and redolent of, the divine presence than the habitations of men and women.

St Antony, the first of the desert fathers, is the first in Christian history since Christ to discover and embrace the potential spiritual power of wilderness. He went to the desert from the city on a quest for spiritual renewal and returned many years later with his face apparently shining with holiness. He also grew to love the place of the desert deeply, and saw this love as the gift of God. He may not be, as Susan Power Bratton suggests, the *original* desert solitaire.[28] Moses, Elijah, John the Baptist, Jesus and Paul of Tarsus all sought and found new revelation and inspiration in their prophetic vocation from spiritual communion in desert places: all returned from such places with new insights into their mission and into the purposes of God, which would be manifest in their lives and teachings in often revolutionary ways. But St Antony is the first after St Paul and John of Patmos to embrace the wilderness ascetic in the early church, and he was the first of many thousands of ascetics who subsequently took to the desert to sit on piles of salt, or to dwell in caves, and to engage in a spiritual struggle for holiness apart from the imperial cities of the newly Christianised Roman Empire. The result over time was that the desert became a city, as individual ascetics began to adopt a rule of life that involved them in submitting their spiritual quests to one another in communities of shared discipline and spiritual authority.[29]

This monastic quest for an escape from the compromises with imperial Rome that the Church was drawn into after the conversion of the Emperor Constantine does not seem to have involved a challenge to the unjust social arrangements that the empire brought in its train. The imperial theologian Ambrose criticised the empire for the same kind of abuses of landlordism, greed, oppression of the poor, that the prophets criticised in the kings and princes of ancient Israel.[30] The monks who took to the desert certainly were seeking to resist the corruption of empire. But did their communities instantiate a real alternative, or were they a spiritual opt out? The judgement of this depends upon the view that we take of the social significance of prayer and the spiritual quest.

Thomas Merton described the prayers and rituals of monks in monasteries, such as his own at Gethsemani in Kentucky, as the spiritual powerhouses of America, keeping the nation from falling apart even as America was prosecuting an imperial war in Vietnam.[31] Merton's claim is borne out in the agricultural and educational, theraputic and social projects that monasteries throughout Christendom sponsored. In its origins monasticism adopted the desert for the same reason that Christ retreated to the mountains – the absence of other people and the bare terrain offered a place for struggle with temptation, and for hearing the voice of God. The monks did not see wilderness as a zone of 'pure nature' but rather as a place where the creator spoke to them with greater clarity. It was the association between the spiritual struggle for discernment and against temptation that was at the heart of the monastic adoption of wilderness. But out of this adoption a new relationship of worship and the earth emerged in monastic history as monks formed communities and began to work on the land in a tradition of agrarian self-sufficiency, which was unbroken in much of Europe until the Reformation. Around the monasteries rural communities and farms grew up, which survived the vicissitudes of wars and revolutions and plague that were the lot of early modern Europeans.

The core work of the monk was not, however, agricultural production or soil conservation but worship of God in community. From the fifth century until the twelfth, all monks in the West belonged to communities ordered by the *Rule of Saint Benedict*. Benedict's rule requires that novices who determine to join a religious community make vows of 'stability, fidelity to monastic life, and obedience'.[32] In the vow of stability the novice commits him or herself to dwell in the *place* and among the people who constitute the monastic house for the rest of their life. The vow of stability, combined particularly with the vow of poverty, was central to the realisation by religious communities of conservation of the property as well as the community of the monastic house.[33] Stability and poverty together required the monks and nuns to find ways to live off their own resources and hence to practise community self-sufficiency. Together these principles enabled

Benedictine monasteries to care, across generations and centuries, for monastic dwellings, and for the geographical places in which they were situated. These places are usually far from centres of human habitation, and were originally chosen because they were wastelands, of no or little value to others. In these wild or abandoned places the monks developed skills in building from locally available materials – usually stone and timber. And in order to provide for themselves, and so not to be dependent on others, and in order to care for visitors, the monks also turned to cultivating these wild places and then to creating gardens, herbariums, as well as crops for wheat and barley, hop fields for beer, and vineyards for wine, olive and apple groves for oil and cider. The rule of stability required that the monks had to be particularly careful to cultivate in such a way as to conserve soil fertility, for they did not have the option of moving on or buying alternative fields.[34] As Abbott Klassen observes:

> As Benedictine monastics we want to be people who "stay in a place long enough that the spirits can influence us". By coming to know a place deeply, the set of overlapping ecosystems, the delicate balance which exists between the number of creatures and available nourishment, the patterns that play themselves out year after year, monastic communities will make decisions with an understanding of their consequences. In the event of a serious mistake the community will be around long enough to recognise it as such.[35]

In a range of interviews with contemporary monks, Martine Vonk finds that the principle in the Rule that contemporary Benedictines identify as the one that commits them to care for creation is that all monastic goods are to be cared for in the same way as the 'sacred vessels of the altar'.[36] The link between worship and nature is also expressed in the interpenetration of the daily ordering of the divine office by the hours of sunrise and sunset, of the mapping of the liturgical year, and the events of the life of Christ, onto the agricultural year, and the stress on simplicity and solitude, all of which attuned the monks to find meaning, and spiritual as well as material sustenance in the natural rhythms and ecological qualities of the places where they dwelled.

The development in Christian history of monastic care for and rootedness in place is the paradigmatic way in which the Prophetic announcement of wilderness giving birth to new communities of justice and shalom is realised in Christian history. But the Reformation dissolution of many monastic communities in Northern Europe unsettled the influence of this monastic pattern of life on the general population and on the land. The ripples of that unsettling from the Dissolution to the Enclosures and the Clearances continue until today. And it is, therefore, perhaps inevitable that some in secular life are trying to identify ways to recommit themselves to the stable and spiritual qualities of the agrarian way of life practised by monastics, but in post-monastic or 'new monastic' settings.

The Dissolution of the Monasteries was not, it must be said, without cause. The monks, as the fourteenth-century cleric William Langland documented, were corrupted by the tendency of the nobles to leave them tracts of land to atone for their sins: 'today Religion is a rider of horses, a rover through the streets, an arbitrator at Days of Settlement, and a purchaser of land.' The result was that the monks 'lived at ease with no pity for the poor' while 'their domains are so wide that they think of themselves only as landlords'.[37] So powerful had the monks become by the time of Henry Tudor that it was not only kings and nobles who feared them, and would bring them down. Nonetheless, the acquisition by the Crown and aristocrats of their lands in the sixteenth century did not see a sudden transformation in the condition of the rural poor. On the contrary, it set in train a historical process that ultimately turned the majority of those who once had a claim to a living from the land, albeit in exchange for tithes to the church and various forms of service to an Abbott or Lord, into labourers with no property other than their bodies, which they were forced to offer for hire to whomever, in country or town, would employ them.

The Christian practice of seeking God in the desert from the third century, and the gradual evolution of enduring cenobitic community and monastic dwelling and cultivation in wilderness, shed valuable historical light on the potential of Land Reform in Scotland, rightly conceived and practised, to heal the post-Clearances rift between people and land in the Highlands and Lowlands of Scotland.[38] One place in Scotland where a new monastic approach to dwelling, care for buildings and land, and their association with an intentional worshipping community is recovered most iconically is the Iona Community. It is possible to see on the Island of Iona the influence over time of the establishment of this worshipping community since the 1930s on this island adopted by Columba as one of the beach-heads for the Christianisation of Scotland. A visitor to the island today will be struck by the many guest houses and hotels, built from local stone and in vernacular style, that cater for visitors who do not want merely to visit the island for a day trip but to experience the quality of light, peace and wildness that first drew Columba there in the sixth century by staying for a while. The island also increasingly reveals efforts at horticulture, as both the Iona community and other residents seek to grow more of their own food. But the dominance of guest houses, retreat houses and holiday homes on the island has had the effect of making it difficult for the children of families who live on the island to find homes for themselves. Consequently, an Iona Housing Partnership was established in 2003, and in 2011 glebe land was purchased from the Church of Scotland with the aim of building a number of low carbon and affordable homes for those who want to live long term on the island.

If it can happen in Iona, it can happen elsewhere in the Highlands. The soils and terrain are similar, although the principal landowners in large areas of the Highlands are not a national church, whose trustees may see the wisdom of repeopling underpopulated rural areas, but the 'lairds' of sporting estates who in many cases are descended from the Chieftains that directed the Clearance of Highland people from the land in the eighteenth and nineteenth centuries, and still vociferously guard their right to prevent the Scots from returning to the lands of their forbears. For the Clearances to be reversed on the mainland will require a new commitment by the Scottish government and charitable agencies, such as the National Trust for Scotland and Scottish Natural Heritage, to a vision of Highland land not as a sublime wilderness but as a ruined land, denuded of trees, indigenous mammals, wild birds, and of people and their gardens, food cultures and woodlands. The failure of these bodies and people to see the potential of the Highlands as repeopled glens in which the descendants of Highlanders replace introduced grazing animals, and recover the dignified self-sufficiency and care for land, and biodiversity, which their forbears practised is in part at least precisely because of the modern aesthetic environmental imaginary of Scotland as most beautiful when wild and largely empty of people.[39] Hence if ecological restoration and land management projects in Scotland fail to address the economic and political forces that prevent the descendants of Highland and crofting families from dwelling in, or returning to, the 'wild' lands of Scotland, then these projects fall far short of a biblical vision of ecological restoration.

6

Food sovereignty from Joshua to La Via Campesina

Agriculture originated 10,500 years ago in the Levant. The region was then covered in forest. Climate change in the early Holocene saw a gradual reduction in precipitation, and a shrinking in the Levantine land area with ocean rise from ongoing glacial melt from the last ice age. The hunter gatherer lifestyle became more difficult and neolithic hunter gatherers responded by forming more permanent settlements near rivers, and raising animals and cultivating plants.[1] Levantine agriculture principally involved seven cultivars: wheat, barley, peas, lentils, chick peas, flax and vetch.

Agriculture was initially practised in small self-sufficient agricultural communities. But a growing body of recent archaeological data from the Ancient Near East reveals that the invention of agriculture was the occasion for the emergence of the first large-scale human societies, in which extended hierarchy, deep inequality, and slavery became possible for the first time in human evolution, since these features were unknown in prior hunter gatherer groups.[2] The first large-scale agricultural society in world history was Egypt in the third millennium BCE, during the reign of Pharaoh Pepy II who died in 2230. Subsequent larger-scale civilisations, involving large monuments, death cults, and hierarchies of wealth and rank, include those of Assyria, Babylon, Egypt, Persia and Macedonia.[3] Slavery was a feature of all five of these ancient civilisations, as also was the emergence of metal money as tokens of exchange.

The Hebrew Bible commences with a cultural critique of large-scale agricultural empire and slavery, and the Pentateuch commends agriculture practices for adoption by the Hebrews in the 'Promised Land', which are frequently contrasted with the practices that had led to slavery in Egypt.[4] Agriculture is described in Genesis 3 as the punishment for the first sin in Eden, which is described as the gathering and eating of a forbidden tree-grown fruit in a forest. Read anthropologically the story represents a cultural memory of the hunter gatherer lifestyle that preceded agriculture in the ancient forests of the Levant. Hence exile from the forests of paradise takes the form of a 'fall into agriculture'. The association of evil with the assertion of human willing over dietary intake of fruits underwrites the suggestion of a link in the mind of the narrator between the origin of evil, violence and slavery, all described as outcomes of the exile from paradise in the remaining chapters of Genesis, and the origin of agriculture.

The tragic consequences of the fall into agriculture are soon revealed in the first murder, of Abel by Cain. Cain raised crops from tilling the earth but his offering of cultivated plants as a sacrifice to Yahweh meets with less favour than a meat offering from Abel, a pastoralist who does not till the ground. Cain killed Abel from envy, and hence envy of the lifestyle of nomadic pastoralists by settled farmers is the occasion for the first murder in the bible. If any doubt remained at the evil potential of agriculture, a neolithic iron agricultural implement was the instrument of the first murder. The narrative then rapidly descends into deeper evil and violence. The first part of Genesis concludes with the flood story, and the agreement of Yahweh not to flood the earth again in the Noahic covenant, which clearly linked regularity of seasons, agricultural harvest and divine blessing on this new lifestyle. The new covenant indicates that agriculture, despite its early ambiguous outcomes, at least had the potential to become a divine vocation, and hence 'Noah began to be a farmer' (Genesis 9: 20). But even this new beginning is immediately threatened by sin since Noah plants vines, becomes drunk with wine, and is shamed before his sons. Things get worse with the descendants of Noah who built a large city and ziggurat reaching to heaven, and hence threatened to overmaster the earth–heaven relationship, usurping the power of Yahweh. Yahweh, therefore, is said to have sent languages among them to destroy this new large-scale unified culture, and to discourage the building of any more cities and towers.

Nomadic pastoralism is the form of agriculture that the Hebrew Bible commends after the descent of Israel at Babel, as is well captured in the ancestral memory 'my father was a wandering Aramean' (Deuteronomy 26: 5).[5] Abraham is described as the original Hebrew, the father of the nation and a nomadic pastoralist The original covenant between God and Abraham required him to graze animals in an area of land to which Abraham was directed by angels. Joseph was also a shepherd but the envy of his brothers. His brothers sold him to Egyptian traders, and his subsequent exile in Egypt resulted in him becoming prince regent to the all-powerful Pharaoh, and in the process initiating the first feudal takeover of the land by a ruler in recorded history. The occasion for the takeover was the famine years in which, in exchange for grain, Joseph took the land of smallholder farmers into ownership by Pharaoh. Having invited his family to reside in this now feudal empire their descendants themselves became bonded slaves. The mythic Exodus from slavery in Egypt therefore becomes the ur-narrative for the formation of the Hebrews as a culturally distinct people called to practise agriculture in a different way than the Egyptians.

Subsequent to the nomadic pastoralism of the Hebrew patriarchs, the next place in the Hebrew Bible where agriculture is 'redeemed' as a divinely intended vocation, rather than a source of oppression, is the book of Joshua. This 'text of terror' describes the violent occupation of Canaan, and the genocidal killing of numerous rulers, their subjects and the destruction of their cultural objects. But the theological heart of the book concerns the establishment of a new agrarian economy among the Hebrews through the equitable distribution of the land as *nachalah* – variously translated inheritance, gift or property – among the families and tribes of Israel (Joshua 13). The gift of land, which in Egypt belonged to the ruler, is the source of economic independence to each household, and hence of freedom from slavery. But this freedom is not the achievement of the Hebrews but a divine gift, and the fulfilment of the original covenantal promise made to Abraham; it is a realisation in history of 'the good thing which Yahweh had spoken to the house of Israel' (Joshua 21: 45).

The settlement of land is also the occasion for a new mode of life for Israel collectively. In her own borders Israel is at last a nation, and hence Deuteronomy portrays a long reflective pause at the Jordan, on the boundary between wilderness and the Land, when Israel thinks aloud about the implications of becoming at last a landed people, and both the opportunities and dangers this new status presented.[6] Deuteronomy celebrates the gift of land as one of pure gift, since the Israelites were to live in cities she 'did not build', and enjoy water from cisterns she had not hewn, and food from olive trees and vineyards she had not planted (Deuteronomy 6: 10–11). But as sojourners and former slaves became settlers, the land was also a source of temptation. Immediately after the settlement described in Joshua the tribe of Reuben constructed a pagan altar to the local Canaanite gods (Joshua 22). To keep the land, the Israelites had to purify it of such pagan idolatry by offering the fruit of the land to Yahweh alone as tithes, temple offerings and sacrifices, and by constantly recalling that they did not own it but only enjoyed it as gift from the one who had given it. The Deuteronomist uses the climatic contrast between rain-fed Canaanite hill farms and river-fed Egyptian irrigated fields to contrast the divine source of the free food economy of Israel with the coercive food economy of Egypt; in Egypt the land had to be managed, the irrigation channels maintained, and watered with the feet of the Israelites 'like a herb garden' (Deuteronomy 11: 10). The new Land is instead cared for by Yahweh and its hills and valleys 'drink water of the rain of heaven' (Deuteronomy 11: 11).[7] Idolatry is described by the Deuteronomist as dangerous to the enjoyment of the land because the gods of the Ancient Near East, other than Yahweh, had not given the land to each household but instead conferred it on the rulers. To worship idols then was to risk the return to an economy of coercion, while also to offend Yahweh who was the giver, and hence the *owner*, of good land. And this was the ambiguity of the *nachalah* economy. The laws on inheritance recorded in Deuteronomy and Numbers describe a property regime designed to sustain equitable land-holdings across the generations. They commend inheritance through male heirs as a device to keep landholdings contiguous and of a reasonable size.[8]

Daughters would inherit, through their husbands, the land of their husbands' fathers. However, in the case where a man had no sons, or died intestate, inheritance by daughters was also permitted (Numbers 27: 4–7).[9]

Over time the ordinance envisaged in Joshua of equitable distribution in Canaan, and the covenantal contrast to coercive landlessness in Egypt, would be forgotten. Along with the temptation of following other gods, the gods of the land, was the temptation that the Israelites would so enjoy their food security and sovereignty in the land that they would forget that Yahweh, and not they, was the true sovereign of the land, and that Yahweh and not they was its owner. The Hebrew history books and prophets describe how the economy of *nachalah* was corrupted, and the land managed so as to become the property of the few and not the many. The prophets argued that the neglect of divine law concerning land distribution by those who coveted and coercively seized the inherited fields and houses of others was the occasion for God's judgement against Israel (Micah 2: 1–2). That coercive land seizure had become the norm in Israel, as it had been in Egypt in the time of Joseph, is indicated in the classic story of King Ahab's theft of Naboth's vineyard. Ahab envies Naboth's vineyard in the rich land of Jezreel and tells Naboth he wants his vineyard so he can turn it into 'a garden of herbs', a conversion of usage that would turn Naboth's *nachalah*, the rain-fed vineyard that was the source of his freedom, back into an Egyptian style dug and irrigated herb garden. Naboth resists Ahab on theological grounds saying to Ahab, 'The Lord forbid it me that I should give the inheritance of my fathers unto thee' (1 Kings 21: 2). But Ahab proceeds to have Naboth charged, falsely, with a capital crime, and takes the land. As Ellen Davis comments, Naboth's conception of inheritance is a collective one; he does not resist the king for coveting his property but for challenging the gift of land from Yahweh to his ancestors as passed down over succeeding generations.[10] The implication of the story is clear: kingship was a form of pagan centralised rule that Yahweh had indicated before the anointing of David was not the preferred model for a covenantal society. But once inaugurated the Israelite historians chart the rise of an inevitable contest between the dispersed economy of *nachalah*, and the centralising economy of kingly rule and its associated cults, because kings, and their frequently foreign wives, are described as the main source of the tendency of Israel in her security in the land to erect altars to other gods. The historians and prophets narrate the disloyalty and disobedience of Israel and Judah to Yahweh as the eventual cause of the Israelites losing their inheritance, just as in the Ancient Near East a father could disinherit a disobedient and disloyal son.[11] In the end Israel is divided into two, and subsequently the two peoples are dispersed in Exile into other kingdoms. The economy of *nachalah*, the unique historical experiment to redeem agriculture from the curse of coercive landlessness and hunger, had failed.

But the story of course does not end there. Nehemiah records that in the period of Persian rule over Israel, Persia was unable to occupy the land of Israel and merely required the payment of money tribute. Hence Jewish wealthy elites and other poorer Jews are described in Nehemiah as resettling the land. But the non-wealthy complain to Nehemiah that their lands and even their daughters are mortgaged to wealthy Jews in order that they can afford to buy corn, and to pay the tribute to Persia (Nehemiah 5: 1–5). Nehemiah, who is both a Jew and the Persian governor, calls the elites and rulers together and challenges them that they are acting contrary to divine law in exacting usury from the people on their debts. He then requires that the wealthy redeem the debts against land that they hold and charges them 'restore I pray to them even this day their lands, their vineyards, their oliveyards, their houses' and the text says that 'the people did according to his *promise*' (Nehemiah 5: 11, 13). Nehemiah in other words requires, perhaps for the first time in Israel, if we can take this as a record of historical events, that Jewish rulers and merchants observe the legal procedures for debt forgiveness, and the periodic fifty year return of land lost through debt to the descendants of those whose *nachalah* it had once been. The Jubilee law represented a major modification to the *nachalah* economy: instead of the land 'belonging' to the Israelites for *nachalah*, the Jubilee law makes clear that the Israelites only enjoy the use of the land for an inheritance so long as they recognise that its true owner is Yahweh. Hence a family's ancestral *nachalah* is inalienable to another precisely because it is not theirs to give away: the land remains the Lord's and only its use is alienable, and that only for a period of forty-nine years.[12]

Arguably Nehemiah describes the third time in the Old Testament when agriculture is redeemed from the curse of inequality and the growth of the potentially hierarchical and oppressive social powers that it had 'owness' of the land evolution. But there is one signal difference: this time the former 'owners' of the land are the rich and wealthy elites of Israel who gave the land back to the landless and indebted without coercion or violence. Hence in this third instance of the redemption of agriculture, the landless are again redeemed by the free gift of land, but this time without the genocidal violence described in Joshua or the theft described by the prophets. Food security was re-established by challenging the sovereignty of money power in the form of accumulated debts, and in the recovery of the Hebrew ideal that the earth belonged not to earthly rulers – as it had in Egypt and still does in today's increasingly cartelised global food economy – but to Yahweh. Food security in other words was only restored in Israel where usurious debts were forgiven, where land reform was initiated, and sovereignty over the earth was again recognised as belonging to Yahweh and not to those who had accumulated legal titles over it.

It is reasonable to envisage that Third Isaiah had pondered on Nehemiah's Restoration project, and that he had it in mind, when he narrated his vision of a 'new heaven and a new earth', whose inhabitants 'shall not build and another inhabit, shall not plant and another eat' (Isaiah 65: 22). In this restored land infant mortality and the death of women in childbirth would decline, and more people would enjoy good health into old age; and these indices are used as statistical measures of progress of human development to this day. For Isaiah, their realisation was made possible not by a repetition of the *nachalah* economy of Joshua, which rested on genocidal violence, but by a new peaceable economy in which there was no more coercion but only gift. In this economy 'they shall build houses and inhabit them; and they shall plant vineyards and eat the fruit of them' (Isaiah 65: 21). And hence 'they will not labour in vain, nor bring forth for trouble' and on such an earth not only will there be peace between peoples and generations, but the easy communication Adam and Eve enjoyed with God in Eden will be restored for 'before they call, I will answer' (Isaiah 65: 24); and the peaceable relations Adam and Eve enjoyed as vegetarians with other animals, who before agriculture were not in awe of humans in Eden when brought before them to be named, will also be restored, and even between predators for 'the wolf and the lamb shall feed together, and the lion shall eat straw like the bullock' (Isaiah 65: 25).[13]

Old Testament associations between coercive food insecurity, imperial food storage and landlessness, and between land reform, debt forgiveness, health and long life find resonances in modern empirical studies of the nature and causes of hunger and famine. They also find resonances in peasant and small producer sponsored projects to resist the global commodification of farming and seed supplies as sponsored by governmental and private agricultural agencies and corporations. Historical research into modern imperial rule reveals a strong correlation between large remote government systems and famine, with the incidence of famine in British India and other parts of the colonised world being far higher than in pre-colonial times.[14] Analogously, Jean Dreze and Amartya Sen's research on the causes of famine in postcolonial Africa and Asia reveals that the cause of malnutrition and famine is not lack of food availability but the inability of subsistence farmers to obtain food when their own crops fail, and the inability of the landless to obtain sufficient cash for food from employment or other sources.[15] Principal causes for lack of entitlement to food include 'alienation of land, or loss of labour power due to ill health' and economic change resulting in 'loss of employment, fall in wages, rise in food prices, drop in the price of goods or services sold by the person, reduction in social security provisions'.[16]

Postcolonial hunger is interconnected with the continuing alienation of land from subsistence farmers, often advanced by development aid projects and farm subsidies, which promote hybrid monocrops for export, with associated reliance on expensive chemical inputs and mechanical tillage. This kind of agriculture often reduces local availability of a healthy variety of nutritious food, in both developed and developing country contexts. Subsistence farmers are persuaded by outside experts to abandon traditional mixed farming and grow cash crops for export, but when the prices of these cash crops do not match the income they are promised, or when hybrid wonder-seeds fall prey to pests or diseases, they have no traditional foods of their own to rely on to feed their families.[17] Postcolonial agricultural interventions by government and international agencies rest upon unproven and misleading assumptions about the advantages, in terms of food security, of large collective farms over small householder-owned farms. But the failure of socialist collectivisation did not stem the promotion by governmental and commercial agricultural agencies of large-scale farming aimed at production for global over local markets. A well known example of the failure of this approach is the promotion of hybrid rice and other 'Green Revolution' technologies in India. Hybrid rice, developed in Western and Chinese laboratories, was ill suited to Indian farming conditions but nonetheless it was foisted on small farmers by government and private agencies although the rice produced was inferior and disliked by local millers and consumers.[18] The widespread adoption of chemical agriculture and biotechnology in India has seen a huge rise in farmer suicides, as farmers mired in debt are no longer able to feed their families.[19]

Corporate and governmental promotion of 'food security', where food security means a rise in surplus grain and other export commodities, results in increased food *insecurity* and reduced quality of nutrition for small and peasant farmers. Government subsidies and commercial interventions result in commercial collectivisation as small farmers lose lands because they cannot afford the monetary costs of new inputs, or because corporations and government agencies forcibly take their land from them in pursuit of increased commercial income from farming.[20] In the developed world such policies have seen a dramatic decline in rural populations in what Wendell Berry famously called the 'unsettling of America'.[21] They foster growing mechanisation and reliance on chemical fertilisers, fossil fuels and irrigation from depleting historic aquifers. These methods suppress nematodal worm and microbial activity in the soil and reduce biodiversity, while also reducing the quality of food available in rural areas, thus contributing to rural food insecurity, obesity and other diet-related health problems.[22] In the developing world those made landless by the commercial collectivisation of farmlands, often involving land theft by foreign and domestic governments and agencies, are forced to migrate to more marginal lands, often cutting forests and scrub in the process and promoting soil erosion and biodiversity loss, while many others are forced into insanitary squatter settlements on the edge of burgeoning and polluted cities.[23] But nonetheless commercial production, storage and global trading of high yield grain varieties remains central to many accounts of the 'solution' to world hunger.[24] This is despite the fact that it was precisely speculative manipulation of centralised grain markets in Chicago in 2008 that led to food price rises in Africa and Asia. Price rises sparked food riots in hundreds of cities globally, and were a major cause of violent conflict in North Africa from Tunisia to Syria, much of it still ongoing. There are similar associations between stored food and hunger in India, which has the largest number of small farmers of any nation in the world. In Uttar Pradesh farmers, whose lands have been 'collectivised' by a government agricultural project from which politicians stole billions of dollars, starve and beg on the streets of rural villages close to government grain stores holding thousands of tons of food, stored for so long that more than 10 per cent of it rots before it is distributed.[25]

Under the ideology of 'food security', governments and private corporations have overseen the growing commercial collectivisation of food supplies on every continent in the last thirty years. Just six seed companies now control the majority of seeds sold commercially worldwide and they have sought this increased control as a way of asserting intellectual property rights in patentable hybrids and genetically engineered seeds, and raising the value extractable from farmers for the use of higher yield varieties.[26] As the costs of commercially supplied farming inputs have grown, the liberalisation of the supply of credit has seen growing farmer and householder indebtedness, and house and land price inflation. The resultant growth in debt and reduced access to good nutrition is not confined to the developing world. High levels of housing-related debt in Europe and North America led to the 2008 Global Financial Crisis. But instead of householder debt forgiveness, and regulatory reduction of risk in the financial system, commercial lenders evicted millions of residents from their homes, while governments imposed a regime of austerity economics on citizens, which has produced a dramatic decline in entitlements to food in low wage and under-employed households. In consequence in the UK a large Christian charitable provider of 'food banks' recorded a tripling in requests for emergency food between 2012 and 2013, and its research estimates that 4.7 million people in the UK, or 8 per cent of the population, were living in food and fuel poverty.[27] Consequently, 600 religious leaders wrote a public letter to the British Prime Minister in April 2014 calling for change in government policy to increase entitlements to food among the unemployed and low waged.[28] The more articulate of sufferers from food poverty in the UK speak of a 'failure of democracy'.[29]

The association of democratic failure with food poverty is significant for it indicates the age old sense that a ruler who oversees large-scale hunger alongside extreme wealth and stores of surplus food has failed in the most basic of governmental responsibilities, which is to restrain the strong from oppressing the weak, a responsibility recognised as the core governmental responsibility in ancient Mesopotamia, the origin of the agricultural phase of human evolution. On the Hammurabi Stele, erected by King Hammurabi of Babylon in the eighteenth century BC, which now stands in the Louvre Museum, Paris, is inscribed the earliest recorded legal code. The purpose of the law is there described as being to 'promote the welfare of the people' and 'to cause justice to prevail in the land, to destroy the wicked and the evil that the strong might not oppress the weak'.[30] Similarly, Psalm 72 describes good government as being associated with the restraint of the strong, with justice for the weak, and with fertile land:

Give the king your justice, O God,
and your righteousness to a king's son.

May he judge your people with righteousness,
and your poor with justice.
May the mountains yield prosperity for the people,
and the hills, in righteousness.
May he defend the cause of the poor of the people,
give deliverance to the needy, and crush the oppressor.

The connection between food, farming and governance, which was clearly captured in the Hebrew covenant, is recovered in contemporary discourse in the concept of 'food sovereignty', which is the orienting policy objective of the food and farming reform movement known as La Via Campesina (LVC). Founded at a meeting of small-scale food producers from Central America held in Managua in 1992, LVC was formally constituted as a global social movement with farmers from four continents at a meeting in Mons, Belgium in 1993.[31] LVC now claims to be the largest social movement in the world, with affiliation from 200 million small-scale peasant farmers, fishers and landworkers worldwide.

The term *Via Campesina* is first associated with a Mexican and non-Marxist movement, which was established to promote peasant-led agriculture as a counter to the growing corporatisation of farming and reliance on imported foods in Mexico in the late 1970s and 1980s. Mexican advocates of a revival of peasant farming, who became known as *campesinistas*, argued that growing problems of rural landlessness, commercialisation of seeds, reliance on imported foods, and the turning of land for food into land for animal feeds, could all be addressed by bottom-up peasant-led, rather than top-down collectivist agricultural initiatives.[32] In this approach, the *campesinistas* resisted *both* capitalist food and farming collectivisation and Marxist collectivisation schemes, which were becoming widely discredited in the 1980s, not least because of large-scale hunger in Mozambique, Cambodia and other enforced Marxist collectivisation schemes. They also resisted the bias towards giantism in both Marxist and commercial approaches to farming collectivisation, and they advocated small-scale agriculture for reasons that included social, ecological, economic and cultural concerns.[33]

Mexican anthropologist Arturo Warman argues that there is a bias against the peasant in Mexican government agricultural policy and that to correct this, *campesinos* and not government agents should oversee land distribution.[34] Mexican agronomist Antonio Turrent argues for a *campesinos*-based agriculture to counter the bias in agricultural research and government farm interventions towards enhancing single crop yields. Turrent observes that the bias of agricultural researchers towards raising single crop yields trains them neither to see nor to research the potential benefits of a traditional peasant farm in terms of food availability, biodiversity and long term sustainability of the mixed ecology, including forest patches, grazing land, horticulture, cereals and fruits.[35] One thousand miles north of Mexico, Wendell Berry makes the same argument about the destructive impacts of state-sponsored agricultural research on soils and on ecologically sustainable and socially just small farms in the United States. Berry shows how Federal Government-funded Land Grant Universities promote unsustainable monocrop agriculture, and destroy traditional mixed family farms; agroomic advice to farmers pushes them towards over-reliance on a few seeds, and on agricultural chemicals and fossil-fuelled machinery that impact and degrade the soil, and destroy biodiversity.[36] The costs of these new inputs gradually overwhelm family farmers, who sell up to large corporate famers. Hence what Paul Thompson calls the 'productionist paradigm' of agricultural research colludes with the commercial collectivisation of farming worldwide, and the gradual capture of seed patents, and value in food growing and marketing, by large commercial corporations and statist agricultural agencies.[37]

In LVC the Mexican-originated 'campesina', or peasant-led and small-scale alternative to commercial and governmental agronomy, takes the form of a new social movement, which has fostered peasant-led agrarian reform in countries as diverse as Honduras and Java. It is also increasingly associated with urban as well as rural food growing, and local food initiatives in developing and developed country contexts.[38] Currently headquartered in Jakarta, Indonesia, the movement has fostered strong regional networks in Central and South America, in South and Southeast Asia and in Southern Europe. It is also increasingly making inroads among smallholders and urban food growers in the United States, Canada and Northern Europe. It aspires to grow an equivalent base in Africa. At the heart of LVC is the belief that small-scale peasant agriculture is not an anachronism, as both Marxist and classical economists believe, but essential to a food supply that is ecologically and economically sustainable into the future.

In a country-level study of peasant farmers in Guatemala, Ryan Isakson describes the variety of locally adapted and bred seeds grown by small subsistence farmers in the South as compared to the small number of high yield variety seeds (HYVs) deployed on large-scale commercial farms in North America.[39] The core crop grown in the region is maize but in traditional agriculture peasants interplant maize with horticultural plants, including legumes, squash and herbs, which together with corn provide a healthy household diet in a practice known as *milpa*. However, peasant-based agriculture is being undermined by the importation of subsidised HYVs and other North American farm products, which suppress local market prices for surplus outputs from subsistence farms.[40] Against a global political economy of free trade that facilitates capital accumulation by the largest market actors, peasant farmers in Guatemala have taken up the stance of LVC that a farmer-based food system that achieves a high degree of self-sufficiency, without dependence on imports, is both culturally and ecologically more desirable. But for a farmer-based system to be maintained requires that subsidised unsustainable imports of food, seed and agrochemicals are restrained at the border. Hence the idea of food sovereignty underwrites the spatial importance of local cultural knowledge and dietary practices, and the role of geographical distance, and related political borders, in resistance to a globalised food system dominated by a small number of powerful agronomic corporations and a diminishing range of seeds.[41]

This analysis, while it resists the Marxist account of the need for the overthrow of capitalism, nonetheless represents a significant revision to conventional neoclassical economics. It indicates that individual and household agency in peasant agriculture and market exchange are not primarily focused on economic value. Instead, they reflect a much larger set of ecological and interpersonal concerns, including culture, diet, household self-reliance, human health, land inheritance rights, plant biodiversity and soil quality. Hence peasant organisation and practices in relation to food growing and land distribution practices are *political*, as defined by Carl Schmitt in *The Concept of the Political*, since they represent a communitarian counter to the universalising borderless economy advanced by classical economists and Northern development agencies and multinational corporations.[42]

The political meaning of peasant agriculture is captured in the phrase 'food sovereignty', which describes a counter-politics to the dominant frame of political economy and agronomy. Food sovereignty resists development agency, governmental and commercial advancement of an agronomy focused on single crop production values and the borderless movement of agricultural commodities. And it resists the transfer of land ownership and power over food production and diet from small farmers and householders to agricultural and industrial food corporations. Ernesto Canada enumerates a range of country-by-country examples, in which the pursuit of this agricultural development model in governmental and commercial interventions to force peasants to grow cash crops such as coffee, cotton, peanuts and wheat produced hunger and destroyed viable indigenous agricultures in countries as diverse as Ethiopia, Nicaragua, Senegal and Vietnam. The concept of food sovereignty was formally adopted as a counter to neoliberal agricultural policy at the annual meeting of LVC in Rome in 1996, and it was defined at a World Forum on Food Sovereignty in Cuba in 2001 as:

> the peoples' right to define their own policies and strategies for the sustainable production, distribution and consumption of food that guarantee the right to food for the entire population, on the basis of small and medium-sized production, respecting their own cultures and the diversity of peasant, fishing and indigenous forms of agricultural production, marketing and management of rural areas, in which women play a fundamental role.[43]

Food sovereignty brings together a range of concerns about land ownership, cultural knowledge, soil conservation, social justice and gender and intergenerational justice into an agrarian vision of political economy that has significant resonances with the Old Testament perspective on food and farming outlined above.

There is, however, a major difference between the politics advanced by food sovereignty and the 'new agrarianism' fostered by Berry and his acolytes. The concept of food sovereignty links the destruction of indigenous farming with neoliberal capitalism, and with what Marxists call 'primitive accumulation' by capital owners, and not only with agricultural methods. Food sovereignty represents an alternative understanding of the relationship between land and sovereignty to the dominant Lockean theology of private property, according to which land ownership *ought* to belong to the one who uses land most productively in money accumulation, and which underwrites classical economic theory and neoliberal interventions in agricultural markets.[44] Its advocates recognise that the tendency of modern agronomy to concentrate the food supply and farmland into fewer hands is opposed both to ecological and human flourishing, precisely as did the Old Testament theologians when they reflected on the causes of agricultural failure and exile.

The time from ancient Mesopotamia to the modern agricultural economy is 8,000 years but the greatest changes in agricultural methods have occurred in the last fifty of these. Conventional agricultural and economic historians describe the gradual evolution from peasant to commercial agriculture as one of growth in human welfare and flourishing, and as a sure path to progress in human development as measured in reduced infant mortality and increased longevity, development indices first proposed by Third Isaiah in his prediction of a messianic age. But this conventional history departs radically from Isaiah when it issues, as it has done in the last fifty years, in the gradual loss by farmers and householders of deliberative power over diet, land and seeds, and the concentration of such power into large statist and commercial corporations. As in the story of Joseph, while the promise of such concentrated power is that famine will be staved off and the people fed, the end result is a loss of political freedom and moral agency. The contemporary rise of poor nutrition, and rising suicides among farmers, the homeless and the unemployed in both developing and developed countries, are therefore not incidental to, but a direct consequence of, the loss of power and agency over the fruits of the earth advanced by neoliberal agronomy.

Against the productionist paradigm that underwrites capitalist accumulation with scientific knowledge, anthropological studies reveal that small farmers and traditional farming methods, including interplanting, saved seeds, composting and the mixed ecology of horticulture, cereals and small animal farming, are more productive, more just and more ecologically sustainable than the 'monocultures of the mind' that are envisaged in scientific laboratories and measured on corporate spreadsheets.[45] Hence a central plank of the LVC policy programme is land reform, and a reversal of the Enclosure of land in the name of agricultural 'improvement', which is the same justification used for the Tudor State and aristocratic land grab of pre-revolutionary England, and which paved the way for the first centralised state, and empire, of modern Europe. As the English agrarian Harold Massingham argued in the 1940s, Britain used the monopolisation of agricultural land to create the first centralised banking system.[46] The new central banks of England and Scotland underwrote the gathering of land and paper titles into fewer hands, and occasioned the aristocratic spending spree in which land titles were used to mobilise credit for the building of grand houses and associated landscaping projects. In the same way, Scots and English governments borrowed against Crown land holdings to fund wars, and to underwrite imperial projects such as the development of colonies opened up by the East India Company, the first modern multinational corporation. Hence the central plank of the restoration of sovereignty to food growers is the reconnection between a rebuilt local exchange economy – at least in food and other locally produced products – and a propertied democracy in which people recover use rights and community ownership of the land.[47]

Jeffrey Stout argues that modern democracy may reasonably be seen as the fruit of the Reformation breakup of the monopoly of religious sovereignty and land ownership of the Roman Catholic Church in the late Middle Ages, and the development at different times in Switzerland, England and Scotland, Northern Germany, Scandinavia, and North America, of a model of federal self-government that replaced the primacy of Peter, and hereditary monarchy, with a localist ecclesiology and a localist politics.[48] In this Reformed ecclesiological politics the *esse* of the church derived from the gathering of the people for the weekly celebration of Word and Sacrament, while the authority of magistrates derived from the associations, guilds and citizens of each city or region.[49] Ironically, however, the acquisition by landowners of the lion's share of the land of Britain in the Dissolution of the Monasteries, and in subsequent Enclosures of agricultural lands and forests (which continue to this day in the developing world) tend historically in the reverse direction. Enclosure and depeasantisation remove deliberation and power over food production from local communities and put them in the hands of aristocratic, and now more often corporate, owners of farmlands and agricultural supplies. The movement for local food and land reform therefore represents the urgently needed recovery of that process of democratic formation, and the underwriting of the rights of the laity over against those of an ecclesiastical elite, that began in Northern Europe at the Reformation. It is a double irony, however, that the genius of this movement for agrarian reform comes not from Protestant Europe but from Catholic Central America, under the influence not of Marxist liberation theology but – as Isakson's genealogical investigation of LVC reveals[50] – of an early twentieth-century economist, Aleksandr Vasil'evich Chayanov who likely worshipped in the Russian Orthodox Church.[51]

In her magisterial two-volume study of the peasant economy, practices and religion of a modern Greek village, Juliet du Boulay describes a sacred culture of land care, family life, bread making and worship that shows remarkable continuity with Greek Orthodox Christian culture going back many centuries.[52] In the Greek village the sense of place, and a self-sufficient agrarian economy, are deeply rooted in the worship of the Holy Trinity: the Father Creator is the providential source of life in the field, Christ crucified and risen is the redeemer of life from death and meaninglessness, and points all life towards union with divine life, while the divine Spirit is immanent in all living things and imbues work with and on them with sacred significance. Central to the milieu of practices and meanings that du Boulay describes is a symbolic materialism that sees everyday practices of dwelling and working in place as imbued with sacred significance. The line, in other words, between sacred and profane is very thin in Greek Orthodox village life. Hence the commonest food, bread, is made both for the home and the altar, and even the bread made to be eaten at home is given, in its making and shaping, marks of its symbolic significance as food given through the life, death and resurrection of Jesus Christ. Similarly, the home itself, and seasonal work in the fields, are marked by the sacred calendar of the Christian year and by the sacred time fostered by the hours of prayer. In the traditional Greek village, dwelling and production are underwritten by the doctrine of a divine Creator whose intention is to redeem human persons made in the divine image through the hallowing of land and labour, and the sacralisation of the everyday economy of life and its interpenetration by Orthodox symbolism and worship.

The central production 'unit' in the Greek village, as in all premodern peasant economies, is the family household. As the Russian economist Chayanov argued, the family unit in peasant agriculture exercises a kind of 'self-exploitation', such that what in a wage economy would be seen as excessive hours of work by most family members, including older children, is the 'price' paid for self-sufficiency, domestic production, and *freedom* from the vagaries of market and state collectivisation of the kind that overtook farming in both capitalist and communist societies in the nineteenth and twentieth centuries.[53] It is for this reason that, provided land prices are not excessive and water sources are reliable, family-based agriculture is usually more productive than large-scale collective farming, whether of communist or capitalist type.

Under the influence of Christian ideals of freedom and dignity, the institution of slavery came to an end in Europe in the late Middle Ages, until it was reinstated in the colonies. But the concentration of wealth and power into fewer hands consequent on the Dissolution of the Monasteries, and the subsequent growth of large private landed estates in Britain, Germany and elsewhere, increasingly elided the lately won freedom of the peasantry.[54] The demise of a self-sufficient peasantry, and their often enforced decanting into industrial towns, saw the rise of a new kind of urban industrial civilisation. In the new industrial cities freedom through self-sufficiency in food growing, and local harvesting of construction, clothing materials and fuel, was a distant memory to the masses imprisoned in overcrowded slums with insufficient sunlight to prevent rickets, and with working hours and poverty wages that were analogous to slavery. The story of these enforced decantations in Britain is narrated in Charles Dickens' London novel *Hard Times*. But while Dickens clearly describes the link between oppressive hours of work, overcrowding, poverty, ill health and early mortality, the predominant view in Victorian Britain was that the reasons for the ills of slum-dwellers were their 'low' morals rather than the material and economic conditions that exiled them from clean country air, green space and the ability to grow their own healthy food.[55]

Under pressure from reformers, which in nineteenth-century Britain included the Christian Clapham Sect of which Wilberforce was a member, and in the twentieth century from trade unions and socialists, industrial societies gradually regulated factory work and reengineered industrial cities to reduce overcrowding, insanitary conditions and polluted skies. The spread of the universal franchise in the early twentieth century underwrote the gradual equalisation in the distribution of the fruits of industrial production so that the gap between capital owners and workers had narrowed significantly by the late 1970s, with correlative improvements in the health and longevity of the urban working classes. However, since 1979 neoliberal capitalism has reasserted the rights of capital owners over industrial workers, and wealth inequality in Britain and North America is now rapidly reverting to that of the late Victorian era. At the same time the myth of the 'undeserving poor' is revived to legitimate the winding down of social security, while entitlements and tax breaks to capital owners have significantly increased. The consequence is a gradual and significant deterioration in the nutrition and housing conditions of the non-rich in both Britain and America, and the return of an oligarchic elite, concentrated in London and Manhattan and dubbed the 'one per cent'.[56] Their extreme wealth promotes an economy skewed towards the provision of luxury goods and services by a growing class of workers whose poverty wages are insufficient to meet their housing and nutritional needs and which are subsidised, albeit inadequately, by the neoliberal State.

These developments recall the moral descent of earlier agrarian civilisations into large-scale hierarchical societies, as narrated in Genesis, in which ruling elites used stored food and concentrated wealth to coerce large numbers of people into slavery, and which led eventually to the economic and political collapse of the Egyptian, Babylonian and Persian empires in the last millennium before the Christian Era. There are nonetheless developed and developing nations in which such tendencies are resisted, and there are even within the UK and North America hopeful examples of rural and city-based agricultural, economic and political projects that successfully resist the oligarchic and centralising tendencies of neoliberal rule, and I review some of these in the next chapter.

7

The moral geography of sustainable communities

In 2014 David Clapson, a 59 year old former soldier and telecommunications worker, died alone in a small apartment in a town in the London Home Counties. He had worked and paid social security contributions and taxes for over thirty years of his adult life. But his semi-skilled employments had not permitted him to build up savings other than payments to Britain's National Insurance fund.[1] Although William Beveridge envisaged that Social Security would be 'a plan of insurance – of giving in return for contributions benefits up to subsistence levels, as of right and without means test, so that individuals may build freely upon it', in reality National Insurance is more analogous to a tax than an actual fund in which individuals have an attributable share.[2] Hence no matter how much is contributed, an individual before pensionable age acquires no correlative rights to social security payments in the event of accident, ill health or other cause of a loss of employment earnings. This deficiency in the UK National Insurance scheme was magnified by the perverse 'austerity economics' of the post-2008 UK economy, in which the poor and unemployed were punished for the mistakes of rich investment bankers. Hence since 2010, social security payments were cut off for periods from weeks to years from more than a million claimants as a way of reducing social security spending and 'incentivising' claimants to find employment. Clapson died with an empty stomach and four pounds in his bank account, having been cut off from social security assistance by the quasi-judicial decision of a social security functionary. The bureaucrat did not think Clapson was serious about looking for work, although he died with a number of printed CVs around him. He had 'saved' for unemployment insurance for thirty years of his working life until he left employment to take up full time care of his mother who was suffering from dementia. After she died he registered as an adult seeking work, which he was urgently doing despite being ill from diabetes and other health conditions. But the 'National Insurance' he had paid for three decades was effectively a chimera: he was cut off without a penny despite his employment 'insurance' after only a few months as a job seeker.

In the same year, a farmer from Essex, England, said to me, at a conference of landowners at Goring in Sussex, that he was beginning to question the wisdom of modern industrial farming, which he described as hydroponics. As he explained, the only function the soil performs for the crop is to hold it up towards the sun and provide a medium for the uptake of rainwater and nutrients from artificial fertilisers. The farmer said he could imagine a situation not many years hence, given the converging crises of climate change, peak oil and peak phosphorous, when people from the towns in Essex nearer London might experience a collapse in the global sourcing of foods that characterises the current supermarket-based food provisioning system.[3] These people would then leave the towns and would approach farmers like him and ask for food. But he would have nothing to give or sell them since currently he is not paid to grow food, but merely crops for utilisation in industrial food factories, and as animal feeds.

More than two hundred years after the industrial revolution it is increasingly apparent that there is a conflict between the global form of industrial civilisation and the health of human and species communities in both rural and urban areas, and the health of the planet as a whole. But resolution of the large-scale problems of species extinction, and of human hunger, remains elusive. This is in part because modern accounts of ethics, and of economy and government, lack an adequate dialectical and phenomenological understanding of the politics and ethics of sustainable habitable communities, resilient economies, and diverse and resilient ecosystems. While economic and bureaucratic forms of organisation have developed an array of quantitative instruments and data sets for procuring resources, producing artifacts, and governing space, they are less sensitive to the specificities of place, ecosystems and local cultures, including the many diverse cultures of farming, because they tend to exclude the anthropic dimension of human dwelling across time in communities with a history.

As we have seen, places of dwelling become *places*, and sacred places, as they are shaped by human experiences and events in interaction with local and specific ecological qualities. The narratives of how people build viable lives and communities in particular places, against the vagaries of climate or disease, or invading warriors, form the patriarchal narratives and heroic stories of ancient civilisations from the Hebrews and classical Greece and Rome to those of Mesoamerica, China and India. What Clifford Geertz calls local knowledge is central to how traditional human communities nurtured and sustained life in place in ways that did not permit the poor to die of hunger, that shared rewards of labour by rules that ensured just prices and wages, and that oversaw common goods such as water, air, grazing land and forests through distributed and participative commons governance arrangements.[4]

Against these traditional, narrated and local forms of knowledge there emerged in the course of the scientific revolution in Europe, and the accompanying depeasantisation of rural life, new forms of universal knowledge – including natural science and political economy – which suppressed local knowledge. Resistance to the social effects of depeasanti-sation in Europe, as in contemporary Asia and Latin America, was therefore weak and ineffective since resistors were said to be on the wrong side of history and against progress. In the course of the British Enclosures and Clearances, few prominent voices were raised against the injustices these represented, and the Churches were often tragically complicit in the eviction of peasants from their ancestral lands.[5] Even the Romantics protested primarily at the ecologically destructive effects of industrial development on rural areas, rather than the toxic and short lives enforced on the poor in industrial cities.

Environmental protests in the industrial era concerned not the shortened lives of the poor but the use of mountain regions as water supply areas for industrial cities. The first such protest in Britain was around the intention of the Manchester Corporation Water Works to flood the beautiful valley of Thirlmere in the mountainous English region known as the Lake District so admired by the English Romantics, including Thomas Gray, William Wordsworth, Robert Southey and John Ruskin. As the Manchester Corporation began to survey and buy up farms in the valley, its plans to flood the valley for Manchester's water supply became known and the Thirlmere Defence Association was born.[6] The TDA proposed that the Lake District be set aside from industrial development as a park, along the lines of the Yellowstone National Park in the United States. The campaign to prevent the flooding of Thirlmere attracted prominent support from local residents, but it also drew membership from artists, essayists, professors and others who visited the Lake District but did not reside there. They did not prevent the building of the reservoir, nor the turning of the rest of the valley into an arborial plantation for fast growing alien trees, such as the Lodgepole Pine and Sitka Spruce by the new landowner, the City of Manchester. But those who organised the defence of Thirlmere set up a nationwide organi-sation, the National Trust, whose purpose was to buy up other precious coastlands, mountains, valleys and rural estates and buildings, set them aside from industrial development, and so preserve them for the enjoyment of the members of the trust and the nation.[7]

The proposal of the City of San Francisco to construct a similar dam at Hetch Hetchy in the equally iconic and beautiful lands of the Yosemite National Park, made famous by the Scots wilderness advocate John Muir, had a similar role in founding the modern environmental movement in the United States. Again the campaign against the dam was unsuccessful but it led to the formation of the Sierra Club, and to campaigns to preserve large areas of wilderness from similar industrial developments.[8] John Muir des-cribed the developers as 'temple destroyers, devotees of ravaging com-mercialism', who 'instead of lifting their eyes to the God of the Mountains, lift them to the Almighty Dollar'.[9] Most environmental historians portray the Hetch Hetchy controversy as 'the difference between a wild Hetch

Hetchy and an artificial reservoir',[10] or as a 'battle over the competing claims of wilderness and civilization'.[11] But in reality it was a contest between competing land uses by outsiders from Yosemite: on the one hand those who wanted the valley developed for nature tourism, and on the other those who wanted to secure San Francisco's water supply, albeit that he also points out that there were nearer and less environmentally damaging alternatives to Hetch Hetchy that the city of San Francisco could have tapped for its water supply.

The Sierra Club, like the National Trust, set the pattern for the early environmental movement in the UK and the USA, which was not so much a critique of industrialism as a more modest reform that set apart certain wild and beautiful areas, including, in the case of the National Trust, buildings and gardens as well as wild places, and preserved them from industrial development or destruction. As we have seen, the danger of wilderness fetishism is that it suggests that environmentalism is primarily about preserving nature from human uses while the human habitat, and human–nature interactions, take second place in environmental campaigns and concerns. But while in America the Sierra Club was a wilderness movement that had little influence on the broader pattern of industrial development and the uglifying spread of strip mall and ribbon development across the American continent, in England the National Trust was one of a number of civic and environmental organisations whose members devoted themselves to the preservation of the landscape, and of historic buildings. Among these are the Council for the Protection of Rural England (CPRE), the Society for the Protection of Ancient Buildings, the Women's Institute, the Youth Hostel Association and the National Council of Ramblers Federations. In different ways these voluntary groups set out to preserve a variety of aspects of English culture and landscape and are, as Roger Scruton argues, more responsible for the remarkable preservation of the diversity and beauty of England's landscape, despite it being one of the most crowded countries in Europe, than action by governmental regulation or environmental agencies.[12]

The establishment of green belts around British cities was also a result of campaigns by the CPRE, and these campaigns culminated in the Town and Country Planning Act of 1946, which imposed national constraints on development in rural areas. But these various initiatives have not spared British cities and rural areas from the spread of ugly municipal and private housing, offices and factories, and indeed since the Second World War the State has used top-down planning powers to impose brutal and ecologically unsustainable forms of development and settlement on towns and rural areas in many parts of the UK. For Scruton, only free association by citizens is capable of reforming industrial development and of restoring 'homeostatic systems' of production and settlement that do not involve ecological destruction.[13] On the other hand, it is the growing power of a centralised and centralising State that has overseen the spread of great destruction both in rural areas and in towns and cities. While the Enclosures had concentrated land ownership, and forced the migration of many rural dwellers to the cities, nonetheless aerial photographs of the UK from the Second World War, taken by the Luftwaffe, show a pattern of fields, hedgerows, woods and copses that had hardly changed over many centuries. But after the war the British government devoted itself in earnest to the industrialisation of agriculture with a view to maximising indigenous food production. Through a regime of subsidies and regulations it imposed a new kind of chemical and mechanistic farming, which saw the widespread destruction of ancient hedgerows and woodlands, and the spread of new prairie style fields in many parts of England and Scotland.[14] The new farming methods were also neglectful of soil quality and encouraged extensive soil erosion, and hence pollution of rivers and shorelines with agricultural run-off, while they also produced a tide of artificial fertilisers and pesticides, which poisoned the same water sources, together with underground aquifers, with consequences which eventually had to be dealt with by filters and other treatment methods in municipal water supplies. As we have seen, Wendell Berry charts the similarly destructive effects of statist agriculture in the United States,[15] and even more terrible results were achieved by top-down statist agronomy in socialist and communist countries, such as that charted by James C. Scott in Tanzania.[16] Sadly, lessons have not been learned from this tragic history, and vast agrarian 'improvement' schemes are still funded by the UK government, and USAid, as development aid intended to alleviate poverty in India and Africa, even though such schemes are a major source of rural poverty, landlessness and farmer suicides.

Scruton is not alone in believing that only bottom-up community action and free association can effectively turn the ecologically destructive tide of modern agricultural and urban industrial development. As we have seen, Elinor Ostrom argues that it is precisely such community-based action to govern and conserve common natural resources, including forests, pastures, soils, rivers, shorelines and water tables, which historically has a better record of sustainably managing habitat, from the rain forests of the Amazon to the montaine pastures of the Alps. But in the contemporary global economy, where the State and the corporation are the dominant agencies in habitat management, rebuilding sustainable habitat governance from the ground up also requires resistance to the imperial and remote procurement and production procedures of the global industrial economy, and it is not clear from Scruton's analysis how such resistance will emerge since he neglects the reemergence of neoliberal oligarchy and the rise of corporate rather than democratic governance.

Many of the problems with habitat that afflict communities in place emanate from the increasingly global nature of the economy. This includes the urban as well as rural habitat, since many of the problems that afflict the urban poor, including poor nutrition and poor housing, reflect an inter-generational history of dislocation from habitats that their ancestors once had control over. When we connect the societal and economic difficulties faced by unemployed and under-employed families and their children in post-industrial cities such as Glasgow and Detroit with the ecological threats to place represented by remote forms of power and rule, whether capitalist or statist, the importance of the relationship of people to land and place comes all the more into relief. That children are being born below normal weight, and with diet-related brain defects, as a result of poor nutrition within hundreds of metres from supermarkets stocked with vast quantities of food in two of the richest countries in human history is a moral tragedy as serious as any that afflicted predecessor civilisations.[17] For whereas in previous eras hunger was the result of natural events such as drought or flood, in 'advanced' industrial societies poor nutrition is the result of maldevelopment, where some have far too much wealth, water, habitat and food available to them, while many others have not enough of these for their full and dignified participation in society as free citizens, nor for their own, or their children's, health.

In the early decades of the twentieth century in Britain there was an informal movement of urban dwellers back to the land, which sought to address nutritional and nature deficits among urban residents. It was not so much an *environmental* movement as a livelihood movement, which nonetheless involved a return to nature. Mirroring similar patterns of informal settlement in Europe, the United States and the developing world, working people in Britain before and after the Great War, and in the midst of the Great Depression, took up an anarchic and populist land grab, which reversed on a small scale the earlier aristocratic and statist land grab of the Enclosures. On the coasts, on riverine scrubland, on hillsides, and on unused land between some of the large enclosed estates, urban families, using the newly constructed railways, sought out waste and uncultivated land within a few hours or a day's travel from the cities. Here they marked out vegetable plots and grew food for themselves and their families. These 'plotlands' were places of informal settlement where families constructed shacks, grew food and so derived some livelihood to supplement their meagre factory wages, or their even more meagre unemployment rations. At the same time, their children could escape overcrowded slums at weekends and in the summers and so experience something of the freedom to move about in nature, and breathe clean air, known by their rural ancestors.

In an historical reconstruction of this rural arcadia, Dennis Hard and Colin Ward trace the extent of informal and temporary settlement and horticulture, which was greatest around the most heavily populated cities of London, Manchester, Newcastle and Glasgow.[18] Ward's fieldwork is strongest in the English Home Counties, and he demonstrates the considerable extent of informal settlement in the twentieth-century interwar period along the English Thames Valley, on the east and south coasts of England and on the North Downs. The movement came to an end with the invention after the Second World War of local authority planning powers. After 1947 many of the informal settlements became permanent suburban dwellings as planning permission was given to their owners or to housing developers who in some cases took them over. In some areas the plotlands were all along intended for permanent settlement. On the Isle of Wight, in South Essex and Dorset, landowners sold small parcels of land to 'smallholders', who moved out from the cities and built small homes on horticultural plots of one to five acres. But in other places plotlands sometimes became places of refuge from the formal propertied economy. In the North East of England miners evicted from mine-owned homes in the Depression sometimes created homes out of their shacks on food growing allotments.

Not all of these shack and plotland developments were born of poverty or slum dwelling. Many urban householders of means also took to rural cottages and vegetable gardens in the summer in a 'back to nature' movement with analogies in the writings of William Morris, Leo Tolstoy, Peter Kropotkin and Edward Thoreau. The anti-urban and agrarian overtones of this movement have deep roots in British history and culture, where fewer peasant farmers had owned their own land since the Norman Conquest than in other parts of Europe, and where in more recent centuries the Enclosures had created a long-standing dispossession of people from common and tenanted land, and an enforced move from the clean air of the country to the coal-infested air of the city. What drove informal settlement was, as Ward argues, 'a sense of seeing justice done – of getting back that to which everyone has a right; and a belief that owning one's plot of land would secure independence and freedom'.[19] The practice has deep roots also in rural squatting, which is a common device by which the law of many nations grants to the poor rights to a parcel of land when they successfully set up a dwelling house in a legally prescribed period, which can be as little as twenty-four hours and as much as twelve or twenty years. The practice was widespread in England from Tudor times and, though outlawed by Elizabeth I, was one of the ways in which paupers responded to population pressures and Enclosure. Many of what are now regarded as traditional English villages originated as informal squatter settlements set up by landless peasants on road side verges and other waste lands.[20] Gerard Winstanley is perhaps the best known English squatter. As informal leader of a seventeenth-century movement that became known as the Diggers, Winstanley held that the ultimate landowner was God, and not the monarch, and that as children of God born of the land, Diggers who took up residence on, and cultivated, a small plot of land acquired the title to that land from God as much as the monarch.[21]

While rural squatting and back to the land movements may be read in Lockean terms as affirming the right of private property to the industrious users of land, they also represent an alternative pattern of dwelling and livelihood to the form of concentrated land and capital ownership, urban dwelling, and factory or office-based employment, which emerged as the dominant form of civilisation across much of the planet in the twentieth century. At time of writing, in the European Union there are more than twenty-five million people who are not in formal employment in the aftermath of the continuing post-2008 Global Financial Crisis (GFC), and more than twelve million in the United States. In Greece, which was the most indebted European nation after the GFC, a back-to-the-land movement began as individuals returned from the cities, where they had insufficient income for food or heating, to the homes of their grandparents to grow food, gather wood for heat in the winter and seek an alternative to the enforced poverty of a vastly depressed formal urban-industrial economy. In Scotland, as we have seen, a campaign for land reform led to a project primarily rural in its location, where residents in the Scottish Highlands and Islands are given rights under the Land Reform Act of the Scottish Parliament to acquire shared title to land in which they already dwell. But there are at least half a million adult residents of Scottish post-industrial cities and towns – or one-tenth of the nation – who lack employment or income sufficient for their healthy participation as citizens in the life of the nation. Land Reform needs to address the dispossession of the urban, as well as the rural, landless if it is to be a genuine movement of social transformation beyond the iconic loci of crofting estates and Hebridean islands.

The project to reconnect land and livelihood has long characterised resistance to the centralising tendencies in ownership of land and wealth characteristic of British political economy since the English Civil War. From Gerard Winstanley to John Ruskin and Hilaire Belloc, a number of radical English political philosophers have argued that to each person made in the divine image belongs a divine endowment of use rights to the divine creation, and more particularly the land in which they are born and their parents dwell. Belloc in particular connects such proprietary use of the divine creation with the Christian (and English) ideal of political freedom, which was at risk in an industrial economy in which wages, and not property, were the principal means of livelihood.

In his essay, *The Restoration of Property*, Hilaire Belloc argued that since under both Capitalist and Communist social arrangements the vast majority of people are denied ownership of the means of production, modern social arrangements represent a reversal of the trend from the late Middle Ages to the seventeenth century of a form of yeoman farming in which the majority of farming families owned their own means of livelihood, and hence slavery was abolished.[22] For Belloc, 'economic freedom' is an essential temporal good for the dignity of persons and for the prevention of tyranny, since only a society in which property is well distributed can resist a tyrannical government or State. Political freedom cannot, therefore, be said to reside in societies the vast majority of whose members merely receive a wage or salary but lack ownership of the tools of a trade, land title or secure use rights to land. Belloc therefore calls for the intervention of the State into the 'natural tendency' of unrestrained competition in capitalist economies to concentrate ownership of land and wealth in fewer hands so that the ownership of property sufficient to guarantee economic independence from either wages from an employer or the largesse of the State may be restored to the majority of households.[23] For Belloc, the restoration of property cannot be achieved by economic redistribution, or 'social credit', as advocated by social creditors in the 1930s and as more or less formalised after the Second World War in the Beveridge 'welfare state'. Only the redistribution of land and titles from large landowners to small or peasant farmers, and of production and sales activities from industrial capitalists to craftsmen and small shop keepers, will suffice to turn back the centralising and servile tendencies of industrial capitalism, which of course are exactly paralleled by industrial communism.

Fifty years on from Beveridge, many people now suspect that Belloc was right about social credit. Welfare payments to poor and unemployed people have declined in real value and are no longer backed by a real fund to which they have contributed and from which they, therefore, have a right to draw in times of necessity. The value of social security assistance has also declined below subsistence so that there are growing numbers of homeless people, including families, living in hostels in London and other large British cities who may have low waged jobs but for whom social security assistance does not provide sufficient supplement to enable them access to decent and secure housing. This is in part because social security is increasingly represented by politicians, and in the media, as undue reward for lack of industry, or carelessness, rather than as insurance for those who have saved through their contributions for assistance in difficult times.

Belloc's distributist programme was a more radical project than National Insurance since for Belloc the maldistribution of a nation's property, where some are unable to properly feed themselves or their children while living close to stores of surplus food, represents a kind of collective theft. Belloc's position has become part of Catholic social teaching in the twentieth century, and is expressed in the idea of the 'universal destination of goods'.[24] In this perspective every person, by being born in a nation with a defined land area and borders, acquires a God-given endowment of the divine creation in the land into which they are born. If their portion was stolen from their peasant ancestors in the business of State-making, and in the creation of large landed estates, corporately owned farms, and collectivised industrial food production, this does not take away their God-given inheritance. Belloc's proposal was to reverse this ancient fault by a modern redistribution not of income but of property rights, with the intention that to individual households would also return economic freedom, and hence responsibility, for their own livelihood, stewardship and use of the gifts of God's good creation.

Belloc also reckoned with the fact that the majority of urban dwellers were unlikely to be able to turn back into peasant farmers, even though some will still have a feeling for working land and soil. Instead, Belloc proposed modifications in income and land taxes, and land sale arrangements, such that the small owner would be treated preferentially over the large, and the large landowner given strong incentives to sell to the small owner. No such modifications were, however, instituted and, to the contrary, after the Second World War, subsidies and taxation arrangements were instituted by the UK government, and subsequently in concert with the European Union, in such a way that the largest landowners are in receipt of the largest public subsidies. At the same time large corporate purchasers of agricultural produce – and especially supermarkets – grant very unfavourable terms to small producers, and even taxation arrangements favour the wealthy, who can employ tax advisors and move wealth to tax havens, over the smallholder.[25] The net effect has been a further emptying out of rural areas of people working on the land, an increase in the use of heavy machinery, and in farm size, and a significant increase in field size in many areas, accompanied by a grubbing up of hedgerows and copses, with a consequent decline in biodiversity as noted above.

The results of this grand social experiment, as we have seen, have been declining nutrition among lower income families, a growing gap between rich and poor, and an increasing maldistribution of wealth and land, which threatens the very social fabric of society. In many urban and rural areas the rich are increasingly living in gated communities where they employ private security guards, and hence even the monopoly of violence on which the modern social contract of the State was founded is undermined.[26] At the same time the expenditures and governance and surveillance regimes of the State have grown vastly beyond the imaginary of early modern political theorists requiring that an ever heavier tax burden fall upon the general non-property owning populace.

According to the Code of Hammurabi, as we have seen, in the first human society organised along agrarian lines, the purpose of kingly rule was envisaged as protecting the weak against the strong. Analogously, the rule of ancient Israel was grounded in the rescue of the ancient Hebrews from slavery in Egypt. Hence in the federal polity of Israelite society, dispersed ownership of land among the tribes and households of Israel was seen as the epitome of the divine project of Israelite freedom. But in late modern societies the State enforces or underwrites, with threat of forfeit of possessions, and ultimately imprisonment, debt and taxation demands on the poorest households, while large multinational corporations and the wealthiest households use global mobility and accounting devices to enjoy a kind of cosmopolitan freedom from the claims of any particular political community to a taxable share, or what in the bible was known as a tithe, of the product of the lands and workers from which their income derives.

In modern social contract theory the consent given by citizens to the State's monopoly of violence is envisaged as being conferred in exchange for the State defending citizens from harms. But increasingly the State abrogates its duty to defend citizens from corporate power and corporate harms. In just the last thirty years large corporations have been responsible for major corporate crimes, in which millions of people lost their lives or livelihoods. To name just three of the most prominent of such events these include: the chemical poisoning of the town of Bhopal in which 15,000 people lost their lives and hundreds of thousands were disabled; the poisoning of a significant part of northeast Japan by TEKPO with the earthquake-triggered meltdowns at three of the reactors at the Fukushima nuclear plant; and the poisoning of the Gulf of Mexico by the BP Horizon oil spill whose toxic effects were significantly magnified by the use of thousands of barrels of toxic chemical dispersants, which poisoned thousands of individuals involved in the clean-up or who live close to the shore line. In none of these instances were individual executives or managers prosecuted for negligence, and financial compensation obtained through the courts was never sufficient for the losses of dwelling, livelihood, or life itself, that these events visited on households, farms, fishers and businesses.

The gravest example to date of the failure of the State to protect citizens from corporate harms was the socialisation of the risks incurred by bankers in the period leading up to the Global Financial Collapse in 2008. Trillions of dollars in bank losses and bad debts associated with fraudulent mortgages and financial derivatives, such as 'securitised debts', were taken over by governments, and hence tax payers. But under 'austerity economics' the poor were required to suffer for these debts with cuts in their already minimal social security benefits while many millions of waged employees lost their jobs. But at time of writing no significant new regulations have been passed to prevent such large-scale fraud from happening again, and in the USA, the UK, Germany, Switzerland and the Netherlands fewer than ten people had been indicted for the wide scale banking, home loan and investment frauds that led to the GFC.[27]

Even this failure to restrain collective and corporate evils will pale into insignificance when viewed from the perspective of the envisaged 4–6°C warming of the global climate from greenhouse gas emissions by the end of the twenty-first century. Deaths and loss of homes, farms and businesses from human induced climate change will far exceed all other corporate harms by the end of the present century. But national governments show no willingness to restrain the licensing of fossil fuel corporations to extract coal, oil and gas in quantities far in excess of the capacity of the atmosphere and the ocean to absorb the waste greenhouse gases from the burning of these fuels.

The failures of the State to protect citizens, or nature, from the related crises of climate change and loss of biodiversity produces a growing clamour among activists and academics for the kinds of environmental action that take back responsibility for environmental protection from the State into the hands of citizens and local communities of place. The turn towards a green politics of place is often identified with the term bioregionalism. James Parsons describes a bioregion as 'a geographical province of marked ecological and often cultural unity', which is 'often delimited by watersheds (water divides) of major streams'.[28] The term bioregion reflects the influence of the counter-culture of the 1960s, and of a 'back-to-the-land, do-it-yourself' movement to resituate human life within the ecological limits of eocsystems within particular geographical regions. Bioregionalism also has a spiritual motive, which Peter Berg defines as 'a spiritual identification with a particular kind of country and its wild nature' as the basis 'for the kind of land care the world so definitely needs'.[29] Along with an emphasis on geographic and ecological community, bioregionalists emphasise in preference to State government the role of local communities and practices in place in promoting a more ecologically sustainable way of life.

The bioregional vision sounds at times anti-modern and anti-urban, and seems to represent Romantic nostalgia for past ways of inhabiting land, such as those of the Native Americans in the West Coast States, where the bio-regional vision first emerged. But ecological scientists Rees and Wackernagel of Vancouver, British Columbia, undergird the bioregional vision with a scientific and planning tool – ecological footprint analysis – to determine the precise area of land and water needed to resource the energy and material consumption of a given city, town, region or nation-state. The collective footprint of a city such as Vancouver is a multiple of the consumption of its individual residents. The land area required to support the consumption of an 'average Canadian' is '4.3 hectares or a 207 metre square', and hence the land area required to sustain a city the size of Vancouver is hundreds of times the city boundaries: hence 'the ecosystems that actually support typical industrial regions lie invisibly far beyond their political or geographic boundaries'.[30]

Modern political economists since Adam Smith assume the existence of a colonial hinterland or 'periphery', from which flow natural resources and other kinds of capital in support of the 'wealth of nations'. Smith and others did not feel the need to justify such arrangements, since they lived in the heyday of European colonialism. Now that cosmopolitan theorists hold that each nation has a right to equivalent natural resource consumption, the ecological multiplier that the colonial powers enjoyed in growing the wealth of their cities through their colonial expropriation of the lands, labour and markets of others is brought into critical focus. Another assumption built into the tradition of political economy inaugurated by Smith is that factors of production are substitutable one for another, so that when one factor becomes scarce, another factor will make up the deficiency.[31] But it is not obvious that fresh water and topsoil are actually substitutable by anything else. Analogously there are global limits to the quantity of fish that can be caught in the ocean, or the capacity of the atmosphere and ocean to absorb carbon dioxide from human activities. Ecological footprinting therefore represents a radical challenge to political economy, which conventionally measures monetary exchanges between countries, but does not consider these as ecological or 'natural capital' exchanges. Exposure of the ecological substrate of global trade flows that sustain contemporary consumption patterns therefore reveals the extent to which, even after the formal end of colonialism, European, American and Asian cities still rely on consumption of forests, agricultural lands, minerals, water and energy resources from former colonial lands, where large multinational corporations continue to source such resources, often on terms that are disadvantageous to the local inhabitants of these lands.

Built into ecological footprint analysis is a consideration of two other factors: the rate at which ecosystems can replace resources harvested from them by human activities, and the capacity of ecosystems to absorb wastes from human activities without being systematically degraded; the resultant figure is sometimes called 'biocapacity' or 'biological capital'. Adding in this temporal element to the spatial and geographic elements, ecological footprint analysis indicates that taken together current human consumption and production activities across the planet would require a planet area roughly three times that of planet earth for them to be sustained indefinitely. Using a range of footprint measurement tools, analogous to the family of footprinting tools developed by Gallia et al.,[32] the Global Footprint Network estimates that current human activities already require 1.5 planets to resource them and absorb associated wastes, or to put this another way that the earth takes 1.5 years to regenerate the biocapacity, and sinks, present human activities require.[33] The resultant overshoot of human activities burdens some human beings, species and ecosystems more than others and these unequal effects are experienced within and between political domains. The poor and propertyless are most at risk of exclusion from environments where resources are being used to support the unsustainable consumption of distant cities and regions.

The European Environmental Agency argues that it is possible to use ecological footprinting to redress inequities and power imbalances arising from access to and use of natural resources between peoples and regions occasioned by contemporary growth in cross-border and international trade.[34] However, the scale and degree of regulation required for such redress is beyond the capacities of individual nations, and would therefore suggest the need for global governance instruments and enforceable treaties, of the kind that the nations have signally failed to realise in relation to biodiversity and climate change. Furthermore, the global agency that legally regulates world trade, the World Trade Organisation, opposes efforts by trading nations to recognise the ecological costs of internationally traded goods through trade regulations designed to limit unsustainable resource depletion.[35]

Others propose that against the trend to concentration and hierarchical upscaling of governance procedures that have accompanied modern political economy and, more especially since the 1960s, exponential growth in the volume of world trade, the only way to redress, country by country, imbalances in access to natural resources is a bioregional politics, where local communities recover greater control over their own ecosystems, and engage in efforts to match their consumption activities to the carrying capacities of their bioregion. The mining engineer and ecological visionary E. F. Schumacher was perhaps the first modern environmentalist to call for 'local production for local needs', and he called this approach 'Buddhist economics'. It is Buddhist because the Buddhist requirement for 'right livelihood' suggests that work ought to lead to the fulfilment of the worker, to enable people to work for the common good, and 'to bring forth the goods and services needed for a becoming existence'.[36] Buddhist economics therefore distinguishes 'between the machine and the tool', and hence between production technologies that enhance the human element in work while reducing human effort, and technologies that replace the human element:

> It is clear, therefore, that Buddhist economics must be very different from the economics of modern materialism, since the Buddhist sees the essence of civilisation not in the multiplication of wants but in the purification of human character. Character, at the same time, is formed primarily by a man's work. And work, properly conducted in conditions of human dignity and freedom, blesses those who do it and equally their products.[37]

For Schumacher, production is primarily for the purposes of human liberation from want, and for human wellbeing and character development, rather than for increasing wealth or ownership of material goods. This indicates an economy organised around 'simplicity and nonviolence' rather than luxury and wealth accumulation by an elite. Schumacher envisaged that the only kind of social organisation that would promote this is one where craftmanship is signally honoured as the indispensable crucible of human character, and where work is organised nonviolently around cooperative and sustainable use of local and renewable biological resources, rather than the purloining of the resources of other places and peoples.

Schumacher's conception of work as a school of character finds a direct parallel in Wendell Berry's account of the character-building nature of agrarianism as a kind of farming that does not deplete soils, nor unsustainably draw water or energy resources from other places to grow food in one place. Such farming depends on careful engagement between the farmer and the conditions of the soil, the slope, the sources of water and the seasons, which determine the crop growing and grazing possibilities of his or her land. It is also reminiscent of the Benedictine theology of work, which goes back to the Rule of Benedict in the fifth century of the Christian Era. Indeed given the extensive development by Benedictine monastic communities of craft technologies, farms, gardens, herbariums, and botanical and medicinal arts it might be said that this approach would be better named Benedictine than Buddhist economics, since Buddhist monasteries have not manifest the same productive tendencies as Benedictine.[38]

A contemporary example of efforts to create, or recover, local and sustainable economies around communities of place is offered by the 'Transition' or 'Transition Towns' movement, which is a response to the perceived energy crisis represented by the declining availability of conventional oil and the problem of climate change. Begun by permaculture and peak oil activist Rob Hopkins in the small market town of Totnes in Devon, England, in 2005, the premise of the Transition vision is that climate change requires a transition from oil and other fossil fuels to renewable energy, and that this can only be achieved by a recovery of local procurement of energy, food and the other essential material inputs of life.[39] Advocates of Transition argue that current forms of globally distant and remote procurement produce societies that are inherently fragile and may be destabilised and cease to function where external 'shocks' such as climatic extremes disrupt these remote supply chains. This is exemplified, for example, by contemporary approaches to food supply. In the course of an eight-day blockade of petrol refineries in the UK in 2000, supermarket executives told the government that the shelves would soon be empty of bread and other perishables if the strike was not ended.[40] The majority of bread in Britain is now sold by just four supermarket chains, and as we have seen world food supply is similarly concentrated in the hands of a small number of companies. This gives these companies an extraordinary power over the ability of people to eat, but the increasingly global logistics structure through which they procure food is extremely fragile and vulnerable to external shocks, and especially extreme weather and non-availability of oil.[41]

Transition represents an effort to relocalise the human economy, and local food and energy provision figure large in Transition projects. Transition is as much about process as results. The core political assumption of Transition is that *participation* in creating community is essential to the recovery of a local economy, where people are again engaged in meeting their own needs for food, shelter, entertainment and personal care, instead of relying on large corporations and government agencies. As Hopkins indicates, Transition has a wide spread of interests, is informed by a wide range of ideas and promotes an array of practices:

> Rebuilding local agriculture and food production, localising energy production, rethinking healthcare, rediscovering local building materials in the context of zero energy building, rethinking how to manage waste, all build resilience and offer the potential of an extraordinary renaissance – economic, cultural and spiritual. I am not afraid of a world with less consumerism, less 'stuff' and no economic growth. Indeed, I am far more frightened of the opposite: the process which took fertiliser sacks to the most fertile fields I will probably ever stand in continues, reducing the ability of communities to support themselves beyond the brief, transitory historical interlude when industry was able to turn natural gas into a fertiliser and when the car was king.[42]

This approach is reflected in the adoption of a wide range of locally based cooperative, charitable and commercial initiatives including plant and seed exchanges, community-owned renewable generation plants, local money, local food markets, local land purchase for community food initiatives, improved local transport provision and cycling initiatives, and urban and rural sustainable design and building projects. Since 2005, the Transition Network has already spawned more than a thousand Transition Initiatives in the UK and around the world and represents one of the fastest growing social movements of recent history. Local exchange arrangements, of which the most far-reaching in its implications is local money, are also a growing part of Transition.[43] The biggest such arrangement in the UK is represented by the Bristol Pound which is a unit of local currency in the form of securely produced bank notes, similar in appearance to national currency, and which are exchangeable within 50 miles of the centre of the City of Bristol for goods and services.[44]

A study of Transition in Belgium found that the key contrast between Transition and government efforts to 'steer consumer behaviour in a sustainable direction' is that Transition engages people as 'subjects instead of objects of change'. Transition is a place-based approach to renewing the connections between nature and culture, land and life, exchange relations and neighbourhood relations that starts in already existing communities and neighbourhoods. But its advocates also claim that it represents a vision of 'emancipatory citizenship', since it returns deliberative decision making over the governance of place, including procurement of energy and food and habitat design, to communities of place. But though it occurs at this local community level it also has the potential to foster 'large scale societal change', since it is being replicated and taken up in thousands of communities around the world.[45] As Madeleine Bunting comments, Transition 'is rooted in a new politics of place: geography matters again as people look to the community immediately around them to devise the solutions for sustainability and resilience.'[46]

Recovering a local economy of place in ways that reconnect economy, ecology and ethical deliberation within bioregions, as defined for example by water catchments, is no small adaptation to modern social arrangements. It was the soil chemist Joseph Liebig in the nineteenth century who first observed the marked change in the human relation to land that allowed the export of the products of fields to distant cities, with the result that nutrients and humus from these fields were not returned to the soil but instead deposited in the ocean, rivers and rubbish tips as effluent or waste.[47] The resultant rift between land and livelihood meant that modern agriculture increasingly relied on imported fertilisers to maintain soil condition and fertility, or on artificial fertilisers created by the Haber-Bosch process from oil or gas and air. An economy that relies on imported materials to substitute for exported waste is an unsustainable economy, whch ultimately destroys the condition of the soil and the farming communities and small farms that once sustained it. Refusing this logic is intrinsic to the idea of 'permaculture', which underwrites the Transition movement: this is an approach to agriculture and design of the built environment, which works 'with, rather than against nature', depends upon 'protracted and thoughtful observation rather than protracted and thoughtless labour', and treats 'plants and animals in all their functions, rather than treating any areas as a single product system'.[48]

The term permaculture was coined in contrast to monoculture, which is the system of agriculture that has grown up since the Second World War and which treats all species and plants other than the single crop as invaders or weeds. Monoculture farming and forestry is a major cause of environmental destruction and waste, from the continuing advance of palm oil plantations into tropical rainforests, to the unsustainable keeping of large numbers of animals and birds in sheds in tropical and temperate regions, where they live in cruel conditions, are fed antibiotics and other drugs just to survive, and create huge amounts of waste. Permaculture treats each plot of farmland as an ecosystem and fosters a mix of animals and plants matched to the ecological conditions of the place in such a way as to improve the condition of the soil and limit artificial imports while also maximising food production. Some of the better established permaculture techniques include efforts to keep ground under planting year round, to grow more perennial crops interplanted with annuals, and to reduce tillage and hence soil erosion. Permaculture techniques are human ingenuity and labour intensive and, therefore, do not benefit from the 'economies of scale' of mechanised and chemical farming, which have driven small farmers out of business, and led to vast soil erosion, pollution of ground water and unsustainable draining of aquifers. But precisely because they require more human input, and less mechanical and chemical input, they are suitable for the realisation of a lower energy local economy, where local employment and land use are prioritised over globally procured imports.

The permaculture ideal is not confined to rural agriculture and has fostered a variety of local food projects in urban areas, including those associated with Transition. Urban agriculture has long been a feature of urban living, and local authorities in Britain have a legal obligation to provide residents with small plots – allotments – where fresh vegetables may be grown. However, allotment provision is far below demand and some citizens are turning to liminal and waste ground, or to indoor hydroponics in empty factories and warehouses, in a movement that is sometimes called 'guerrilla gardening'.[49] This reflects a major resurgence in urban food growing among city residents in parts of North America and Europe in the last thirty years. The rise of urban vegetable growing, urban local food cooperatives, and farmers' markets reveals a growing desire in cities for people to reconnect with the food and land that nourish and sustain them.

The quest for locally grown food also represents a response to the growing exclusion of disabled, poor and unemployed people from healthy or even adequate nutrition, as illustrated above. It also resists the tendency of large State and corporate food agencies to promote and subsidise industrial foods which rely on refined fats, sugars and starches and strip out essential plant and soil-derived minerals, nutrients and fibre. The low price of such foods, relative to fresh vegetables and fruits, reflects the fact that in both North America and Europe the largest agricultural subsidies are directed at cereal growers and domestic animal husbandry. Public subsidies to fat, salt, starch and sugar-laden food contribute to growing epidemics of obesity, diabetes and other diet-related diseases, and these are more prevalent in lower income groups for whom food choices are most price dependent.[50] The bureaucrats and corporations who promote the unhealthy industrial diet underwrite the disconnections between food and health, nutrition and neurology, soil and soul that accompany the demise of traditional local food economies.[51]

Another approach to poor access to fresh food in cities, which is still widely practised in Russia and parts of Eastern Europe, is the 'dacha' system, which mirrors the English plotlands but has continued through the end of Communism and the emergence of post-Yeltzin anarcho-capitalism. Millions of residents of Russian and East European cities return in the spring and summer months to small summer houses on plots of land outside the city where they grow food, and this makes 'an important contribution to urban dwellers' food security and livelihoods especially during times of economic uncertainty'.[52] In the UK, Western Europe and North America the creation of a dacha-style city hinterland of summer plots would require significant land and planning reform, but it would provide a sustainable and resilient approach to the related ills of urban poverty and underemployment, lack of access to fresh food and nature, and the fragile, energy-intensive character of industrial food provision.

The idea that sustainable urban agriculture requires a new approach to land use and ownership is resisted by Lockean political economists for whom private property remains sacrosanct. But reversing what Marx calls the 'metabolic rift' between land and livelihood does require the recovery of local ownership of the means of production, including land.[53] For it is the centralisation of the factors of production in cities that has driven the growing disconnnects between land and livelihood, city and countryside, and the wasteful character of modern industrial food and energy supply systems. Hence Transition, permaculture and local food movements aim not only to relocalise food production, but other core aspects of the economy including construction, energy, mobility, and personal services such as health and social care. In this way economic exchanges are reintegrated into the relational economies and face-to-face exchanges of local communities and neighbourhoods, and the 'society of strangers', promoted by anonymous global market exchanges, is resisted and replaced with an economy of neighbours.[54]

Bioregionalism, Guerrilla Gardening, Permaculture and Transition represent not small adaptations to an existing political economy but radical challenges to mainstream political economy.[55] In liberal economic orthodoxy the provision of goods and services that is said to maximise human wellbeing is that which provides these at lowest market price to individual market actors, regardless of local affiliation or democratic or ethical deliberation. The spread of this newly atomised and geographically and morally blind 'liberal' economy was influentially described by Karl Polanyi as the 'Great Transformation', which, while it began in Britain, has spread to most of Europe, the Americas and much of Asia in the last fifty years. For Polanyi, the origins of the Great Transformation lay in the turning of land from customary and community use into its primary economic function as the provision of rent to landowners, and the subsequent and related turn of human work into labour compensated for by 'wages'.[56] Economies in which rent and wages are the principal determinants of productive relationships and procurement strip out the place-specific and ecologically dependent character of human work, including craft and agriculture. The ultimate telos of such economies becomes a centralised global market, in which even health services and education become merely services that can be bought and sold by 'investors', whose principal aim is to extract the public value of such services as private wealth rather than to sustain or enhance their humanitarian purposes.[57]

Many apocalyptic and fictional readings of post-collapse societies envision the future of human civilisation as a return to the small-scale, place-based and locally provisioned patterns of the past. But most such accounts envision that this return only comes about after large-scale civilisational collapse, in which urban residents engage in desperate and often violent struggles to find food and shelter when machine-dependent provisioning systems break down from extreme weather and related catastrophes.[58] Some hint of what such breakdown looks like in the largest and most imperial economy on earth, that of the United States, was revealed by the reduction of first New Orleans in 2005, and then parts of New York City and other coastal cities in 2012, to chaos following extensive storm and flooding. The turn back to the local from the global will come too late to prevent such collapses happening more frequently, and causing the abandonment of many coastal cities, unless it happens soon enough to prevent the vast increase in the mining and use of coal and unconventional oil and gas currently planned by fossil fuel companies and governments. With one metre of sea level rise much of New York City's residential and downtown areas will be uninhabitable, absent vastly expensive sea defences. The same holds true for the majority of coastal cities around the world.

Growing extremes of weather threaten the fragile global supply chains on which modern urban industrial provisioning systems rely. But there are strong ecological and ethical reasons for resisting these long procurement chains, even if they prove more resilient than some fear. The remoteness of these systems enables their ecological and social costs to be buried in the many links in global supply chains. And while the Fair Trade movement works to return transparency to internationally traded agricultural goods such as coffee, cocoa and bananas, a broader reform of capitalist procurement strategies along these lines is resisted by corporations and liberal politicians, and by economists who argue that economic efficiency is maximised where market actors are able to trade with the minimum of social and ecological regulation. In this book, and elsewhere, I have argued that what I call 'parochial ecology' represents a morally and ecologically viable alternative to the placeless drift of the global market, and that this would also go some way to repair the relational and spiritual deficit of the individualism and loneliness that the market-based societies of strangers promote. But critics of what is sometimes called a 'communitarian' turn argue that there are dangers of exclusion and even racism in efforts to recover parochial, local and self-sufficient, even if ecologically more resilient, communities and economies.

It is valuable, in assessing the merits of this argument, to recall the evolutionary origins of morality in human history, including its biological and geographical origins. Communitarian philosopher Alastair MacIntyre traces the history of ethics from the evolutionary origins of morality in kinship and small tribal groups to the emergence in medieval Europe of an increasingly cosmopolitan, mobile and hence pluralist civilisation, characterised by a 'conflict of too many ideals, too many ways of life'.[59] In tribal societies, and in city states such as those that characterised ancient Israel, or Homeric Greece, moral codes were related closely to the spatial setting, and social relations, of relatively small scale human groups, which rarely exceeded five thousand souls gathered in a particular place. In most of these early settings moral life was rarely codified into formal legal or morally prescriptive principles. Instead, 'heroic ethics' emphasised the duties and roles individuals performed in relation to kith and kin. Hence there was no clear distinction in Greek or Anglo-Saxon between 'ought' and 'owe', and in heroic sagas 'a man is what he does'.[60] Even where attempts were made to formally codify the moral life, such as the Ten Commandments of the Hebrews, the moral code was closely related to the agrarian and communitarian context of the land of Israel, and the agrarian and familial duties and property rights that emerged therein.

For MacIntyre, the transition from the classical to the modern world through the Middle Ages involved the gradual detachment of moral and legal codes from particular customs and traditions situated in place. Roman law and classical philosophy, and not least the philosophy of Aristotle, were rediscovered by Christian canon lawyers in an attempt to codify a new universal set of laws and moral rules, which transcended familial or customary traditions situated in place. This is reflected in the efforts of canon lawyers, and the Roman church hierarchy, to impose uniformity in ecclesiastical government, which was an important stimulus to the breakup of Rome's religious monopoly at the Reformation.

The emergent tensions between the local and the universal were also felt between the increasingly powerful mercantile cities of the late medieval era and their rural hinterlands. In what was arguably the first modern nation-state, that of England, these tensions took the extreme form of a land grab by the English court in London, and subsequently by landowners in the English parliament, which began with the Dissolution of the Monasteries, and proceeded through many hundreds of Acts of Enclosure passed by successive parliaments between the seventeenth and nineteenth centuries. The outcome, as we have seen, was a monopolisation of power over land, place and politics by a small elite of landowners and aristocrats, who gradually dispossessed peasant farmers, and created a forced move from rural to urban areas of a population, which was then conscripted into the new factories and workhouses of the industrial revolution.

There was a gradual evisceration of the communitarian and customary powers that resided in place in these political developments, which had their analogies in the industrial development of other regions in Northern Europe including Germany's Rhineland, Northern Italy, France and the Netherlands. At the height of this process of concentration of cultural power in cities and the nascent nation-states of modern Europe, Enlightenment philosophers began to represent the nature of human morality as a universal and law-like phenomenon rather than one that evolved in gatherings of families and households in communities of place. Thus Immanuel Kant adopted the spatial metaphor of a man looking out on the world from a foggy island to characterise moral judgement, and argued that every man has within him the intuitive awareness of a moral imperative or law such that he will always treat another person as an end and not a means.[61] Reflecting the increasing tendency of urban societies to gather large numbers of people in space and under one law and rule, John Stuart Mill adumbrated a utilitarian philosophy in which quantitative estimates of the sum of human goods take priority over harms done to particular places or individuals by the quest for the greater good. The Enlightenment thus paradoxically promoted the ideal of the sovereign, autonomous and individual moral agent, while at the same time advancing a tendency for the agency of individuals to be increasingly subject to the collective will of the masses as expressed in statist governmentality, or corporately dominated markets, and where the good is subject to a quantitative hedonic calculus of consequences measured increasingly in the monetary balancing of harms (or costs) and benefits.

MacIntyre argues that the erasure of particular cultural narratives, and familial and community roles, from modern philosophical descriptions of the moral life is the reason moral values and practices are increasingly contested in modern societies. This erasure makes it more difficult for moderns to understand and even to agree on the nature and ends of the moral life and hence to train young people in what the ancients called virtues, or moral excellences. This is manifest in a growing tendency in Anglo-Saxon cultures, and beyond, to assume that for most purposes individuals interact together as *Homo economicus,* and out of self-interest, rather than community interests and moral regard for others. It is not surprising in this context that what moderns call 'altruism' is increasingly problematised, such that moral behaviours are increasingly seen as 'unnatural' and as needing to be sustained by collectively imposed rules and sovereign power, rather than evolving spontaneously in familial, kinship and local community relationships. Hence modern States sponsor an increase in positive law, through which a vast array of behaviours are represented as formal infractions of moral and legal norms, while at the same time public places, and personal communication devices, are increasingly subject to technological surveillance by the 'big brother' State and its agents, including the United States National Security Agency and Britain's GCHQ.

The modern *displacement* of morality from local cultures and geographic contexts, represented by the quest for a universal, or even a 'global', ethics also participates in the modern divide between nature and culture. Moral values and practices are conceived by most modern philosophers as uniquely human cultural traits that have no analogy with landscapes or species. This is why morality is represented increasingly as an *unnatural* phenomenon, and hence one in which human beings have to be educated and even coerced for, left to themselves, individuals will pursue their own interests without regard for others. Morality is therefore characterised by both Kantian and utilitarian philosophers as constituted by the promotion of *rules* that govern the interaction of autonomous human agents, rather than as an ethos or way of life that arises naturally in the context of relationships of care and nurture, such as those of the family.

Against this view communitarians argue that morality evolved in relation to particular cultural, biological and relational contexts and that human moral consciousness cannot be adequately understood without consideration of the formative role of these contexts. The family for MacIntyre is the primary moral community for human persons, and there is strong analogy between the moral features of nurture in human families and those that pertain to other mammals, such as dolphins and chimpanzees.[62] A similar critique of the idea of morality as response to authority or rules is sustained by feminist philosophers, including Carol Gilligan and Virginia Held, whose empirical studies clearly reveal that appropriate nurturing behaviours in human families are the source of empathic and caring responses on the part of children and young adults to other individuals.[63] They argue that the preference for a description of morality as rule-governed behaviour reflects a gendered bias in moral philosophy and moral psychology arising from patriarchal patterns of child nurture in modern European societies.

If morality describes familial as well as species relations, it is a biological, emplaced and natural phenomenon as much as a cultural one. This explains why immorality grows in human exchange and trade relationships between parties remote from one another. Human beings are not well adapted to act ethically towards people who do not live in their bioregions, and who live thousands of miles away. Hence environmental destruction and unjust working conditions are often hidden in chains of subcontractors and outsourcing arrangements. And while it is in principle possible to create trade laws that promote socially just and ecologically responsible practices, the Federal government of the United States, the European Commission and a number of European national governments have created a network of trade partnership agreements with developing nations which prioritise the profits and practices of European and American multinational corporations over the social and environmental regulations of national developing country governments.[64]

For communitarian philosophers, and philosophers of place, morality is a biological and geographically situated phenomenon, and not only a feature of human brain capacity or human social interaction. On this account the *places* where people reside, the living creatures and the landscape, as well as the built environment, which surround them, play a significant role in the nurture and development of morally sensitive individuals. On this account playing in a tree, planting bulbs in the garden, watching beetles or birds close to home, feeding a squirrel, are activities that contribute to the development of adult moral agents, as well as interactions with other creatures.[65] As Val Plumwood puts it, the sensory rhythms of place are ways in which 'the land itself can speak to us and place anchor our lives.'[66]

There is a growing belief among child psychologists that deprivation of such experiences in childhoods in urban environments that are increasingly denatured can give rise to a diminished sense of self. Darcia Narvaez and her collaborators argue that the growing recognition of the role of environment as well as genetic inheritance in moral development enables a more sophisticated account of the evolution of ethical behaviours in human groups than was available to Enlightenment philosophers.[67] Ironically, it was the intention of Enlightenment philosophers such as Hume, Kant and Mill to define morality as a discrete kind of human experience, which was not subject to the dominating urge to engineer and reorder nature characteristic of the scientific revolution and industrial societies. But by attempting to secure a special set of human capacities – emotion, forward thinking, intuition, reason, willing – as the source of moral behaviours, philosophers constructed a reductionist account of human moral behaviours that underwrote the nature–culture divide, locating morality exclusively in culture. Precisely by seeking to secure morality against the controlling will-to-power over nature of a scientific culture, morality was reductively shorn of its biological, embodied and familial roots and represented as an abstract sphere of emotional or rational responses to authority, law or rules. The Enlightenment project thus underwrote a growing division between both nature and culture, and science and ethics, which moral and evolutionary psychologists are only now beginning to challenge and overcome.

The work of Narvaez and other evolutionary child psychologists reveals how central are embodied experiences in early childhood to the formation of healthy and morally empathic adults. Rich sensory experiences related to breast-feeding, touch, nutrition and the visual and auditory environment of home are all indicated as crucial determinants of moral flourishing and empathic capacities in growing children and young adults. These findings resist the tendency to emphasise linguistic interaction and rational thought processes as the principal crucible of moral behaviours. They also reveal the potential for denatured urban environments and industrialised foods to arrest or depress the development of creative, empathic and morally sensitive individuals. Some of the most troubling implications of this research are in the area of the diet available to low income mothers in communities affected by global procurement chains that have led to a loss of local employment opportunities. Epidemiological research reveals that low income mothers who have limited access to fresh foods, and to fish and fish oils essential for healthy brain development in the womb, often give birth to babies with low birth weight, and to babies more prone to have cognitive defects including cerebral palsy.[68] At the same time low income mothers are the most likely to be persuaded by the baby formula industry that artificial baby milk is better than breast milk, although science reveals that human milk has omega 3 and 6 oils, lactobacilli, and fat-processing proteins in far greater abundance than industrial formulae.[69]

Nature deprivation in modern childhood takes many forms, from deprivation of healthy foods and breast milk to deprivation of experiences of the sound of running streams, the sight of trees and shrubs, involvement in food growing, or interactions with animals. At the same time the growing mobility and placelessness of life in modern residential and urban neighbourhoods promotes a loss of trust and of a sense of communitarian guardianship of exterior space. This leads in turn to a fear of strangers on the part of parents who may respond by over-supervising their children and prevent them having unsupervised access to parks, woodland, river banks and other wild areas, which again psychologists have found are vital to human development and the sense of wellbeing in children and young adults. Narvaez and her colleagues therefore argue that the denatured character of much childhood experience in modern industrial societies explains the rising extent of anxiety and mental illness in modern industrial societies, and suggests the urgent need to renaturalise child nurture and domestic, built and educational environments as ways to grow morally and mentally healthy adults and hence reduce both mental illness and crime.

That it should be necessary to invent a name for a condition, 'nature deficit disorder', to describe the loss of sensory interaction with the environment in the places in which modern children grow up indicates the extent to which modern urban and industrial civilisation is increasingly characterised by a division between culture and nature. Aldo Leopold argues that this division originates in the failure to include land and place in the field of ethical considerability, which he argues goes back to the Abrahamic traditions, whereas the evolution of modern moral consciousness has grown the moral field gradually to include not only humans but other animals, and most recently land.[70] However, it is precisely *modernity*, not premodern religion, that divided nature from culture, creation from ethics, since 'being modern' meant being in control of, and independent of, nature.[71] It is *modern* cultures that exclude land and creatures from the sphere of moral consciousness: premodern cultures rarely did this.

The single most influential social process that has led to the exclusion of nonhuman creatures from moral considerability in modernity is the growing concentration of human dwelling in the artificial environs of large urban-industrial cities. While much of the discussion in the previous chapters has concerned place and economy in rural areas, the loss of economic and political power in rural areas drove the majority of humans to dwelling in cities by the turn of the third millennium. In the bible the emergence and rise of cities is viewed with ambiguity, which indicates on the one hand the great opportunities for human advancement that the possibility of the division of labour in cities makes possible. But at the same time the social power conferred on urban merchants and rulers by this newly evolved and concentrated form of human dwelling raised ethical and spiritual questions that had not been encountered before and that are clearly reflected in biblical history, and moral teaching. In the final chapter I will consider the spatial turn in ethics and its implications for the rapid urbanisation of humankind.

8

Re-placing ethics in the city and the countryside

In 1971 an inspiring history teacher bravely took a party of schoolboys from their school in Cranbrook, Kent on a tour of Venice, Florence, Siena and Rome. For me the most memorable part of the fortnight was Florence. I walked under the Romanesque arches of the Piazza del Annunziata there, and stood before Michelangelo's 'unfinished' granite figures in the Galleria dell' Academia, in states of ecstasy. Something in me resonated deeply with the extraordinary beauty of the architecture and sculpture of Florence. I returned to my studies convinced that, against the atheist philosophies of Jean-Paul Sartre and Albert Camus, which had captivated me in the intellectual ferment of the late 1960s, there must be a God, and soon after I adopted a Christian faith that set the course of my life. I have not been back, but Florence remains the place on earth where I first encountered such an abundance of beauty that it turned my mind and heart towards the possibility of a divine Creator. Subsequently, I had similar experiences in natural environments. The most memorable of these were in the landscapes of my childhood, including an ancient oak that stood a hundred yards from my boarding house in Cranbrook, and a view of the Weald of Kent from the North Downs, near Shoreham where I lived for some months on leaving school; the view was made famous by the painter Samuel Palmer in *The Golden Valley*.

My early experiences of the sublime in Florence, and in Kent, recall the characterisation of religious experience by Rudolf Otto as a 'numinous' encounter, which is not reducible to rational description.[1] The depth and quality of beauty resonated with me at a deeper level than reason, and what Francis Dubay calls 'the evidential power of beauty' led me from atheist existentialism to belief in the existence of a divine Creator, and of a divine Spirit in those who had created the architecture and art of Florence to which my soul or spirit responded.[2]

My encounter with sacred place in Florence was a response to the monks and Christian craftsmen and merchants who had shaped its built environment so as to enhance the goodness, beauty and truth of the larger created order.

Beauty is a standard of truth that was recognised throughout Christian history and that is being repristinated by contemporary theologians, and by some natural scientists.[3] The belief that there is contiguity between truth and beauty was recognised by Plato, and this belief informed the design and building of Solomon's Temple. In the cosmogony of the Hebrews the beauty, harmony and order of the sacred place of the Temple paralleled the divine imposition of order on the original chaos of the primeval elements of the earth.[4] For the Hebrews the crafting and care of sacred place, and the offering of sacrifice and worship there, affirmed and underwrote the divine place-making project that had given them a good land in which to dwell.[5] As Margaret Barker argues, the Temple was a microcosm of the macrocosm of the earth and was designed to uphold the sacred order of Creation.[6] There was a related belief in many premodern cultures that domestic dwellings were the meeting point between their inhabitants and other beings, both earthly and heavenly, and that their aesthetic design should symbolise this sacred purpose, and express beauty and not merely utility.[7] This can be seen in neolithic dwellings, such as those at Orkney in Scotland, which are clearly oriented with reference to earthly and heavenly beings, including ancestors, the moon and the sun.[8]

The cosmogony that is reflected in the art and architecture of Florence was the fruit of a combination of the influence of medieval Catholicism and the civic humanism of the Italian Renaissance. There is a tendency among art and architectural historians to attribute more influence to the Italian Renaissance than to the medieval church.[9] But the medieval core of Florence, its basilica, churches and piazzas, such as Annunziata, were first and foremost the fruit of Christian humanism, and not the Renaissance;[10] for it was the monks and the guilds of medieval Florence who built and laid out much of the city scape it is still possible to encounter today.[11] The shaping influence of Christian culture on the medieval cities of Europe is one of the most enduring aesthetic marks of Christianity in the West. As discussed above, Benedictine monasticism represented a unique approach to sacred place, not only through the establishment of enduring communities of worship and work, but through its particular care of the sacred goods of the monasteries – including not only the abbey itself but the monastic house, its furniture, gardens, fields, hostels, mills and storehouses. Monastic influence was also strong in cathedral building, which shaped many medieval cities.

Philip Bess argues that the Christian practice of sacred architecture includes elements found in most sacred architectures: a sense of verticality, a concern for light as symbolic of the divine, care and delight in durable and well-crafted material things, the use of geometric measurement as representing natural order, the quest for artistic unity in a structure, and a sense of hierarchy expressed in the monumental quality of a sacred building.[12] For Bess justice, knowledge and healing power are attributes of most sacred structures, and in early modern 'secular' architecture the building of universities, libraries and hospitals drew upon these attributes. Hence the traditional aesthetic of the sacred remained influential although the buildings were not expressly Christian in commission or design.[13] However, modern buildings and the modern urban environment are mostly lacking in these guiding principles. Instead, contemporary architecture intentionally transgresses sacred and classical architectural elements and attributes. Hence modern space is 'characteristically nonhierarchical, abstract, rational, universal, and undifferentiated; i.e. shapeless, not purpose-specific, and not characterised by the specific formal and figural qualities found in traditional spaces' such as the public piazzas of Florence.[14]

Nowhere is the resultant amorphousness of the modern city more evident than in the car, mall and skyscraper dominated character of North American cities, from Baltimore to Los Angeles.[15] This is the reason so many American tourists travel to the medieval cityscapes of Florence, Siena, the Ile de France, Canterbury and York on their travels to the 'Old World'; these places represent a city aesthetic that is hardly visible in North America. Whereas in the medieval Christian tradition the good city represented an earthly parallel world to Paradise, in the modern era the city is primarily a site for economic consumption, and production, and for the rapid movement, by mechanical means, of goods and persons. The resultant car, mall and office block dominated cityscape frequently lacks public and personable space where people can interact without a commercial purpose and security surveillance.

By contrast cities in Christian Europe were 'moral center(s), the locale of privileges, civil rights and liberties' and places where tribal and kinship bonds and cultures were superseded by great beauty, high culture, the rule of law and the practice of virtue.[16] It was because of these higher purposes, and above all the idea that beautiful buildings and harmonious public places pointed those who entered them to the divine, that medieval cities such as Florence and Siena, the Ile de France and central London fostered an aesthetic of public squares, gardens and walkways between sacred and other public buildings designed for civil, cultured and moral interaction between persons.

Bess's account of the ways in which Christian ethics and Christian Platonism shaped the good city contrasts with Richard Sennett's claim that Augustine's *City of God*, the single most important text in the Christian appropriation of Plato, is marked by admiration for homeless and wandering gods and saints, including Christ himself, which set up an opposition to the importance of the material in the life of the senses.[17] Sennett is right that there was a critique of the cult of the domestic in the life and teachings of Christ, who was born in an animal byre and not a home, and who described himself as 'having nowhere to lay his head' (Luke 9: 58).[18] Hence for Augustine sense experience, materiality and the domain of human action, were unreliable as pathways to God without the correcting light of *theoria*, of seeing with the inner eye of conscience and the Spirit. But this did not mean that for Augustinian Christianity there was a necessary division between the inner world of the spirit and the outer world of the places of human dwelling. On the contrary Augustine, above all in his writing on music, argued that aesthetic beauty, harmony and order are means by which the divine is mediated to human souls in the good city.[19]

There is also considerable evidence from the built environment of medieval Europe that Christian doctrine, ethics and worship fostered a symbolic aesthetic of the medieval cityscape beyond church buildings themselves. This influence can clearly be seen in Florence. There is no alienation between the 'secular' piazza adjacent to the Duomo in Florence and the 'sacred' cathedral; the wonder of the domed sacred building extends its hallowing power into the city beyond through the great public square adjacent to it, as does the Piazza San Marco next to the basilica of St Mark in Venice, or Westminster Square next to Westminster Abbey, albeit in the latter case the two are now divided aurally and visually by a noisy, car-dominated road.

John Milbank argues that the symbolic marking of European cities by the ecclesial body of Christ resisted the alienation between private order and social immorality that increasingly characterises the modern urban environment:

> The church as a whole was not an enclosed, defensible realm like the antique *polis*, but in its unity with the heavenly city and Christ its head, infinitely surpassed the scope of the state, and the grasp of human reason. At the same time, what was fundamentally the same excess could be glimpsed in the single person and the Christian association (monastery or guild) whose activities are legitimised by the quest for salvation, not by human law.[20]

This shaping aesthetic of Christian art and worship did not end at the Reformation. London from the seventeenth to the nineteenth centuries grew in size principally through aristocratic commissioning of residential squares of town housing set around a central garden, in which a parish church was often a centre-piece of the design.[21] However, it is the case that the alienating spaces and social exclusions of modernity are an unintended consequence of the attack on the civic associations, such as guilds and monasteries, which shaped the medieval Christian city, but which were gradually suppressed by the emergent nation-states of modern Europe in the pursuit of the Enlightenment ideal of a universal liberty detached from bonds to kin, locale or religion. Against the complex mediated places of late medieval Europe, the Enlightenment fostered the concept of 'simple space', in which both the sacred and the associational are marginalised as the law of contract overtakes the rule of charity.[22] Simple space is open, on one hand, to domination and coercion by the State and the private corporation even though, on the other hand, simple space sustains the private morality of the individual as citizen, consumer, home-builder, and lover.

At the centre of Christianity's aesthetic shaping of dwelling and place through its history is the practice of sacramental worship, in which Christians are reconstituted, renamed, not as sovereign individuals or as outcasts – excluders or excluded – but as members of a diverse community subject to the sovereignty of God. In the Eucharist Christians experience their reconstitution as members of the one body of Christ. In the Eucharist Christians rediscover the character of all created things, including that which sustains human life, as gift in the transformation of bread and wine.

This *location* of the new creation, the new community, in the celebration of the Eucharist has important spatial implications. As William Cavanaugh argues, the Christian understanding of space is focused on the 'localisation of the sacred in the Eucharist host', and hence the Eucharist and the local church together constitute 'the contemporary performance of the historical body, the unique historical event of Jesus. Christians are the *real* body of Christ and the Eucharist is where the church *mystically* comes to be.'[23] However, from the fourth century in the West the idea that the Church was constituted in essence by local eucharistic assemblies gradually gave ground to the dogma of the universal church, from which local churches were said to derive their validity, and in tandem with this the primacy of the Roman See. Hence whereas in the East the doctrine persisted that the Eucharist makes the church, in the West this deeply local ecclesiology gave ground to a centrist ecclesiastical polity.

By the Middle Ages, and in combination with the scholastic theology of the Mass, and of priestly authority, the Pope as head of the Church claimed dominion not only over all priests and eucharistic gatherings, but over ecclesiastical property. This claim of the propertied dominion of Rome was a major cause of the Reformation. It also laid the foundations for modern secular assertions of the powers of *this* world in the emergence of the market economy and the nation-state as the twin loci of authority and power, and the related loss of a sense of the submission of political and social power to the transcendent lordship of Christ.[24]

Although the Reformers intended to return power and authority to the local church from the supremacy of Rome, the division of Church and State had the unintended consequence of permitting the rise of political absolutism and the accompanying doctrine of private property. This is illustrated in the history of the Church of England, which since the Reformation underwent a gradual process of delocalisation, where the authority of place, vested in the parish, passed into the hands of episcopal and Diocesan authorities. This process was accelerated by the depopulation of rural communities, which meant that much of the wealth of rural parishes ended up in the hands of the Church Commissioners. The nadir of their resultant powers was the creation of a series of temples to consumerism in the form of giant shopping malls built as speculative developments by the Church Commissioners in England and Scotland, such as the St Enoch Centre in Glasgow and the Metrocentre in Gateshead. This investment of the formerly localised wealth of the church in temples to consumer fetishism is a revealing indicator of the extent to which the modern church partners rather than critiques the idolatry and false ontology of the sovereign individual that reproduces social exclusion in the contemporary global economy.[25] The ecclesiastical economy is at risk of mirroring the processes of centralisation and accumulation that underlie present-day experiences of social exclusion, such as those at risk of hunger in contemporary Britain, and the contemporary dissolution of local communities of place where neighbour love is practised in neighbourhoods. But as the State in Britain, as in the United States, gradually eviscerates the Statist forms of welfare and care, which supplanted local charitable action, local churches again find themselves on the front line of the return of real hunger and destitution to the streets of both countries.

The shopping mall is the antithesis of the human-scale, mixed-use urban habitat that characterises the medieval cities that world tourists visit in their millions in Europe, including the Old Town in Edinburgh where I teach, to escape their own placeless mall and motorcar dominated urban environments. The mall is arranged for mostly global brands, and for shopping outlets to purvey placeless goods that reflect no culture other than the universal world culture of consumerism and the celebrity-fuelled cult of fashion. These cathedrals to the new universalism of shopping are a perversion of a deeper quest for the universal movement of goods and people that promotes the placelessness of modern culture, and that threatens the continuing habitability of the home planet because of climate change and biodiversity loss. The quest for a universal culture that supersedes the regional characteristics of kinship, place or religion, while it has roots in the Catholic ideal of a 'universal' church centred in Rome, is fuelled even more by the Lockean ideal of private property, and the imaginary of 'homo economicus' who, with the aid of jet planes and hotel chains, is the ultimate global nomad.[26]

The Catholic dogma of the Church as a universal society, above any necessary ties to place, was accompanied in the Middle Ages, as Oliver O'Donovan points out, with the recovery by civil lawyers of the Roman idea of a polity as a form of constitutional association that, because it was universal and even eternal, was not tied to any particular territory. The colonisation of the New World enhanced this tendency since with the appearance of New England, New France and New Spain, political constitutionality did seem to be post-territorial.[27] This post-territorial character of politics also infected moral philosophy. At the Enlightenment Immanuel Kant influentially described the moral life in terms of a moral law which is innate to the individual reasoner and independent of the particularities of religious revelation or cultural or geographic context. Analogously, Adam Smith attributed the wealth of nations not to their cultural or geographic circumstances but to the principles of political economy, and in particular the division of labour and the 'law' of comparative advantage.

The quest for a universal philosophy, and a universal politics, has deep roots in Western Christianity, and before that in Platonism, and it has been advanced in modernity by the Lockean institution of private property, and the Enlightenment ideal of a universal ethic. But human beings are pheno-menologically place-bound, even although they move around more than other species. It is not possible for persons to thrive without access to food and water, clean air and places to walk around and take exercise. Corpo-rations or individuals may claim to own all these things, but such claims of ownership must be bracketed by the fact that land cannot be removed from the map – land, whether private or public, remains in public view.[28] Similarly, all human beings inhabit geographical areas with certain defining and place-specific features. One of these, and perhaps the most fundamental, is water catchment. All cities, towns and villages are situated in water catchments, and rely upon topography, rivers and streams to gather water in sufficient quantities to make human life possible. If a city cannot govern its water sources, then its citizens will either lack water or be required to devote considerable resources to making it fit for human consumption. But it is increasingly the case that cultural tendencies and economic processes that are beyond the control of city authorities, or in some cases even nations, are rendering water more scarce in many parts of the world.

A lifestyle that requires 120 gallons of water a day per person, as does the North American suburban lifestyle, is not replicable throughout the planet: there just is not enough water, and particularly as increasing atmospheric heat renders water scarcer in many locations. Similarly, people need to be able to breathe clean air and to walk if they are to remain physically fit, and to interact with other people and other species, such as trees and birds, in their neighbourhood. And people need to be able to eat fresh, and not only industrial manufactured, and hence stale, food. By definition truly fresh food has been recently picked and is, therefore, local. Clean air and water, walkability, local food – these might prove to be universals from which it should be possible to speak about the design and care of a habitable city. But when left to their own devices and professional training, city planners, architects and owners of commercial and public property rarely succeed in bringing all these elements together in ways that foster habitable neigh-bourhoods in modern cities. The question then is how might the recognition of such universal needs shape the politics of urban design and the broader governance of particular towns and cities?

Paradoxically, while the needs for clean air and water, walkability and local food may be universal, they cannot be made universally available; they are not 'rights' that can be guaranteed to persons by constitutional fiat, nor even by successive individual choices in a consumer market: it is only when communities and neighbourhoods are arranged so as to provide them in particular places that these elements come together to create truly habitable places. This requires places to be governed in ways that recognise that morality and politics are geographical – that there are customs, duties, practices and virtues that when shared by citizens in particular locations together make for habitable places. But for citizens to be able to shape their neighbourhood by such practices there need to be boundaries to the neighbourhood that, for example, restrain constant movement into and out of the neighbourhood, including restraints on speeding vehicles, economic extraction and pollution.[29] To put this more abstractly, there is a relationship between habitable neighbourhoods and moral and political community. Community is a boundaried concept. Despite frequent reference to the 'international community', this is a cosmopolitan chimera; communities are by definition constituted by *some* people, people who are known to each other as colleagues, friends or neighbours, and not by all people everywhere.[30]

Michel Serres argues that the loss of a sense of care for place, and for what moderns call 'nature', or the 'environment', is related to the rise, since the Enlightenment and the French Revolution, of the social contract.[31] In modernity, the social contract replaces local attachments to communities of place with a broader attachment of citizens to the State. In exchange, citizens are said to gain the protection of the State from conflict, such as the conflicts that arose between different confessional communities after the Reformation.[32] In practice, as we have seen, the State often fails to keep its side of the bargain and permits large landowners or corporations to steal common property, farms or homes from peasant farmers or poor urban squatters. One of the ways in which this theft now takes place in contemporary cities in North America and Britain is the sale of public housing, public land and public utilities to private corporations so that housing areas, hospitals, schools, shopping malls, communications networks, ports, buses and trains are places where people are surveilled and taxed by multinational corporations, in the governance of which they have no say.[33] The rise of electronic surveillance, and of unaccountable corporate ownership of land and public utilities in cities, produces growing alienation between city residents and the elites who govern them, and promotes the rise of segregated housing areas, such as gated communities. It also corrodes political participation and civic responsibility, and risks provoking the return of xenophobia and parties of the extreme right, which scapegoat migrants and refugees as though these incomers, and not the maldistribution of wealth and power, are responsible for the growing sense of powerlessness among the low waged and unemployed, and increasingly among citizens in general.

The modern or postmodern city is at risk of losing the moral and political ideals and practices that evolved from the Christendom ideal of the godly, and charitable, city, through the cities of the Italian Renaissance to the public and democratic corporations of modern industrial cities, which, through public works, gradually ameliorated the poor housing, lack of sanitation and social care that characterised many industrial cities in the nineteenth century. As more power leaches from local communities and cities to the State and private corporations in the name of the social contract, not only political but ecological governance is affected. Serres argues that our ancestors knew how to love their neighbour sometimes but, because their lives depended on it, they loved the land more often. As Christian civilisation evolved into modern civic humanism, love of neighbour developed into 'love of humanity', and political arrangements such as social security and public works – including housing, hospitals, roads, sewers and schools – reflect this evolution. But there has been no equivalent universalisation of love for the land on which we dwell to love for the earth.[34] This problem is compounded with the demise of civic humanism, the privatisation of public services, and the dismantling of social security or welfare. Some argue as we have seen that the solution in the sphere of 'nature' is to cost nature's ecosystem services and so incorporate these as 'natural capital' into economic markets.[35] But given the corrosive effects of the marketisation of human services on the charitable public service ethic that once underwrote these, it seems unlikely that the marketisation of ecological services will promote the love of 'nature'.[36]

I began this book by observing the growing disconnect between people and 'nature', or the environment, and in the last chapter I traced the growing scientific evidence of the ill effects of this disconnect on human health, including psychological as well as physical wellbeing. There is also growing evidence of the harmful effects on people of economic and political disempowerment. Correlatively, there is growing scientific evidence that when people spend more time outside, when they are in green spaces, and when they participate in the governance of the places where they live, these factors all contribute significantly to wellbeing.[37]

In the city of Edinburgh, Scotland, where I work, a number of projects have been established that engage people with food growing and horticulture in order to promote wellbeing and to provide therapy. Within the city limits these include an eighteenth-century walled garden at Redhall, run by a mental health charity,[38] and an NHS health project on Bridgend Allotment at Craigmillar, to which patients with mental health problems are referred. On a field visit to Bridgend that I made, the project manager described a woman who had experienced physical and sexual abuse from an early age, and who had had her own children taken from her into care because of her mental health problems. The woman had been referred to Bridgend by her general practitioner, and after planting seeds and nurturing, she cried with joy when they successfully grew into vegetable plants. She had not been able to nurture her own children but through nurturing plants, she rediscovered her ability to care for other life. In a survey conducted in 2013 respondents said that the project 'helped them to keep active, made them feel happier, helped them feel more part of things, let them make a contribution to something worthwhile and made them feel better overall'.[39] There are also horticultural projects that engage people with disabilities on farmland around Edinburgh. One of these is Ormiston Grows, which receives people with a range of disabilities, and others undertaking community service in the criminal justice system, and gets them involved in growing organic food.[40]

Food-growing projects that reengage city dwellers with nature and farming are examples of a larger project to address the growing alienation between the modern market economy and the primarily urban dwelling places of corporations and consumers, as well as the rural hinterland in which cities are situated. This alienation is ultimately the fruit of a market economy in which money and contract are the principal media of procurement relationships, and where biological and emplaced relationships make little impact on market instruments and product prices. But as the resource extraction of the global economy presses down on available water sources and reduces the resilience of ecological communities, food prices rise, and fresh food and even potable water become catastrophically out of reach for those on low incomes. It was such food price rises, combined with water shortages, which sparked food riots and protests across North Africa and the Middle East in 2010, and led to a series of civil conflicts that are in many cases still unresolved.

As Peter Sloterdijk observes, the global market economy, in which the supply of money is the principal driver, is a 'horizontal Babylon', where human existence is increasingly focused on consumption and penetrated by flows of money.[41] The result is a world in which people feel less at home, and experience growing alienation from their dwelling places. Sloterdijk sees this as the end result of a global economy that began in the fifteenth century with the first circumnavigation of the globe by European explorers and colonists, and he proposes a new turn away from the global to the local. Space is about distance between beings; it makes possible their individual dwelling places. But modern transportation and the related flows of money, both physical and digital, erase distance, and this has the paradoxical result of subjecting all places to the penetrating invasion of money power.[42] Bruno Latour argues that the result is a perverse alienation between two 'great narratives' in human history, 'one of emancipation, detachment, modernisation, progress and mastery, and the other, completely different, of attachment, precaution, entanglement, dependence and care'; and the healing of the alienation between these two narratives is design, or *dasein as design*.[43]

Heidegger's philosophical strategy to resist the dissolution of place in modernity, and the turn of nature into a mere store or 'standing reserve' of energy and value, was to reemphasise the dwelling of beings in place. Being involves not only individuation but gathering, and places are places where, as in Durisdeer, the gathering constitutes a habitat that feels true and looks beautiful. The error of the humanities since the seventeenth century has been to imagine humans apart from the Christian doctrine of Creation, which describes the background elemental conditions in which the divine Spirit brought and brings forth life on earth. But 'to define humans is to define the envelopes, the support systems, the *Umwelt* that make it possible to breathe'.[44] Whereas the modern humanities and social sciences exclude this essential dimension from human being and the social, theologians before modernity saw the 'envelope' of air, earth and water as a divinely created cosmos, which made possible a gathering of spiritual and material forces apart from which the human person lacked being. For the composers of the Nicene Creed, it was not only the persons of the Trinity who were consubstantial, but human beings. Hence for the desert fathers, and the monastics who were their heirs, this consubstantiality was not confined to persons; as they dwelt in their cells and began to cultivate the land around, they discovered the redeeming potential of their dwelling with other, nonhuman, creatures.

In the modern secular world the mediators of this relation between humans and nonhumans, between the built environment, where human interiority is increasingly situated in screen-filled consumer cells, and the envelope of air, earth and water, are designers. But because so much of the materiality of design has been digitised, and emerges from computer screens, designers increasingly pay less attention to the *places* where their designs will be situated.[45]

Sloterdijk, and Christian monastics, are the inspiration for a remarkable project in the Netherlands to reconnect and redesign urban and rural places, human and nonhuman creatures, consumers and food growing, economy and ecology. The Eemlandhoeve is a farm-based business and sustainability project situated near Amersfoort, which won an award as 'the greenest city in Europe' in 2007. This award recognised the efforts of city planners and councillors to create a city that broke down the boundaries between the urban and its surrounding rural environment, and to increase the availability and beauty of green spaces within the city.[46] Eemlandhoeve is a farm established in the Middle Ages by Saint Paul's Abbey in Amersfoort. The present farm owner, Jan Huijgen, realised that with the growing pressures of the global market on farmers, and the growing disconnect between consumers and food and farming, there was an opportunity for a new farming model, inspired by the monastic reforms of Bernard of Clairvaux. Bernard reformed corrupt monasteries with a renewed emphasis on *ora* and *labora*, prayer and work; Bernard got the monks out of the chapel and the library and back into the fields. At the same time he travelled around Europe, challenging kings and feudal lords who behaved immorally and oppressed the people. Huijgen describes how a wealthy businessman has bought up most of the land surrounding his farm, and treats the locals, including Huijgen, with contempt. Against this new version of feudalism, Huijgen aims to create an ecological and spiritual oasis at Eemlandhoeve, where the increasing individualism and loneliness of modern urban existence is challenged in a non-hierarchical community of people caring for a place as their monastic ancestors did:

> The Eemlandhoeve stands in stark contrast to the big multinationals who continually move in search of profit; never settling in any one place. On the contrary, the Eemlandhoeve is connected with one specific place, with my ancestors and the inheritance I draw from. If you cut yourself off from your cultural background, you start drifting. It is obvious today that many people are not securely rooted anywhere. The more one is exposed to the wider world, the more one may encounter difficulties, which in turn bring a longing for peace, solitude, being looked after, and

being at home. Settling and putting down roots is achieved by exploring the past, and being nourished by the knowledge of being somewhere where people have been living and working for a long time.[47]

Eemlandhoeve uses ecological and organic farming methods designed to increase the biodiversity and beauty of the land, while producing food in a way that engages people from the nearby city. It manages a range of arable, forested, grazing, horticultural and wetland habitats, a team of co-workers and an extensive range of volunteers. The farm is also an educational centre that welcomes local schoolchildren to encounter and study farmed and wild species, and a place of retreat for people seeking to escape the fast pace of city life.

The Netherlands is the second largest exporter of agricultural products in the world. Given the small land area, and the risk of flooding from its proximity to sea level, this is a remarkable achievement. But it comes at a cost. It is for the most part a highly urbanised society, and the land footprint of homes is small, even although they are much better built, and with lower energy requirements, than most homes in the UK and North America. However, the consequence is that people in cities have a sense of detachment from food growing, and from the countryside. Eemlandhoeve is responding to this detachment by using agriculture to enable people to reconnect with Holland's rural past, and its highly agriculturally productive present.

Eemlandhoeve is an example of a 'care farm' where care is no longer exclusively for monetary income. Huijgen has investigated what people want from countryside and farming and sought to respond to this in the values and species and habitats he aims to foster, and to do so in a way that represents a new sustainable business model. Care for animals, care for cereals, grasses, fruit and vegetables, care for birds, trees and non-domesticated species, care for the land of local parishes beyond the boundaries of the farm, care for neighbouring residents in the city and the countryside are all included in the farm's circles of care. This approach represents a new economic model for farming, where farmers rediscover their ancestral role in giving people healthy nutritious food while also connecting them to the land.[48] It is an approach that has also been embraced by the city of Amersfoort. The city's aldermen, local residents and farmers, and the Netherlands minister for agriculture, met at Eemlandhoeve in 2007 and concluded the 'Amersfoort Agreement', which set out a vision for a new approach to the rural hinterland of the city, where farmers, city planners and local residents would work together to create a range of facilities that would break down the rural–urban divide. These include canoeing routes, hiking trails, ditches that are friendly to wildlife, and eco-educational projects.[49]

For Huijgen, the success of the project in overcoming the rural–urban divide, while developing biodiversity, rural employment and sustainable food production, is not only because his vision attracted followers, but because the land and the city have a sacred history of care for place. There was a hermit who lived and prayed on the 'mount of the saints' where the Amersfoort monastery was built in the Middle Ages, which built up the farming and food growing potential of the surrounding land. At the same time the hermitage and the monastery became a place of pilgrimage. Prayer, and care for food and land, hallowed the place centuries ago, and that hallowing has endured and is being rediscovered in the ecological community of care that Huijgen has nurtured. Consequently, the region is now recognised in the Netherlands as a Heritage Landscape. And the region is also drawing a growing number of creative artists and writers from the city into the countryside, and inspiring a range of new works of art that draw on natural materials and in the creation of sculptures, paintings and useful artefacts, such as furniture and household utensils.

The disconnect between nature and people, as we have observed, is a consequence of a global economy, where aesthetic and ethical care and repair of dwellings, habitats, materials and species in place is displaced by the over-arching goal of monetary growth and growth in consumption of industrially produced artefacts, clothing, devices and foods. Global out-sourcing means that there is a growing gap between consumers and producers, so that a cheap item of clothing may result in the death of workers in a poorly maintained factory in Bangladesh, and a packet of biscuits cooked with palm oil in the destruction of a Sumatran rainforest. The idolatrous universal – monetary accumulation – commits city-based corpora-tions, financiers and governments to the destruction of places both far and near. Challenging this idolatrous universal is a project that must also take place in the city, and not just in rural areas and parklands on the edge of cities. This project is also about the aesthetics of design, and it involves the redesign of city buildings, businesses, habitats, and even money itself.

I chose the story of Eemlandhoeve as a representative example of a much larger move to reconnect farming and food throughout the developed world, which is building momentum.[50] This movement resists the continuing neoliberal global trade project of industrial food corporations, mainstream politicians and bureaucrats to pursue trade in food, manufactures and even human services, which completely ignore the emplaced character of human and other-than-human dwelling, and hence continue to destroy and degrade the dwelling places of people and species in both rural and urban areas. By a perverse logic, economic neoliberalism treats human beings and businesses as intrinsically discrete units or individuals, and intends to establish anonymous markets ruled solely by price, where these individuals come into contractual relationships. The idol of a global placeless economy, therefore, also sustains a new universal, and a new cosmology, in which the individual is 'sovereign' and no longer viewed as intrinsically in relation to other persons, species or the earth itself. This new economy is a borderless economy and its principal agents and promoters no longer consider that human beings and their business activities are 'earthbound'.

In a 'foreword' to his monumental *Spheres* project, Sloterdijk argues that economic globalisation commits human beings to a false metaphysics, which he sets out to pierce by engaging Lacan's psychoanalytic description of the development of consciousness of self in children. Infants have no sense of separation between themselves and other bodies: individuation is acquired, and one of the ways in which it is acquired is through the reflected image. The child looks in a mirror and learns to see him/herself as a distinct one who is not directly connected to others. But the image in the mirror and the child are a couple: they are not one but two and they are connected by atmospherics, organic lenses, refracted light and retinal nerves. Sloterdijk's project, which is one of the inspirations for Eemlandhoeve, is to describe 'the intense relations between individuals and the construction of the resonant space inhabited by lovers and creators'.[51] Sloterdijk argues that conventional metaphysical descriptions of being in space, where space is a container, are wrong and that it is more accurate to describe the way in which persons inhabit space as a 'ball of care (*sorge*) in which existence has spread out in an original being-outside-itself'.[52] German it seems does not distinguish between 'place' and 'space', but Sloterdijk's insistence on the intimate con-nectivity of persons to that which sustains and surrounds them – atmosphere, wind, rain, earth, buildings, artefacts, screens, persons, animals – is reminiscent of Edward Casey's philosophy of place in the rejection of descriptions of human habitation that conceive of space as container.

Most modern humans are 'contained' in cities. Cities are also the spaces in which the corporations and bureaucracies reside, which advance the disconnecting, disempowering and spatialising trends of the global economy. Hence if a vision for reconnecting the city with the mode of human dwelling in place is to be consistently pursued it must also be pursued through a new vision of industrial economy and production, and of dwelling, in urban places. Of course, it will not be possible to review in this final chapter the whole history in the last two hundred years of efforts to create and sustain such a vision. Instead, I will conclude with the story of two approaches, one Christian-inspired and one secular, to the repair and redesign of industrial production and urban-industrial dwelling places.

Christianity, as I have argued, was the key source in Western history for moral and spiritual visions of the city that advanced human freedom and community, and care for other life. The emergence of a form of civilisation in which humans were enslaved to a merciless factory regimen, incarcerated in polluted, unhygienic and cramped dwelling places where the sun was obscured and clean water and nutritious food were scarce, was therefore a dramatic challenge to the Christian vision of a 'New Jerusalem', in which freedom from suffering, and the beauty and fecundity of the earth were both sustained.

The terrible suffering of the majority of the inhabitants of the new industrial cities was less of a challenge to the newer philosophies of the industrial era, including the political economy of Adam Smith, the idea of progress and the evolution of species. For eighteenth- and nineteenth-century *laissez faire* political economists, if commercial activities required that the majority of persons in a country suffered to make them profitable, then this was a price worth paying. Government interference in manufacturing conditions on this view would be against the 'natural law' of commercial markets, and would act as deterrent to wealth creation.[53] The idea of progress promoted the belief that it was necessary for human beings to suffer, and their traditional ways of life to be destroyed, in order to 'advance' the human material condition and promote a new science-informed and technologically sophisticated civilisation. This belief underwrote, or at least offered a flimsy justification for, the incarceration of fifteen million people, or three-quarters of the population of Britain, in industrial slums in the nineteenth century, where they never saw the sun and average life expectancy was just 25. Similarly the theory of evolution promoted to a social ethic the idea of the 'survival of the fittest', and Thomas Malthus, Charles Darwin and others therefore argued it would be against the progress of evolution of species if societies were ordered in such a way as to rescue the suffering and weak from the life-shortening conditions of slum living, deficient diets and polluted air. Against these beliefs a small group of Christian urban visionaries in the nineteenth and early twentieth centuries set out to adapt the new factory-based method of production, the division of labour, and urban living to the biblical vision of the good city in which people are freed from coercion and suffering. In these earthly but industrious New Jerusalems, the factories drew power from the rivers on which they were situated, so freeing the residents from polluting skies. At the same time, because they were built outside the confines of the cities, their founders were able to afford to buy sufficient land to provide decent housing, horticultural plots and parklands for their inhabitants.

In Britain the founders of model industrial villages were in the main non-conformist Christians.[54] They included Robert Owen, who founded a utopian community in Indiana, and then took over the water-powered mills and worker houses of New Lanark in Scotland; Titus Salt who built the model industrial village of Saltaire at Shipley, three miles distant from the polluted skies and overcrowded slums of Bradford, West Yorkshire; Henry Lever who, with his brother, constructed a model worker village at Port Sunlight on the Wirral, across the water from the slums and transatlantic docks of Liverpool; and George Cadbury who built an arts and crafts inspired 'chocolate factory in a garden', surrounded by attractively laid out houses and gardens three miles south of the sprawling slums of Birmingham at Bournville.

The non-conformist Protestant beliefs and values of these Victorian businessmen are referred to by some of them as a major motive for their desire to relieve the suffering of the working classes by building factories and worker housing in a healthy environment. New Lanark remains perhaps the most influential of all these villages. It was originally founded by David

Dale, who owned a number of mills throughout Scotland, to take advantage of the considerable water power of the Falls of Clyde. In addition to four cotton mills, Dale built good stone tenement apartments for the workers, and houses for himself and the factory manager. But while Dale ran the settlement on 'enlightened' lines for the time, he nonetheless required children as well as adults to work thirteen-hour days in the mills. Robert Owen visited New Lanark twice before buying it from Dale in 1799. He later observed critically of Dale's factory regime, which was the norm for the time, that it resulted in child apprentices being stunted in growth with deformed limbs, even though they received a limited education at night and a diet that included meat. He also observed that the adults of New Lanark under Dale's ownership lived in debt, misery and poor health.[55] Owen became the proprietor of New Lanark when Dale agreed to sell it to the New Lanark Twist Company, of which Owen was a leading partner. Owen's work regime was, however, by no means relaxed, and involved careful surveillance and recording of the daily performance of every worker, and at times when the cotton price was low, increased hours of work. As his ownership endured, and financial security grew, Owen introduced further ameliorating features into the factory regimen and earned the loyalty of his workers. He gradually reduced the hours of work of apprentices and he built nurseries, educational institutes, and even an indoor swimming pool, and through these and other measures he intended to turn this industrial village into a model utopian community.

In his *New Society* essays Owen appealed to the utilitarian ideal of happiness, and the relief of suffering, as his motive for establishing a kinder industrial regime at New Lanark, and he linked these aims with belief in a divine creator, even though he later took up strongly anti-religious views[56]:

> For that power which governs and pervades the universe has evidently so formed man, that he must progressively pass from a state of ignorance to intelligence, the limits of which it is not for man himself to define; and in that progress to discover, that his individual happiness can be increased and extended only in proportion as he actively endeavours to increase and extend the happiness of all around him.[57]

Owen believed that the environment formed character, and that a place of work and dwelling that was invested with aesthetic and moral qualities, while also permitting its residents access to clean air, parks and woodlands, would therefore improve those who lived and worked in it. Owen's project was the origin in Britain of the idea of urban planning as a means to improve the quality of dwellings, factories and the appearance of the towns and cities in which they are situated.

The idea of planned settlements was also influenced by the building of new towns and villages in nineteenth-century North America. Ebenezer Howard, who originated the concept of the Garden City, was inspired by new settlements in North America on visits there. But his idea of planned settlements was not so much a *new* way to build cities; in house plot size and housing density Howard took his lead from the Middle Ages. Rather, what Howard pioneered was the idea that an urban settlement ought not to be built in opposition to, but in symbiotic relation to, its rural surroundings.[58] Hence his plan for a new town was an area of six thousand acres, which included agricultural land as well as dwellings, factories, warehouses, railway sidings and roads. He envisaged that the wastes from the town would be 'utilised on the agricultural portions of the estate', which would constitute a mix of large arable farms, horticultural smallholdings, orchards and dairy farms.[59] Hence Howard intended to overcome a range of problems thrown up by industrial cities, including sewage and the disposal of household refuse, as well as the depletion of nutrients from soils, through his concept of Garden Cities. He also intended that proximity of city and agriculture would promote a greater range of foods being grown by farmers, including fruits, which before the invention of refrigeration declined in availability, as well as cereals and animal products. He planned that the ready availability of a market for a diverse range of produce would make the city's farms more profitable and hence provide good rents to the city, which would underwrite and maintain its infrastructure and social institutions, including schools and hospitals.[60] At the Edwardian planned town of Letchworth, near London, Howard created something close to his garden city ideal, although the area was smaller and did not include farmland and horticultural land to the extent he had earlier intended. Other garden cities followed and the movement had a considerable influence on suburban development around London and beyond.

Edwardian garden cities and suburbs, including Cadbury's Bournville and Howard's Letchworth, remain as testament to a built style of urban settlement, which while reasonably high in density provided residents with their own gardens as well as good access to green space. However, the town planning movement that these settlements inspired, and the post-Second World War turn to 'new towns' in Britain, did little to continue Howard's ideal of an approach to city and countryside that would heal the rift between urban industrial economy, dwelling and production and the sustainability of habitats and ecosystems either within or beyond urban environments.

In the last two decades a city design movement emerged, the 'New Urbanism', whose advocates intend to capture some of the moral and even utopian spirit of the Garden City and industrial village movements. The aim, against the economic hollowing out and privatisation of industrial cities in North America and related suburban sprawl, is to recover a sense of place and of public and civic values and ownership in the redesign of urban centres and their peripheries. Architects and planners in this movement intend to design settlements that enable the development of place-based communities where people are able to live, work, walk, play and shop, to provide space for civic activities, to prioritise pedestrians over moving vehicles, to provide diverse and affordable housing, and to improve environmental sustainability.[61]

'New urbanism' has promoted a number of planned small town settlements in North America, from Arizona and Florida to British Columbia. But the small town nature of most new urbanist projects fails to promote enduring communities of place because they lack the range of employment opportunities that enable intergenerational community, where children can settle when they become adults.[62] Design alone, in other words, cannot redeem the city from the global division of labour and a local economy that has been ravaged by an extractive economy. If significant numbers of manufacturing jobs are out-sourced to China, if food is flown or trucked in from California, and if even water belongs to a private company who turn off the supply to indebted poor residents, as in Detroit in 2014,[63] then the redesign of a few housing areas is not going to redeem things.

The Aristotelian architect Philip Bess argues that it is possible to design in such a way as to facilitate community. But architects, designers and planners often fail to understand that city-making, like agriculture, the arts and all cultural endeavours, is about the human relation to the more-than-human world, and that it also needs constant reference both to the more-than-human world of 'nature' and to the origin of all life in the creative work of the divine Spirit. Human nature is part of creation, or 'nature', and design is one of the arts through which humans interact with creation. As Aristotle and Saint Paul argued, all human beings in order to realise the good life need to pursue excellence in aesthetic and moral qualities, since in so doing they honour their divine and transcendent origins. But this means that people need to participate in the design and making of their place on earth, and it is not sufficient merely for a developer or a bureaucrat to provide them with already designed 'community towns' in order to enable them to live the good life.[64] This means that it is not sufficient for a city to be designed to be walkable, to have plenty of green space and diverse housing; it means that those who make and dwell in the city need to do so in ways that are moral, and that honour the biblical 'New Jerusalem' vision of a city free from coercion and suffering, where charity rules, where there is no violence, and which is at peace with the waters, atmosphere, plants and other species that sustain life on earth in all their God-given creaturely diversity. This vision for Bess means a city:

> the inhabitants and guardians of which understand and respect the cycles of nature; that in its practical pedestrian qualities is scaled to the physiology of the human person; that is economically healthy; that is more rather than less just, and more rather than less inclusive; that promotes individual freedom, respect for others, the life of the mind, and the life of the spirit; that is beautiful . . . I think of this as something like the City of God.[65]

The greatest cities are labours of love; they are not designed in advance from a set of aesthetic, engineering and technical specifications. In practice, this vision means a *participative* city, where people are engaged in the design and governance of homes and of mixed-use streets, which are also socially diverse and walkable, and where the consumption and production activities of the city are governed by justice, including to the city's citizens and citizens and creatures beyond the city. Such a city will be designed to preserve and not to pollute the water catchment in which it is situated; it will be governed in such a way as to permit all its residents to breathe pollution free air, to drink clean water, to eat nutritious food and to dwell in dry, warm and safe houses; it will draw sustainably on the surrounding bioregion for its food, construction materials and energy.

In the history of the West, after the collapse of the Roman Empire, the city, the village and the parish for at least a millennium before the nation-state were the primary agencies of government. But as first Britain and then other countries formed a central, national government, the tendency was to draw the governing powers, and property rights, from parishes, villages and towns to the central State. In the mid-twentieth century it was widely believed that the function of the State could only preserve common order where adequate income and natural resources were made available to all citizens. For this reason, local arrangements for mutual support – such as cooperative insurance and friendly societies – were drawn into national schemes of social insurance by the mid-twentieth century. However the rights of capital owners were reasserted by *laissez faire* neoliberal economists, most influentially Ferdinand Hayek and Milton Friedman, in the 1970s. Their influence has bequeathed forms of nation-state governance in the United States, the UK and beyond, which systematically set out to undermine common property rights and democratic participation in systems of procurement and provision by the sale of water, farmland, forests, ports, housing, power generation, schools, health and social care, transportation and telecommunications infrastructure, and justice, military and policing services, to private corporations. These corporations, though mostly headquartered in capital cities such as Frankfurt, London, New York and Paris often seek to offshore their profits in tax havens and hence refuse to enable the cities in which they operate to provide the necessities of life to their citizens. Consequently, citizens in post-industrial cities find themselves subject to corporate levies for basic services in which they have no democratic participation, and when their jobs are out-sourced and their social security cut off, they have no means to pay for water or warmth or food. Rickets and other indicators of malnourishment are, therefore, reappearing in significant numbers of children in cities in affluent 'developed' nations; in Britain there were 350,000 hospital admissions for malnutrition in 2012.[66] In cities subjected to neoliberal forms of governance, agency in the politics of place is passing from citizens and local democratic institutions in cities to private corporations, which, though licensed by the nation-state, refuse that they have duties other than to their owners or shareholders.

At the origins of modern democracy in Britain and North America, only citizens with property – which meant land – were able to vote. This was true of elections to the British House of Commons, and of State government elections in what is now the United States. It was envisaged by early advocates of universal suffrage that citizens would also be given rights to meet their bodily and cultural needs by the newly democratised nation-states. Tom Paine was the single most influential political advocate of the universal franchise in Britain, France and the United States, and he made precisely this point: 'the earth, in its natural, uncultivated state was, and ever would have continued to be, the common property of the human race'.[67] It is only 'the value of improvement' and not the earth itself that ought to be claimed as individual property, and hence every proprietor 'owes to the community ground-rent for the land which he holds'. This idea was taken up by Henry George and other advocates of land taxes and citizen income.[68] It was also reflected in Ebenezer Howard's original plan for Garden Cities, in which ground rent from farms owned by the city would support the infrastructure of the city, which benefited farmers as well as urban residents.

The idea that all who are born into a land are owed either a share of the land, or of its fruits, including food, clothing, fuel, housing and water, even if circumstances have left their parents landless, is in the Hebrew Bible and is closely connected to the Jewish and Christian doctrine of divine creation. As we have seen Joshua's original distribution of the land of Israel is said to have given an *allotment* of the land sufficient to provide a living for each family. Basing his argument on biblical precedent, Pope Leo XIII in *Rerum Novarum* argued that the newly industrialised and urbanised masses had a right to the earth's fruits by their birth into the land, which is God's creation, an ethical principle which came to be known, as we have seen, as the 'universal destination of goods'.[69] Leo XIII also asserted the right of urban workers to associate and so ensure just wages. It is no coincidence that the rise of neoliberal economic policies was accompanied by a systematic attack on worker associations and trade unions, whose origins lie in the Guilds that governed product prices and wages in the medieval city. Centuries before universal suffrage, and the modern nation-state, participation in the governance of cities was directed by Guilds of craftsmen and merchants whose officers were elected. [70] The decline of the powers of cities to govern their own affairs is directly related to the centralisation of power and property by the modern nation-state, and the grant of subsidiary powers to licensed private corporations. This is why, as we have seen, in the early decades after the American Revolution, cities retained the right to license and govern economic corporations. The loss of this right was a critical moment in the birthing of the now oligarchic character of American society, and the gradual economic bankrupting of America's cities. Detroit's bankruptcy was the excuse given for cutting off water supplies from tens of thousands of its citizens in 2014; there was no shortage of water since Detroit is situated on a river that links Lake Erie and Lake Huron, which are part of the Great Lakes, the largest body of fresh water on earth.[71]

Austerity economic programmes, which punish the urban poor for the mistakes of urban financial elites, drove urban residents in Greece back to abandoned rural farms and villages in the hundreds of thousands. But many more migrated to cities in other nations, lacking ancestral lands to which to return. Millions of other urban residents in Europe and the United States are forced by neoliberal policies and 'austerity' economics to attend food banks, buy bottled water, and wash themselves and their children in public baths as their own domestic incomes and utilities are cut off. Renewing the capacity of persons, made in the divine image, to live as beneficiaries and carers of the creaturely habitats in which their dwelling places are situated is the central means to address the economic and ecological crises that afflict advanced industrial civilisation in the twenty-first century. Reconnecting persons and nature is not then so much an *environmental* project as it is a civilisational project. If farms and forests are owned by private landowners and corporations, school playing fields and parklands are sold by bankrupt cities to commercial developers, and public squares turned into privately owned retail spaces, there will be no common and accessible 'nature' in the vicinity of cities where urban residents can reconnect. These increasingly inhuman trends in the design and governance of neoliberal cities are indicative of a perverse materialism, which neglects that the earth is a divine creation, and that all persons, and not only kings or the elite, are made in the divine image.

In the midst of the twentieth century the prophetic voice of Harold Massingham argued that the natural law of Christianity, which had fostered the careful and just governance of cities and nature, was being replaced with the mercantile rule of a technocentric elite, who were everywhere overseeing the destruction of soils and forests, and hence the thin biological covering of the land, which is the source of life on it. The key institution in the origins of this new kind of disenfranchising rule was the emergence in the seventeenth century of a new kind of city institution, the Central Bank, which, in the form of the Bank of England and the Corporation of London, in 1694 took over the right of the king to issue money, and oversaw the gradual demise of the peasantry and the concentration of power and nature's wealth into few hands.[72] The parish had been 'the cradle of the nation' and its overthrow led to the dissolution of the ties of place that had bound lord, priest, craftsman and peasant in a community where property and skill were sources of freedom. As R. H. Tawney put it:

> Whatever the future may contain, the past has shown no more excellent social order than that in which the mass of the people were the master of their own holdings which they ploughed, and of the tools which they worked.[73]

The loss of this propertied equality and mutual governance, more than any other factor, was the reason for the decline of the love of God and the love of nature, which together had so clearly defined the English people and nation until the eighteenth century.[74] And this form of civilisation was underwritten both by good husbandry of soil and soul, since the monastery and parish churches were at the heart of the seasonal round of farming and food growing, and the cathedral central to the city-based institutions of Guilds, just price and just wage. Land and craft, yeoman farms and smallholdings, city cathedrals and Guilds, were therefore the organic *and* spiritual foundations of the form of civilisation that ended slavery and serfdom, and where the ideas of liberty, equality and fraternity first flourished without need of violent revolution:

> This is the due and proper explanation of why the intercourse between the temporal and the eternal was symbolically represented in the drama of a peasant and a craftsman, and why the village community and the craft-guilds were dual manifestations, in terms of the social complex, of the primitive natural law. It also explains why, when both of them disappeared, it was not by decay from within but by destruction from without.[75]

This is why John Steinbeck, in *The Grapes of Wrath*, linked the exploitation of small farmers by the banks and the mechanical destruction of the soils of the American prairies. The settlers were in the main driven from Britain by the centralising forces of the Bank of England and the Enclosures, and they attempted to grow in the mid-west cheap cereals and cotton to feed and clothe the newly disenfranchised masses in British cities.[76] But ultimately this colonial project foundered in the dust storms of the 1920s, which helped bring on the Great Depression. The American ethicist Reinhold Niebuhr understood this more clearly than most when he wrote of the roots of the social crisis in mid-twentieth century North America:

> Speaking in social terms, one might say that man lost his individuality immediately after establishing it (after the Renaissance) by his destruction of the mediaeval solidarities. He found himself the artificer of a technical civilization which creates more enslaving mechanical dependencies and collectivities than anything known in an agrarian world.[77]

Romantics and environmentalists since the nineteenth century have sought to resist and repair a mercantile civilisation that treats nature as a machine, and refuses the organic connections between health of the soil and health of citizens by reigning in the impacts of industrialism on air, water, forests, moorlands and coastal areas. But the fetishisation of nature, which often accompanied this project, failed to address the degradation of humans and nature by a civilisation that has rent apart consumption from production so thoroughly that many city dwellers know not where their food or clothing come from, while they are also deprived of opportunities to grow their own food, or develop craft skills of the kind that freed their ancestors from penury. As climate change, habitat destruction, land and ocean desertification and species extinction are advanced by city-based corporations and investors who are impervious to the suffering of people or the earth, the 'safe space' for humanity to dwell on the earth is declining.[78] Some envisage that as the remote harvesting systems of collectivised corporate capitalism collapse, cities and towns later in the present century will again become the governance agencies that organise food growing and the supply of timber, energy and water, to their citizens, since the corporate systems that have collectivised these functions will break down under the dual weight of ecological and social collapse. Given the clear failure of nation-states to stem the climate crisis and the extinction of species, or the social crisis which followed in the wake of the Global Financial Crisis of 2008, with record levels of fossil fuel extraction, deforestation, soil erosion, youth unemployment and hunger in cities throughout Europe and North America, the rebirth of city-based, and hence place-based, economic and political governance has never been more urgent.

Absent reform of the economic and political institutions that drive industrial civilisation to erode the 'safe operating space' conferred on humans by planetary boundaries, the efforts of bioregionalists, urban and guerrilla gardeners, artist and craft cooperatives, local churches, credit unions, energy, housing and food cooperatives, and 'transition' initiatives – some of which I have described above – begin to look like the only alternatives to the Gaderine madness of neoliberal corporate and collectivised rule. It is hard to be hopeful, given the present 'signs of the times', that the madness will end until mother earth herself calls time on it. Some thought the Global Financial Crisis would be sufficient to turn the neoliberal tide but instead economists and politicians have used the crisis as an excuse to impose even more draconian thefts of common property and public services on citizens. The collapse of the seemingly impervious edifice of global neoliberal economy will, therefore, not come in my lifetime. But it will likely happen when the melting of Greenland and the West Antarctic Ice Sheet flood the financial centres and trading infrastructures of the major capital cities including New York City, London, Tokyo, Singapore and Paris, and so render the old model of the centralised city-based corporate economy non-viable. The speed at which the Cryosphere is already melting, and the great acceleration in fossil fuel extraction and deforestation that is currently proceeding, means that this collapse may come within fifty years, though it will more likely come in the next century.[79]

There will be a place on earth for humanity after the collapse. Most visions of collapse envisage that cities will require more concentrated living than they do now, that they will be much more closely related to their agrarian hinterlands, and far more conserving of their water catchments, and of locally available energy sources than present cities.[80]

The irony is that the ecological redesign of urban-industrial cities that mimic rather than destroy nature, and that reduce their footprint to their bioregion, would both help to prevent civilisational collapse, while also enabling healthier, less car- and meat-dependent lifestyles in cities and rural areas, greater citizen participation, increasing urban and rural employment opportunities, and conservation of soils and species.[81] The 'environmental' movement should have a pivotal role in promoting this urgently needed second 'Great Transformation' from a polluting corporatised and money-driven civilisation to a global network of bioregional cities and farms, where most exchanges are local and all are based on full knowledge of their impacts on people and species. But it will not have this role without radical transformation of the 'environmental' message itself.[82] Wilderness fetishism is as attractive to corporations and marketers as it is to wilderness walkers and sea kayakers. This is why it is rare to see a car advertisement that places a car in a city jam, but common to see cars depicted on a mountain ledge or driving alone through a beautiful and de-peopled rural landscape.

Against wilderness or nature fetishism, humanity and the earth need the holistic vision of compassion for people and creatures that first emerged in the small wilderness gardens of the Christian desert fathers and spread from there to the edible landscapes, smallholdings and common fields and grazing lands of late medieval towns and villages. Every action, every community, every household, that turns away from heedless consumption towards mindful care and compassionate use of earth and species, and to just reward for the labour and craft of other persons, contributes to the recovery of this vision. Such actions though apparently small and weak are growing in number in every city, town and village on earth as consciousness spreads of the causes of ecological and social crisis and psychological alienation. It was from such small beginnings that the messianic 'shepherd of the catacombs' founded a spreading network of local churches and monastic cells. As I argue elsewhere, Christian messianism has as its central meme the capacity of the apparently weak 'local hero' to overturn the remote and apparently all-powerful influence and rule of the strong.[83] The network of communities that worshipped Christ as Messiah ultimately outlasted the first global empire, which burned out in the spreading deserts and eroded soils of North Africa and Southern Italy.[84] But if those who engage in these mindful but severally weak activities are not to burn out or lose hope they also need the sustenance of a spirituality of place that again connects them to the genius of place and the religion and spirits of the ancestors.

For people in the 'West', that religion was Christianity. It is possible that indigenous religions, and other world religions, may have the potential also to turn the tide of our currently suicidal civilisation. But given Christianity's seminal role in birthing Western modernity, capitalism and the nation-state since the Reformation and the Renaissance, it is hard to envisage how any other religion than Christianity could underwrite the civilisational turn that is urgently needed.[85] Principal among the practices that will promote this turn are the reconnection of human life, body and spirit, to the places where we dwell, and to the communities of people and species, and the places of worship, that are near us.

Thomas Traherne observed at the dawn of the restless modern era that gratitude for the air we breathe, the sunlight on our faces, the trees and plants, birds and insects that we will encounter, even in cities, if we look for them, will help us recover that connection between created order and ethical sensibility that the modern era threatened to pull apart:

> Therefore hath God created living ones, that by lively motions, and sensible desires, we might be sensible of a Deity. They breathe, they see, they feel, they grow, they flourish, they know, they love. O what a world of evidences! We are lost in abysses, we now are absorpt in wonders, and swallowed up of demonstrations. Beasts, fowls, and fishes teaching and evidencing the glory of their creator. But these by an endless generation might succeed each other from everlasting. Let us therefore survey their order, and see by that whether we cannot discern their governor.[86]

The modern failure to see the visible and audible order of the universe as divinely created, as well as evolved, and therefore *meaningful* in its order, is centrally implicated in the refusal of Western civilisation to either respond to the signs of ecological collapse, or to remodel its destructive processes on nature's ways.

Traherne, like Orthodox theologians to this day, understood that the senses are the doors to the divinely created order through which human consciousness and rationality interact with a material and organic order. This order for Traherne was as important an educator of the spirit and mind of humanity as the school room, the library and the laboratory.[87] And this is especially so for children:

> For nothing is so easy as to teach the truth because the nature of the thing confirms the doctrine: As when we say the sun is glorious, a man is a beautiful creature, sovereign over beasts and fowls and fishes, the stars minister unto us, the world was made for you, &c. But to say this house is yours, and these lands are another man's, and this bauble is a jewel and this gew-gaw a fine thing, this rattle makes music, &c., is deadly barbarous and uncouth to a little child; and makes him suspect all you say, because the nature of the thing contradicts your words. Yet doth that blot out all noble and divine ideas, dissettle his foundation, render him uncertain in all things, and divide him from God. To teach him those objects are little vanities . . . yet better and more glorious things are more to be esteemed, is natural and easy.[88]

For Traherne the created order was a moral and relational, as well as an aesthetic and evolved, nexus of being, which, being divinely originated, is peculiarly suited to the education of young children who have yet to lose the wonder of young souls in the world around them. And for this reason it is a source of great hope that environmental and outdoor education are becoming more central to school curricula, even in church Sunday schools, and that educational psychologists and others are beginning to appreciate that nature herself plays a vital role in morally forming young people in the ethics of care for persons and creatures, and the places in which they dwell.[89]

NOTES

Introduction

1. For a classic essay on the origins of urbanisation see Kingsley Davis, 'The urbanization of the human population' (1965) reproduced in Richard T. LeGates and Frederic Stout (eds.) *The City Reader* (Abingdon: Routledge, 2011), 22–9.

2. Hence when the working classes, confined to the city, took to the new trains from London at weekends and grew informal vegetable gardens and created huts on waste land in coastal and rural areas they were condemned by conservationists and the 'Bloomsbury set': Colin Ward and Dennis Hardy, *Arcadia for All* (London: Mansell, 1984), 24–9.

3. The phrase 'edible landscape' was first coined by Rosalind Creasy in her *The Complete Book of Edible Landscaping* (San Francisco: Sierra Club Books, 1982).

4. Linking Environment and Farming, *Confused about the countryside*, 7 June 2011 at http://www.leafuk.org/resources/000/615/221/Confused_about_the_Countryside.pdf [visited 20 May 2014].

5. Nancy L. Galambosa and James Garbarinob, 'Adjustment of unsupervised children in a rural setting', *Journal of Genetic Psychology: Research and Theory on Human Development* 146 (1985), 227–31.

6. R. S. Ulrich, 'View through a window may influence recovery', *Science* 224 (1984), 420–1.

7. Sylvia Samborski, 'Biodiverse or barren school grounds: their effects on children', *Children, Youth and Environments* 20 (2010), 67–115.

8. Public Health England reported to the UK parliament in 2014 that 30% of children have 'sub-clinical' mental health problems: http://data.parliament.uk/writtenevidence/committeeevidence.svc/evidencedocument/health-committee/childrens-and-adolescent-mental-health-and-camhs/written/7562.html [visited 21 June 2014]. For international evidence, see Jane Hurry, 'Deliberate self-harm in children and adolescents', *International Review of Psychiatry* 12 (2002), 31–6.

9. Expert witnesses were unable to explain it in oral evidence to the UK Parliament's Health Committee hearing on Children's and Adolescent Mental Health and CAMHS, HC 1129, 1 April 2014 and at http://data.parliament.uk/writtenevidence/committeeevidence.svc/evidencedocument/health-committee/childrens-and-adolescent-mental-health-and-camhs/oral/8443.html [visited 21 June 2014].

10. Richard Wilkinson and Kate Pickett, *The Spirit Level: Why Greater Equality Makes Societies Stronger* (London: Bloomsbury, 2010).

11. Richard Louw, *Last Child in the Woods: Saving Our Children from Nature-Deficit Disorder* (Chapel Hill, NC: Algonquin Books, 2008).

12. Aldo Leopold, 'Land pathology', in Susan L. Flader and J. Baird Callicott (eds), *The River of the Mother of God and Other Essays by Aldo Leopold* (Madison, WI: University of Wisconsin Press, 1991), 212–17.

13. Robert Burns, 'Scottish Ballad', in Hamilton Paul (ed.), *The Poems and Songs of Robert Burns, with a Life of the Author* (Ayr: Wilson, McCormack and Carnie, 1819), 245–6.

14. I am indebted to Michael Polan for introducing me to a few basic elements of *feng shui* in his *A Place of My Own* (London: Bloomsbury, 1990).

15. Henri LeFebvre, *The Production of Space*, translated by Donald Nicholson-Smith (Oxford: Blackwell, 1991), 179.

16. Oliver Rackham, *The Deserted Village: A Poem* (London: W. Griffin, 1770).

17. On how Scots landowners got the land, and how the public now subsidise them to keep them on it, see Andy Wightman, *The Poor Had No Lawyers: Who Owns Scotland and How They Got It* (Edinburgh: Birlinn, 2013).

18. Gwen K. Neville, 'Community form and ceremonial life in three regions of Scotland', *American Ethnologist* 6.1 (1979), 93–106.

19. An example of an early estate book is the *Day Book of the Duke of Buccleuch, with annotations by Francis Farquarson, accountant*, Drumlanrig, 1760–73, National Archives of Scotland, GD 234.

20. Michael Foucault, *The Order of Things: An Archaeology of the Human Sciences*, (London: Tavistock, 1970), 130–2.

21. Foucault, *Order of Things*, 132.

22. Michel Foucault, 'Two Lectures', in *Power-Knowledge: Selected Interviews and Other Writings, 1972–1977*, edited by Colin Gordon (NY: Pantheon Books, 1980), 104.

23. Edward Relph, *Place and Placelessness* (London: Pion, 1974).

24. R. A. Skelton, 'The military survey of Scotland 1747–1755', *Scottish Geographical Magazine*, 83 (1967), 5–16.

25. On a visit to the village, Alastair McIntosh observed the symbolic significance of the war memorial placed in the village square where the maypole would once have been erected.

26. See further Carolyn Marvin and David W. Ingle, *Blood Sacrifice and the Nation* (Cambridge: Cambridge University Press, 1999) and Michael S. Northcott, *An Angel Directs the Storm: Apocalyptic Religion and American Empire* (London: I. B. Tauris, 2004).

27. Wes Jackson, *Becoming Native to This Place* (Lexington, KY: University Press of Kentucky, 1994).

1 Losing and finding sacred place

1. Lynn White Jr, 'The historical roots of our ecologic crisis', *Science* 155 (1967), 1203–7.

2. George Grant, *Technology and Empire: Perspective on North America* (Toronto: House of Anasi Press, 1969).

3. R. R. M. Verchick, 'Dustbowl blues: saving and sharing the Ogallala Aquifer', *Journal of Environmental Law and Litigation* 14 (1999), 13–23.

4. Joy McCorriston and Frank Hole, 'The ecology of seasonal stress and the origins of agriculture in the Near East', *American Anthropologist* 93 (1991), 46–9.

5. See fuller discussion of the Joseph saga in Chapter 7 below.

6. Kent Flannery and Joyce Marcus in *The Creation of Inequality: How Our Prehistoric Ancestors Set the Stage for Monarchy, Slavery and Empire* (Cambridge, MA: Harvard University Press, 2012) argue that the evolution of agriculture presented new moral and social challenges that the human species had not previously encountered, and in particular the possibility of large scale and systematic subjugation of some humans by others, as instanced in the institution of slavery. Hence slavery, and release from it, is central to the early books of the Hebrew Bible, which also describe the origins of agriculture: see further Chapter 6 below.

7. Economist Herman Daly argues that agrarian and economic regulations in the Hebrew Bible would have had the effect of restraining inequality, and represented in effect an 'eleventh commandment' proscribing deep inequality: H. E. Daly, *Beyond Growth: The Economics of Sustainable Development* (Boston: Beacon Press, 1997).

8. Giambattista Vico, who has a good claim to be the first anthropologist, argues that Israel's calling was the origin story of the peoples of Western Europe from the first to the seventeenth centuries in the Christian Era in *The New Science of Giambattista Vico*, translated by Thomas Bergin and Max Fisch (Ithaca, NY: Cornell University Press, 1988); see also Donald Kunze, 'Giambattista Vico as a philosopher of place: comments on the recent article by Mills', *Transactions of the Institute of British Geographers*, New Series 8 (1983), 237–48.

9. Jacob Nuesner, *An Introduction to Judaism: A Textbook and a Reader* (Nashville, TN: Westminster John Knox Press, 1991).

10. Craig G. Bartholomew, *Where Mortals Dwell: A Christian View of Place for Today* (Grand Rapids, MI: Baker Academic, 2011), 80.

11. Walter Brueggemann, *The Land: Place as Gift, Promise and Challenge in Biblical Faith* (Philadelphia: Fortress Press, 1977).

12. Gordon Strachan, *Green Spirituality in Romantic Poetry and Painting* (Edinburgh: Floris Books, 2008), 39.

13. Strachan, *Green Spirituality*, 41.

14. Donald Senior and Carroll Stuhlmueller, *The Biblical Foundations for Mission* (Maryknoll, NY: Orbis Books, 1983).

15. Mircea Eliade, *The Sacred and the Profane: The Nature of Religion*, translated by W. R. Trask (New York: Harcourt, Brace and World, 1968), 26.

16. Eliade, *The Sacred and the Profane*, 29.

17. For a detailed survey of the biblical evidence, and some doctrinal approaches see Bartholomew, *Where Mortals Dwell*.

18. See especially John Inge, *A Christian Theology of Place* (Farnham, Hants: Ashgate, 2004) and Philip Sheldrake, *Spaces for the Sacred: Place, Memory, and Identity* (London: SCM Press, 2001).

19. A largely contemporary survey of the relationship of Christianity and the built environment is available in Timothy J. Gorringe's *A Theology of the Built Environment: Justice, Empowerment and Redemption* (Cambridge: Cambridge University Press, 2002).

20. Susan Power Bratton, *Christianity, Wilderness and Wildlife: The Original Desert Solitaire* (Scranton: University of Scranton Press, 1993), 28.

21. Hebert Butterfield, *Writings on Christianity and History* (Oxford: Oxford University Press, 1979).

22. Bratton, *Christianity, Wilderness and Wildlife*, 132–8.

23. Bratton, *Christianity, Wilderness and Wildlife*, 140–7.

24. Oliver O'Donovan, 'The loss of a sense of place', in Oliver O'Donovan and Joan O'Donovan, *Bonds of Imperfection: Christian Politics Past and Present* (Grand Rapids, MI: Eerdmans, 2004), 296–320.

25. John Inge, *A Christian Theology of Place* (Farnham, Hants: Ashgate, 2004); Philip Sheldrake, *Spaces for the Sacred: Place, Memory, and Identity* (London: SCM Press, 2001). See also Michael Northcott, 'The desire for speed and the rhythm of the earth', in Sigurd Bergmann and Tore Sager (eds), *The Ethics of Mobilities: Rethinking Place, Exclusion, Freedom and Environment* (Aldershot: Ashgate, 2008), 215–332.

26. Michael S. Northcott, *A Moral Climate: The Ethics of Global Warming* (London: Darton, Longman and Todd, 2007).

27. Oliver O'Donovan, 'The loss of a sense of place', *Irish Theological Quarterly* 55 (1989), 39–58.

28. In this event the Ethiopian Church claims an ancient lineage back to the first century.

29. Roland Allen, *Missionary Methods: St Paul's or Ours* (London: Robert Scott, 1912). Allen argued that it was the failure of Western Christian missions to adopt Paul's methods that explained their poor results in much of Asia.

30. Mary McClintock Fulkerson, *Places of Redemption: Theology for a Worldly Church* (Oxford: Oxford University Press, 2007).

31. Dwelling and place are core themes in Martin Heidegger, *Being and Time*, translated by Joan Stambaugh (Albany, NY: State University of New York Press, 1996) and in Maurice Merleau-Ponty, *The Phenomenology of Perception*, translated by Donald A. Landes (London: Routledge, 1996).

32. Peter Verbeek and Frans B. M. de Waal, 'The primate relationship to nature: biophilia as general pattern' in Peter H. Kaan and Stephen M. Kellert

(eds) *Children and Nature: Psychological, Sociocultural and Evolutionary Investigations* (Cambridge MA: MIT Press 2012), 1–27.

33. See further Edward Casey, *The Fate of Place: A Philosophical History* (Berkeley, CA: University of California Press, 1997).

34. See further Robert Pogue Harrison, *The Dominion of the Dead* (Chicago: University of Chicago Press, 2003).

35. Sheldrake, *Spaces for the Sacred.*

36. There is considerable empirical evidence of an association between sacred place and species richness, though which came first is harder to establish: see for example Jan Salick, Anthony Amend, Danica Anderson, Kurt Hoffmeister, Bee Gunn, Fang Zhendong, 'Tibetan sacred sites conserve old growth trees and cover in the eastern Himalayas', *Biodiversity and Conservation* 16 (2007), 693–706; Bruce A. Byers, Robert N. Cunliffe and Andrew T. Hudak, 'Linking the conservation of culture and nature: a case study of sacred forests in Zimbabwe', *Human Ecology* 29 (2001), 187–218.

37. Miguel B. Araujo, 'Biodiversity hotspots and zones of transition', *Conservation Biology* 16 (2002), 1662–3.

38. The area is a UNESCO World Heritage Site, described at http://whc.unesco.org/en/list/850 [visited 4 August 2014].

39. Mechtild Rossler, 'Linking forests and cultural diversity: The World Heritage Convention', in *Forestry and Our Cultural Heritage: Proceedings of the Seminar 13–15 June 2005, Sunne, Sweden* (Warsaw: Ministerial Conference on the Protection of Forests in Europe Liaison Unit, 2006), 13–22.

40. For an influential account of the lack of regard for nature among Christian monastics, see Roderick Nash, *Wilderness and the American Mind* (New Haven: Yale University Press, 1982); Bratton's *Christianity, Wilderness and Wildlife* is in part an extended and highly effective disproval of Nash's argument.

41. Athanasius, *Life of Antony*, English translation by Robert T. Meyer (NJ: Paulist Press, 1950), 62; see also Bratton, *Christianity, Wilderness and Wildlife*, 164–5.

42. Athanasius, *Life of Antony*, 63.

43. Bratton, *Christianity, Wilderness and Wildlife*, 165.

44. Helen Waddell, *The Desert Fathers* (Ann Arbor, MI: University of Michigan Press, 1957), 129, and cited Bratton, *Christianity, Wilderness and Wildlife*, 165.

45. I have written on the story of Jerome plucking a thorn from a lion's paw in Kyle S. Van Houtan and Michael S. Northcott, 'Nature and the nation-state: ambivalence, evil, and American environmentalism', in Kyle S. Van Houtan and Michael S. Northcott (eds), *Diversity and Dominion: Dialogues in Ecology, Ethics, and Theology* (Eugene, OR: Wipf and Stock, 2010), 138–56.

46. See further E. A. Wallis Budge, *The Paradise of the Holy Fathers*, Vol 1 and 2 (London: Chatto and Windus, 1907); see also Rita Nakashima Brock and Rebecca Parker, *Saving Paradise: How Christianity Traded Love of This World for Crucifixion and Empire* (Boston: Beacon Press, 2008).

47. John Cassian, *The Conferences of John Cassian*, Book 8, 16, translated by Edward C. S. Gibson, *Christian Classics Ethereal Library* at http://www.ccel.org/c/cassian/conferences/cache/conferences.pdf [visited 4 August 2014].

48. Bratton, *Christianity, Wilderness and Wildlife*, 169.

49. Bratton, *Christianity, Wilderness and Wildlife*, 178.

50. Bratton, *Christianity, Wilderness and Wildlife*, 184.

51. Christopher Dawson, *The Making of Europe: An Introduction to the History of European Unity* (Washington DC: Catholic University Press of America, 1932), 179.

52. Bratton, *Christianity, Wilderness and Wildlife*, 185.

53. *Two Lives of Saint Cuthbert*, translated by Bertram Colgrave (Cambridge: Cambridge University Press, 1940), 81, cited in Bratton, *Christianity, Wilderness and Wildlife*, 188.

54. *Two Lives of Saint Cuthbert*, 85–7, cited in Bratton, *Christianity, Wilderness and Wildlife*, 188.

55. Mary Donatus MacNickle, *Beasts and Birds in the Lives of Early Irish Saints* (Philadelphia: University of Pennsylvania Press, 1934), 182, cited in Bratton, *Christianity, Wilderness and Wildlife*, 193.

56. Bratton, *Christianity, Wilderness and Wildlife*, 196.

57. Quoted in Christopher Bamford, 'Introduction', in *The Voice of the Eagle: John Scotus Eriugena's Homily on the Prologue to the Gospel of St John* (Great Barrington, MA: Lindisfarne Books, 2000), 41.

58. Terence L. Nichols, *The Sacred Cosmos: Christian Faith and the Challenge of Naturalism* (Eugene, OR: Wipf and Stock, 2003), 31.

59. Jacques Chevalier, *Essai*, cited Louis Gougaud, *Christianity in Celtic Lands: A History of the Churches of the Celts, Their Origin, Development, Influence and Mutual Relations* (Dublin: Four Courts Press, 1992), 56.

60. Gougaud, *Christianity in Celtic Lands*, 89.

61. Harold J. Massingham, *The Tree of Life* (London: Chapman and Hall, 1943), 35.

62. Massingham, *Tree of Life*, 35.

63. Michael W. Herren and Shirley Ann Brown, *Christ in Celtic Christianity: Britain and Ireland from the Fifth to the Tenth Century* (Woodbridge: Boydell Press, 2002), 41.

64. Tim Gorringe argues that the lack of shared engagement in common tasks is the main reason that not only towns but rural villages in contemporary Britain lack communities of place capable of acting together for tasks such as community energy procurement: Gorringe, *Theology of Built Environment*, 169.

65. Elinor Ostrom's work in describing enduring but, in origin, pre-modern (pre-capitalist *and* non-State) commons governance institutions was rewarded with a Nobel prize for economics: see her *Governing the Commons: The Evolution of Institutions for Collective Action* (Cambridge: Cambridge University Press, 1990); on craft guilds, see S. R. Epstein, 'Craft guilds in the pre-modern economy: a discussion', *Economic History Review* 61 (2008), 155–74.

66. Bede, *The Ecclesiastical History of the English People*, translated by Judith McClure and Roger Collins (Oxford: Oxford University Press, 1969).

67. The classic record of the Benedictine and Cistercian orders, and their spread from France to England, and of the Dissolution of the Monasteries under Henry VIII and Wolsey, is William Dugdale, *Monasticum Anglicanum: or the history of the abbies, monasteries, hospitals, Cathedral and Collegiate Churches with their dependencies in England and Wales, Vols 1–3* (London: 1718).

68. Massingham, *Tree of Life*, 38.

69. Massingham, *Tree of Life*, 39.

70. *The Holy Rule of St Benedict*, translated by Priest of Mount Melleray [sic] (London: Paternoster Press, 1865), 48.2.

71. Rembert Sorg, *Holy Work: Towards a Benedictine Theology of Manual Labour* (Santa Ana, CA: Source Books, 2003).

72. Sorg, *Holy Work*, 38–9.

73. On the many unintended consequences of the Reformation, see further Brad S. Gregory, *The Unintended Reformation: How a Religious Revolution Secularized Society* (Cambridge, MA: Harvard University Press, 2012).

74. Juliet du Boulay, *Portrait of a Greek Mountain Village* (Oxford: Clarendon Press, 1974), 6.

75. On the relation between linguistic and biological diversity, see D. Harmon, 'Losing species, losing languages: connections between biological and linguistic diversity', *Southwest Journal of Linguistics* 15 (1996), 89–108.

76. For a fuller response to White, see Michael S. Northcott, *The Environment and Christian Ethics* (Cambridge: Cambridge University Press, 1996).

77. Edward Casey, *The Fate of Place: A Philosophical History* (Berkeley, CA: University of California Press, 1996), 106–8.

78. Casey, *Fate of Place*, 115.

79. Casey, *Fate of Place*, 137.

80. Alfred North Whitehead, *Science and the Modern World* (Cambridge: Cambridge University Press, 1996), 72, cited in Casey, *Fate of Place*, 138.

81. For a fuller discussion of the role of medieval nominalism in erasing the human mediation of place, see John Milbank, 'On complex space', in John Milbank, *The Word Made Strange: Theology, Language and Culture* (Oxford: Blackwell, 1997), 268–92.

82. Casey, *Fate of Place*, 141.

83. On the role of nominalist accounts of nature and species in the origins of modernity, see John Dupré, *Passage to Modernity: An Essay in the Hermeneutics of Nature and Culture* (New Haven: Yale University Press, 1993).

84. Casey, *Fate of Place*, 147.

85. Casey, *Fate of Place*, 150.

86. On More's idea of the extension of the divine Spirit in nature, see Henry More, *Letters to Descares &C.*, in More, *A Collection of Several Philosophical Writings* (London: James Flesher, 1662); on Benedict Spinoza's account of God as filling bodies and space, see Part One of Spinoza, *Ethics*, translated by Edwin Curley, in *The Collected Writings of Spinoza* (Princeton: Princeton University Press, 1985), vol. 1.

87. See further my fuller discussion of Locke's theology of land and redemption in Michael S. Northcott, *An Angel Directs the Storm: Apocalyptic Religion and American Empire* (London: I. B. Tauris, 2004) 47–50.

88. For a fuller account of Schmitt's political theology, see Michael S. Northcott, *A Political Theology of Climate Change* (London: SPCK, 2014).

89. Karl Polanyi, *The Great Transformation: The Political and Economic Origins of Our Time* (Boston, MA: Beacon Press, 1944).

90. Ostrom, *Governing the Commons.*

91. Max Weber was the first to argue that the monopoly of violence is the precondition for the successful organisation of a modern state in his *Political Writings*, trans. and edited Peter Lassman and Ronald Speirs (Cambridge: Cambridge University Press, 1994), 21–2.

92. Martin Heidegger, *Poetry, Language, Thought*, translated by Albert Hofstadter (New York: Harper and Row, 1971), 149.

93. Simone Weil, *The Need for Roots* (London: Routledge & Kegan Paul, 1952).

94. R. H. Tawney, 'The rise of the gentry', *The Economic History Review* 11 (1941), 1–38.

95. Michel de Certeau, *The Practice of Everyday Life*, English translation by Stephen Randall (Berkeley, CA: University of California Press, 1984), xix.

96. de Certeau, *The Practice of Everyday Life*, xx.

97. Dumfries and Galloway Employability Partnership, *Briefing Pack for Meetings with Potential Work Programme Prime Contractors* (Dumfries: Dumfries and Galloway Council, 2010).

98. For a fuller discussion, see Michael S. Northcott, *A Political Theology of Climate Change* (Grand Rapids, MI: Wm. B. Eerdmans, 2013), 129–33.

99. Environmental exclusion is a phrase first coined in Brett Stephenson and Susan Power Bratton, 'Martin Luther's Understanding of Sin's Impact on Nature and the Unlanding of the Jew', *Ecotheology* 9 (2000), 84–102. The exclusion of African Americans from green space is one of the central concerns of the African American account of Environmental Justice: see further W. Malcolm Byrnes, 'Climate justice, Hurricane Katrina, and African American environmentalism' in *Journal of African American Studies* (2013) DOI 10.1007/s12111-013-9270-5.

100. Michael S. Northcott, 'The failure of Neo-Liberalism and the despotism of numbers: a political and theological critique', *Modern Believing* 52 (2011), 27–41.

101. Jaques Ellul observes that the economic efficiency of the United States has made it the capitalist hub par excellence of the modern world; but it is won at the aesthetic cost of its persistent uglification, a cost that is not included in the balance books of companies and the nation: see further Jaques Ellul, *The Technological Society* (New York: Knopf, 1968).

102. Tim Ingold, *Lines: A Brief History* (Abingdon: Routledge, 2007), 81.

103. Ingold, *Lines*, 85.

104. Ingold, *Lines*, 81.

105. Ingold, *Lines*, 81.

106. Henry D. Thoreau, 'Walking', *The Atlantic Monthly* 9 (1862), 657–74.

107. Thoreau, 'Walking', 668.

108. Rob Hopkins, *The Transition Handbook: From Oil Dependency to Local Resilience* (Totnes: Green Books, 2008).

109. Iamblichus, 'Distinctions of the superior races', in Iamblichus, *Theurgia*, translated by Alexander Wilder (London: William Rider, 1911).

110. E. F. Schumacher, *Small is Beautiful: Economics as if People Mattered* (New York: Harper and Row, 1973).

2 Lament for a silent summer

1. Norman Maclean (ed.), *Silent Summer: The State of Wildlife in Britain and Ireland* (Cambridge: Cambridge University Press, 2010).

2. Robert S. Robinson, 'State of bird populations in Britain and Ireland', in Maclean, *Silent Summer*, 281–318; RSPB, *The State of the UK's Birds 2013* (Bedfordshire: RSPB, 2013).

3. David Attenborough, 'Foreword', in Maclean, *Silent Summer*, ix.

4. Christopher Rootes, 'Nature protection organizations in England', in C. S. A. (Kris) van Koppen and William T. Markham (eds), *Protecting Nature: Organizations and Networks in Europe and the USA* (Cheltenham: Edward Elgar, 2007), 34–62.

5. See further Richard Body, *Our Food, Our Land: Why Contemporary Farming Practices Must Change* (London: Rider, 1991), 96–136, and Graham Harvey, *The Killing of the Countryside* (London: Vintage, 1998).

6. Wendell Berry, *The Unsettling of America* (San Francisco, CA: Sierra Club Books, 1977), 26.

7. The UK ecological footprint was estimated at 5 hectares per person in 2012: *Living Planet Report 2012: Biodiversity, Biocapacity and Better Choices* (Geneva: WWF International, 2012). Ecological footprinting as a way of assessing ecological sustainability was first proposed by M. Wackernagel and William Rees in *Our Ecological Footprint: Reducing Human Impact on the Earth* (Gabriola Island, BC: New Society Publishers, 1996).

8. Helena Norberg Hodge, Todd Merrifield and Steven Gorelick, *Bringing the Food Economy Home: Local Alternatives to Global Agribusiness* (London: Zed Books, 2002).

9. Berry, *Unsettling of America*, 26.

10. Berry, *Unsettling of America*, 26.

11. Rachel Carson, *Silent Spring* (London: Hamish Hamilton, 1963).

12. M. Jimmie Killingsworth and Jacqueline S. Palmer, *Ecospeak: Rhetoric and Environmental Politics in America* (Carbondale, IL: Southern Illinois University Press, 1992), 74–5.

13. Carson, *Silent Spring*, 100.

14. Carson, *Silent Spring*, 121.

15. For an influential ecofeminist critique of Bacon, see Carolyn Merchant, *The Death of Nature: Women, Ecology and the Scientific Revolution* (San Francisco, CA: Harper Collins, 1990); for a more nuanced account of Bacon, see Michael S. Northcott, *A Political Theology of Climate Change* (London: SPCK, 2014), 100–18.

16. See further Catherine Rigby, *Topographies of the Sacred: The Poetics of Place in European Romanticism* (Charlottesville, VA: University of Virginia Press, 2004).

17. Roderick Nash, 'The American invention of national parks', *American Quarterly* 22 (1970), 726–35.

18. On the seminal role of efforts to conserve the Lake District in the British environmental movement, see Harriet Ritvo, *The Dawn of Green: Manchester, Thirlmere and Modern Environmentalism* (Chicago: Chicago University Press, 2009).

19. Jonathan Bate, 'The Picturesque Environment', in Bate, *The Song of the Earth* (London: Picador, 2000), 119–52.

20. Theodore Adorno, *Aesthetic Theory*, translated by C. Lenhardt (London: Routledge Kegan Paul, 1970), 96.

21. Bates, *Song of the Earth*, 97.

22. Bates, *Song of the Earth*, 100.

23. Bates, *Song of the Earth*, 104.

24. Bates, *Song of the Earth*, 106.

25. Bates, *Song of the Earth*, 109.

26. On communities of place in the Romantics, see further Catherine Rigby, *Topographies of the Sacred: The Poetics of Place in European Romanticism* (Charlottesville, VA: University of Virginia Press, 2003), 57–60.

27. See further Nigel Leask, *Robert Burns and Pastoral: Poetry and Improvement in Late Eighteenth-Century Scotland* (Oxford: Oxford University Press, 2010).

28. Roger Lovegrove, *Silent Fields: The Long Decline of a Nation's Wildlife* (Oxford: Oxford University Press, 2009), 29.

29. Lovegrove, *Silent Fields*, 87.

30. Lovegrove, *Silent Fields*, 92.

31. The finest account is Keith Thomas, *Man and the Natural World: Changing Attitudes in England 1500–1800* (London: Penguin Books, 1983).

32. For a fine study of the Dissolution see David Knowles, *Bare Ruined Choirs* (Cambridge: Cambridge University Press, 1976).

33. Kevin Cahill, *Who Owns Britain* (Edinburgh: Canongate, 2002).

34. On Scottish land ownership, and the case for land reform and other measures, such as land taxation, to redistribute landed property, see Andy Wightman, *The Poor Had No Lawyers: Who Owns Scotland and How They Got It* (Edinburgh: Birlinn, 2013).

35. For a stirring first-hand account of the pioneering Eigg buyout see Alastair McIntosh, *Soil and Soul: People versus Corporate Power* (London: Aurum, 2004).

36. H. Ali Saleem and Richad Paradis, *Transitioning Land Tenure in Scotland: A Comparative Study of Public, Private and Community Arrangements* (Burlington VT: Instritute for Environmental Diplomacy and Security, 2010).

37. Fredric Jameson, *Archaeologies of the Future* (London: Verso, 2005).

38. I discuss the case for the revival of local food economies more fully in Chapter 6.

39. Julian Cribb, *The Coming Famine: The Global Food Crisis and What We Can Do About It* (Berkeley, CA: University of California Press, 2010).

40. Paul Maeder, Andreas Fliessbach, David Dubois, Lucie Gunst, Padruot Fried and Urs Niggli, 'Soil fertility and biodiversity in organic farming', *Science* 296 (31 May 2002), 1694–6.

41. Alasdair MacIntyre, *After Virtue: A Study in Moral Theory* (London: Duckworth, 1981).

3 Artificial persons and the political economy of place

1. M. Zhao and S. Running, 'Drought-induced reduction in global terrestrial net primary production from 2000 through 2009', *Science* 329 (2010), 940–3.

2. Gregory P. Asner, Scott R. Loarie and Ursula Heyder, 'Combined effects of climate and land-use change on the future of humid tropical forests', *Conservation Letters* 3 (2010), 395–403.

3. J. Raven, K Caldeira, A. H. Elderfeld and O. Hoegh-Guldberg, *Ocean Acidification Due to Increasing Atmospheric Carbon Dioxide* (London: Royal Society, 2005).

4. Sampled Red List Index for Plants 2010 at http://threatenedplants.myspecies. info/ [visited 5 February 2014].

5. Stuart H. M. Butchart, Matt Walpole, Ben Collen, Arco van Strien, Jörn P. W. Scharlemann, Rosamunde E. A. Almon, Jonathan E. M. Baillie, Bastian Bomhard et al., 'Global biodiversity: indicators of recent declines', *Science* 328 (2010), 1164–8.

6. S. B. Hecht, 'Environment, development and politics: capital accumulation and the Eastern Amazonia', *World Development* 13 (1985), 663–84.

7. G. S. Hartshorn, 'Ecological basis for sustainable development in tropical forests', *Annual Review of Ecology and Systematics* 26 (1995), 155–75 and N. Myers, 'Tropical forests: much more than stocks of wood', *Journal of Tropical Ecology* 4 (1988), 209–21.

8. Jai Ranganathan, R. J. Ranjit Daniels, M. D. Subash Chandran, Paul R. Ehrlich and Gretchen C. Daily, 'Sustaining biodiversity in ancient tropical countryside', *Proceedings of the National Academy of Sciences* 105 (2008), 17852–4.

9. J. E. M. Arnold and M. R. Perez, 'Can non-timber forest products match tropical forest conservation and development objectives?' *Ecological Economics* 39 (2001), 437–47.

10. J. M. Vadjunec, 'Extracting a livelihood: institutional and social dimensions of deforestation in the Chico Mendes Extractive Reserve, Acre, Brazil', *Journal of Latin American Geography* 10 (2011), 151–74.

11. R. Black, 'EU and Indonesia sign deal on illegal timber', *BBC News*, 4 May 2011: http://www.bbc.co.uk/news/science-environment-13272393 [visited 5 February 2014].

12. J. Harwood, 'Marine mammals and their environment in the twenty-first century', *Journal of Mammalogy* 82 (2001), 630–40.

13. D. Pauly, 'Beyond duplicity and ignorance in global fisheries', *Scientia Marina* 73 (2009), 215–24.

14. Boris Worm, Edward B. Barbier, Nicola Beaumont, J. Emmett Duffy, Carl Folke, Benjamin S. Halpern, Jeremy B. C. Jackson, Heike K. Lotze et al., 'Impacts of biodiversity loss on ocean ecosystem services', *Science* 314 (2006), 787–90.

15. Richard Leakey and Roger Lewin, *The Sixth Extinction: Patterns of Life and the Future of Humankind* (New York: Doubleday, 1996) and Stuart L. Pimm and Thomas M. Brooks, 'The sixth extinction: how large, where and when?' in Peter H. Raven (ed.), *Nature and Human Society: The Quest for a Sustainable World* (Washington DC: National Academy Press, 2000) and D. B. Wake and V. T. Vredenberg, 'Are we in the midst of the sixth mass extinction? A view from the world of amphibians', *Proceedings of the National Academy of Sciences* 105, Supplement 1 (2008), 11466–73.

16. Kai M. A. Chan, Robert M. Pringle, Jai Ranganathan, Carol L. Boggs, Yvonne L. Chan, Paul R. Ehrlich, Peter K. Haff, Nicole E. Heller et al., 'When agendas collide: human welfare and biological conservation', *Conservation Biology* 21 (2007), 59–68.

17. *Attitudes of European Citizens Towards the Environment* (Brussels: Directorate General Environment, 2008).

18. A. Franzen and R. Meyer, 'Environmental attitudes in cross-national perspective: a multilevel analysis of the ISSP 1993 and 2000', *European Sociological Review* 26 (2010), 219–34.

19. 'Cap, trade and block', *The Economist* 393 (2009), 51–2 and at http://www.economist.com/node/15019980 [visited 5 February 2014].

20. Holmes Rolston, *Conserving Natural Value* (New York: Columbia University Press. 1994).

21. T. W. Luke, 'Environmentality as green governmentality', in Eric Darier (ed.), *Discourses of the Environment* (Oxford: Blackwell, 1999), 121–51; Michel Foucault, 'Governmentality', in Michel Foucault, G. Burchell, C. Gordon and P. Miller (eds) *The Foucault Effect: Studies in Governmentality* (Hemel Hempstead: Harvester Wheatsheaf, 1991), 87–104.

22. Garrett J. Hardin, 'Concessionary politics: property, patronage and political rivalry in Central African forest management', *Current Anthropology* 52 (2011), S113–125; J. P. Brosius, 'Green dots, pink hearts: displacing politics from the Malaysian Rain Forest', *American Anthropologist* 101 (1999), 36–57; L. Tuck-Po, *Changing Pathways: Forest Degradation and the Batek of Pahang* (Oxford: Lexington Books, 2004).

23. Berry, *Unsettling of America*.

24. A. Franzen, 'Environmental attitudes in international comparison: an analysis of the ISSP Surveys 1993 and 2000', *Social Science Quarterly* 84 (2004), 297–308.

25. Gus Speth, *The Bridge at the End of the World: Capitalism, the Environment, and Crossing from Crisis to Sustainability* (New Haven, CT: Yale University Press, 2008).

26. F. W. Maitland, 'Moral personality and legal personality', *Journal of the Society of Comparative Legislation* 6 (1905), 192–200; J. Ferguson and A. Gupta, 'Spatializing states: towards an ethnography of neoliberal governmentality', *American Ethnologist* 29 (2002), 981–1002.

27. US Supreme Court. 1819. *Trustees of Dartmouth College v. Woodward*, 17 U.S. 4: 518.

28. House of Lords. 1897. *Salomon v. Salomon and Co Ltd*. London: House of Lords, A.C. 22.

29. P. Hughes, 'Can governments weather the storm in the new communications climate?' *Australian Journal of Public Administration* 56 (1997), 78–86; D. Domke, *God Willing? Political Fundamentalism in the White House, the 'War on Terror' and the Echoing Press* (London: Pluto Press, 2004).

30. T. Holmes, 'Balancing acts: PR, 'impartiality' and power in mass media coverage of climate change', in T. Boyce and J. Lewis (eds), *Climate Change and the Media* (New York: Peter Lang, 2009), 92–100.

31. Joel Bakan, *The Corporation: The Pathological Pursuit of Profit and Power* (New York: Free Press, 2004).

32. Norman Myers and Jennifer Kent, *Perverse Subsidies: How Tax Dollars Can Undercut the Environment and the Economy* (Washington DC: Island Press, 2001).

33. N. Willams, 'Tar troubles', *Current Biology* 20 (2010), R260.

34. Environmental Law Institute, *Estimating U. S. Government Subsidies to Energy Sources: 2002–2008* (Washington DC: Environmental Law Institute, 2009).

35. Environmental Protection Agency. *EPA's Budget and Spending* (2011) at http://www.epa.gov/planandbudget/budget.html [visited 16 May 2011].

36. Aldo Leopold, *A Sand County Almanac and Sketches Here and There* (New York: Oxford University Press, 1964), 262.

37. Holmes Rolston, *Environmental Ethics: Duties to and Values in the Natural World* (Philadelphia, Temple University Press, 1987), 186–7.

38. J. Baird Callicott, 'On the intrinsic value of nonhuman species', in Bryan Norton (ed.), *The Preservation of Species: The Value of Biological Diversity* (Princeton NJ: Princeton University Press, 1986), 138–72; Michael J. Zimmerman, *The Nature of Intrinsic Value* (Lanham, MD: Rowman and Littlefield, 2001).

39. US Senate, *Endangered Species Act of 1973* (Washington, DC: House of Congress, 1973), Sec. 2. 1–5.

40. New Zealand Legislation: Acts, *Resource Management Act 1991* (Wellington: Parliament of New Zealand, 1991), 2. 1 (l).

41. R. Arnoux, R. Dawson and M. O'Connor, 'The logic of death and sacrifice in the resource management law reforms of Aotearoa/New Zealand', *Journal of Economic Issues* 27 (1993), 1059–96; K. J. Grundy and B. J. Gleeson, 'Sustainable management and the market: The politics of planning reform in New Zealand', *Land Use Policy* 13 (1996), 197–211.

42. A. Austin and L. Phoenix, 'The neoconservative assault on the Earth: the environmental imperialism of the Bush Administration', *Capitalism, Nature, Socialism* 16 (2005), 25–44; Michael S. Northcott, 'The dominion lie: how millennial theology erodes creation care', in Kyle S. Vanhouten and Michael S. Northcott (eds), *Diversity and Dominion: Dialogues in Ecology, Ethics, and Theology* (Portland, OR: Wipf and Stock, 2009).

43. S. F. Gavin, 'Stealth tort reform', *Valparaiso University Law Review* 42 (2008), 431–9.

44. Cass R. Sunstein, *Worst-Case Scenarios* (Cambridge, MA: Harvard University Press, 2007).

45. Kyle S. Vanhouten and Michael Northcott, 'Nature and the nation-state: ambivalence, evil and American environmentalism', in Vanhouten and Northcott, *Diversity and Dominion*.

46. John Muir, *My First Summer in the Sierra* (Boston: Houghton Mifflin, 1911), 189, 331.

47. H. D. Thoreau, 'Walking', *Atlantic Monthly* (1892).

48. Roderick Nash, *Wilderness and the American Mind* (New Haven, CT: Yale University Press, 1967), 44–9.

49. C. Margules and M. B. Usher, 'Criteria used in assessing wildlife conservation potential: a review', *Biological Conservation* 21 (1981), 79–109.

50. B. G. Carruthers and W. N. Espeland, 'Accounting for rationality: double-entry bookkeeping and the rhetoric of economic rationality', *American Journal of Sociology* 97 (1991), 31–69.

51. J. B. Geijsbeek, *Ancient Double-Entry Bookkeeping: Luca Pacioli's Treatise* (Houston, TX: Scholar's Book Co., 1972); Alfred W. Crosby, *The Measure of Reality: Quantification and Western Society, 1250–1600* (Cambridge: Cambridge University Press, 1997).

52. J. B. Krautkraemer, 'Nonrenewable resource scarcity', *Journal of Economic Literature* 36 (1998), 2065–107.

53. Robert Costanza, Ralph D'Arge, Rudolf de Groot, Stephen Farber, Monica Hannon Grasso, Bruce Limburg, Karin Naeem, Robert V. O'Neill, et al., 'The value of the world's ecosystem services and natural capital', *Nature* 387 (1987), 253–60.

54. S. C. Farber, Robert Costanza and Matthew A Wilson 'Economic and ecological concepts for valuing ecosystem services', *Ecological Economics* 41 (2002), 375–92.

55. V. Girolami, L. Mazzon, A. Squartini, N. Mori, M. Marzaro, A. Di Bernardo, M. Greatti, C. Giorio, and A. Tapparo, 'Translocation of neonicotinoid

insecticides from coated seeds to seedling guttation drops: a novel way of intoxication for bees', *Journal of Economic Entomology* 102 (2009), 1808–15; Penelope R. Whitehorn, Stephanie O'Connor, Felix L. Wackers and Dave Goulson, 'Neonicotinoid pesticide reduces bumble bee colony growth and queen production', *Science* 336 (2012), 351–2.

56. R. A. Morse and N. W. Calderone, 'The value of honey bees as pollinators of US crops', *Bee Culture* 128 (2000), 1–15; J. E. Losey and Mace Vaughan, 'The economic value of ecological services provided by insects', *Bioscience* 56 (2006), 311–23.

57. Tim Kasser, *The High Price of Materialism* (Cambridge, MA: MIT Press, 2002) and Tim Kasser and Aaron Ahuvia, 'Materialistic values and well-being in business students', *European Journal of Social Psychology* 32 (2002), 137–46.

58. Ronald Coase, 'The problem of social cost', *Journal of Law and Economics* 3 (1960), 1–44.

59. Heidi Bachram, 'Climate fraud and carbon colonialism: the new trade in greenhouse gases', *Capitalism Nature Socialism* 15 (2004), 1–16; L. Lohmann, 'Carbon trading: a critical conversation on climate change, privatisation and power', *Development Dialogue* 48 (2006), 3–328, at http://www.thecornerhouse.org.uk/sites/thecornerhouse.org.uk/files/carbonDDlow.pdf [visited 9 November 2014].

60. Michael S. Northcott, 'The concealments of carbon markets and the publicity of love in a time of climate change', *International Journal of Public Theology* 4 (2010), 294–313.

61. G. E. Anscombe, ' Modern moral philosophy', *Philosophy* 33 (1958), 1–16.

62. Iris Murdoch, *The Sovereignty of Good* (London: Routledge, 1970).

63. Alasdair MacIntyre, 'Social structures and their threats to moral agency', in A. MacIntyre, *Ethics and Politics: Selected Essays*, vol. 2 (Cambridge: Cambridge University Press, 2006), 186–204.

64. Michael S. Northcott, *The Environment and Christian Ethics* (Cambridge: Cambridge University Press, 1996), 314–6.

65. Rachel Carson, 'From the sense of wonder', *Landscape Journal* 7 (1966), 1–17; E. O. Wilson, *Naturalist* (Washington, DC: Time Warner, 1995).

66. Herman Daly and John Cobb, *For the Common Good: Redirecting the Economy Toward Community, the Environment and a Sustainable Future* (Boston: Beacon Press, 1989).

67. Robert C. Solomon, 'Corporate roles, personal virtues: an Aristotelean approach to business ethics', *Business Ethics Quarterly* 2 (1992), 317–39.

68. Geoff Moore, 'Corporate character: modern virtue ethics and the virtuous corporation', *Business Ethics Quarterly* 15 (2005), 659–85.

69. D. Barboz, 'String of suicides continues at electronics supplier in China', *New York Times* (25 May 2010).

70. Cass R. Sunstein, *Laws of Fear: Beyond the Precautionary Principle* (Cambridge: Cambridge University Press, 2005).

71. A. O'Rourke, 'A new politics of engagement: shareholder activism for corporate social responsibility', *Business Strategy and the Environment* 12 (2003), 227–39.

72. *Green My Apple Archive* 2007, at http://www.greenpeace.org/international/en/news/features/green-my-apple-gossip/ [visited February 10 2014].

73. Paul S. Giller, *Community Structure and the Niche* (London: Chapman and Hall, 1984).

74. Anthony Paul Smith, *A Non-Philosophical Theory of Nature: Ecologies of Thought* (New York: Palgrave Macmillan, 2013), 139.

75. Smith, *Non-Philosophical Theory of Nature*, 139.

76. E. F. Schumacher, *Small is Beautiful: Economics as if People Mattered* (New York: Harper and Row, 1973), 66.

77. Kevin J. O'Brien, *An Ethics of Biodiversity: Christianity, Ecology, and the Variety of Life* (Washington, DC: Georgetown University Press, 2010), 82.

78. William E. Connolly, *The Fragility of Things: Self-Organizing Processes, Neoliberal Fantasies, and Democratic Activism* (Durham, NC: Duke University Press, 2013).

79. Hans Bosma, Michael G. Marmot, H. Hemingway, A. C. Nicholson, Eric Brunner and Stephen A. Stansfield, 'Low job control and risk of coronary heart disease in Whitehall II (prospective cohort) study' *British Medical Journal* 314 (1997), 558–61.

80. Richard G. Wilkinson and Kate E. Pickett, 'Income inequality and population health: a review and explanation of the evidence', *Social Science & Medicine* 62 (2006), 1768–84.

81. Ara Norenzayan, *Big Gods: How Religion Transformed Cooperation and Conflict* (Princeton, NJ: Princeton University Press, 2013).

82. Jacques Ellul, *Anarchy and Christianity*, translated by Geoffrey W. Bromiley (Grand Rapids, MI: Eerdmans, 1991), 50–1.

83. The role of the remote extractive and trading procedures of neoliberal globalisation in the destruction of ecological *places* is a major theme in Val Plumwood, *Environmental Culture: The Ecological Crisis of Reason* (Abingdon: Routledge, 2002).

4 Place, religion and resistance to corporate power

1. Alastair McIntosh, 'Public inquiry on the proposed Harris superquarry: witness on the theological considerations concerning superquarrying and the integrity of creation', *Journal of Law and Religion* 11 (1995), 757–92.

2. Fiona Mackenzie, '"The Cheviot, the Stag . . . and the White, White Rock?" Community, identity and environmental threat on the Isle of Harris', *Environment and Planning D: Society and Space* 16 (1998), 509–32.

3. Alastair McIntosh, Andy Wightman and David Morgan, 'Reclaiming the Scottish Highlands: clearance, conflict and crofting', *The Ecologist* 24 (1994), 64–70.

4. Fraser Darling, *Pelican in the Wilderness: A Naturalist's Odyssey in North America* (New York: Random House, 1956), 180; see also T. C. Smout, 'The Highlands and the roots of green consciousness' in T. C. Smout, *Exploring Enviornmental History: Selected Essays* (Edinburgh: Edinburgh University Press, 2009), 21–52.

5. Andy Wightman, *The Poor Had No Lawyers: Who Owns Scotland: And How They Got It* (Edinburgh: Birlinn, 2013).

6. Wightman, *Poor Had No Lawyers*.

7. Scottish Office, *National Planning Policy Guidelines: Land for Mineral Working* (Edinburgh: Environmental Department, Scottish Office, 1994); Department of the Environment, *The Mineral Planning Guidance 6: Guidelines for Aggregates Provision in England and Wales* (London: HMSO, 1994).

8. Friends of the Earth Scotland, *The Case Against the Harris Superquarry* (Edinburgh: Friends of the Earth Scotland and Link Quarry Group, 1996).

9. Martin and Abercrombie, QCs, 'Final submission to the public enquiry on behalf of Redland Aggregate Limited', cited in MacKenzie, 'The Cheviot, the Stag . . . and the White, White Rock?', 514.

10. MacKenzie, 'The Cheviot, the Stag . . . and the White, White Rock?'

11. 'Massive swing of opinion against superquarry', *West Highland Free Press*, 26 May 1995.

12. 'Massive swing of opinion against superquarry'.

13. David Ross, 'Council Rejects Superquarry', *Glasgow Herald*, 6 June 1995.

14. Michael Scott and Sarah Johnson, *The Battle for Roineabhal: Reflections on the successful campaign to prevent a superquarry at Lingerabay, Isle of Harris and lessons for the Scottish planning system* (Perth: Scottish Environment LINK, 2006), 66–8.

15. James Hunter, *On the Other Side of Sorrow: Nature and People in the Scottish Highlands* (Edinburgh: Mainstream, 1995), 16–17.

16. MacKenzie, 'The Cheviot, the Stag . . . and the White, White Rock?', 512.

17. Scott and Johnson, *The Battle for Roineabhal*, 107–8.

18. Jason Allardyce, 'Media out in force for "transatlantic cultural psychotherapy session"' *West Highland Free Press*, 11 November 1994.

19. Callum Brown, *Religion and Society in Twentieth Century Britain* (Harlow: Pearson, 2006), 27.

20. Alesia Maltz, 'Commentary on the Harris Superquarry Inquiry', *Journal of Law and Religion* 11 (1995), 793–833.

21. Maltz, 'Commentary on the Harris Superquarry Inquiry'.

22. Scott and Johnson, *The Battle for Roineabhal*, 6, 41.

23. Alastair McIntosh, *Island Spirituality* (Edinburgh: Birlinn, 2013).

24. McIntosh, 'Public inquiry on the proposed Harris superquarry', 776.

25. McIntosh, 'Public inquiry on the proposed Harris superquarry', 779, note 64.

26. McIntosh, 'Public inquiry on the proposed Harris superquarry'. 778.

27. Donald MacLeod, cited in McIntosh, 'Public inquiry on the proposed Harris superquarry', 783.

28. McIntosh, 'Public inquiry on the proposed Harris superquarry', 784.

29. Sulian Stone Eagle, cited in McIntosh, 'Public inquiry on the proposed Harris superquarry', 786.

30. Maltz, 'Commentary on the Harris Superquarry Inquiry'.

31. On Cartesianism, Enlightenment rationality and the nature–culture divide, see further Michael S. Northcott, *A Political Theology of Climate Change*, (London: SPCK, 2014), 62–73, 168–90.

32. Val Plumwood, 'Nature, self and gender: feminism, environmental philosophy, and the critique of rationalism', *Hypatia* 6 (1991), 15–27.

33. For an excellent account of the deficiencies of utilitarianism from an environmental perspective, see Mark Sagoff, *The Economy of the Earth* (Cambridge: Cambridge University Press, 1988).

34. James C. Scott, *Weapons of the Weak: Everyday Forms of Peasant Resistance* (New Haven, CT: Yale University Press, 1985).

35. Plumwood, 'Nature, self and gender'; see also John MacMurray, *Persons in Relation* (London: Faber and Faber, 1961).

36. Carol Gilligan, *In A Different Voice: Psychological Theory and Women's Development* (Cambridge, MA: Harvard University Press, 1981).

37. See further Brian Wilson, *Contemporary Transformations of Religion* (Oxford: Oxford University Press, 1979) and David Martin, *A General Theory of Secularisation* (Oxford: Oxford University Press, 1978).

38. José Casanova, *Public Religions in the Modern World* (Chicago: Chicago University Press, 1994).

39. Anthony Giddens, *The Consequences of Modernity* (Cambridge: Polity Press, 1993).

40. Mackenzie, '"The Cheviot, the Stag . . . and the White, White Rock?"', 529.

41. See further Roger Gottlieb (ed.), *This Sacred Earth: Religion, Nature, Environment* (New York: Routledge, 1994).

42. Max Oelschlaeger, *Caring for Creation: An Ecumenical Approach to the Environmental Crisis* (New Haven, CT: Yale University Press, 1994).

43. J. Baird Callicott, *Earth's Insights: A Multicultural Survey of Ecological Ethics from the Mediterranean Basin to the Australian Outback* (Berkeley: University of California Press, 1994).

44. Michael S. Northcott, *The Environment and Christian Ethics* (Cambridge: Cambridge University Press, 1996).

5 Wilderness, religion and ecological restoration in the Scottish Highlands

1. James Hunter, 'Wilderness in North America and Scotland: the human dimension', in D. Mollison (ed.), *Wilderness with People: The Management of Wild Land* (Musselburgh: John Muir Trust, 1992), 28–49.

2. John Ruskin, *Modern Painters Vol. IV: Of Mountain Beauty* (London: Smith, Elder & Co., 1856).

3. John Muir, *My First Summer in the Sierra* (Edinburgh: Canongate Classics, 1988 (1911)).

4. Robert MacFarlane, *Mountains of the Mind: A History of Fascination* (London: Granta Books, 2003), 75.

5. Muir, *My First Summer in the Sierra*, 32.

6. Alexander Carmichael, *Carmina Gadelica: Hymns and Incantations* (Northumberland: Lindisfarne, 1992), 242, 245: in her *Celtic Christianity and Nature: Early Irish and Hebridean Traditions* (Edinburgh: Edinburgh University Press, 1996) Mary Low argues Carmichael captured an authentic echo of an ancient Celtic oral tradition but Donald Meek argues that the *Carmina Gadelica* is a Romantic reinvention and lacks a genuine connection to historic Celtic Christianity; see Meek's review of Mary Low, *Celtic Christianity and Nature* in *Studies in World Christianity* 5 (1995), 98–101.

7. Alastair McIntosh, *Soil and Soul: People Versus Corporate Power* (London: Aurum Press, 2001), 89.

8. John Prebble, *The Highland Clearances* (Harmondsworth: Penguin, 1969).

9. Max Oelschlaeger, *The Idea of Wilderness: From Prehistory to the Age of Ecology* (New Haven: Yale University Press, 1991), 92–7.

10. Adam Bewell, *Wordsworth and the Enlightenment: Nature, Man, and Society in the Experimental Poetry* (Yale: Yale University Press, 1989), 141.

11. Oelschlaeger, *Idea of Wilderness*, 181.

12. Edward Abbey, *Desert Solitaire: A Season in the Wilderness* (London: Robin Clark, 1992 (1967)).

13. Abbey, *Desert Solitaire*, 247.

14. Wallace Stegner, 'This land', reprinted in T. H. Watkins and Patricia Byrnes (eds), *The World of Wilderness: Essays on the Power and Purpose of Wild Country* (Niwar, CO: Rinehart, Wilderness Society, 1995), 19–33.

15. Howard Clinebell, *Ecotherapy: Healing Ourselves, Healing the Earth* (Minneapolis: Fortress Press, 1996).

16. Catherine Albanese, *Nature Religion in America* (Chicago: Chicago University Press, 1990).

17. Tal Scriven, *Wrongness, Wisdom and Wilderness: Toward a Libertarian Theory of Ethics and the Environment* (Albany, NY: State University of New York Press, 1997), 183.

18. Robert Elliot, 'Faking Nature', in Robert Elliot (ed.), *Environmental Ethics* (Oxford: Oxford University Press, 1995), 76–88.

19. Clifford Geertz, 'Local knowledge: fact and law in comparative perspective' in Geertz, *Local Knowledge: Further Essays in Interpretative Anthropology* (New York: Basic Books, 1983), 167–235.

20. Eric Katz, 'The big lie: human restoration of nature', in David M. Kaplan (ed.), *Readings in the Philosophy of Technology* (Lanham, MD: Rowman and Littlefield, 2009), 443–51.

21. Roy Rappaport, *Pigs for the Ancestors* (New Haven: Yale University Press, 1968).

22. On the problems of scientific forest knowledge, see James C. Scott, *Seeing Like a State: How Certain Schemes to Improve the Human Condition Have Failed* (New Haven: Yale University Press, 1998), 11–19.

23. Andrew Light, 'Ecological restoration and the culture of nature: a pragmatic perspective', in Andrew Light and Holmes Rolston (eds), *Environmental Ethics: An Anthology* (Oxford: Blackwell, 2003), 398–411, at 407.

24. The absence of a justice discourse from ecological restoration projects is noted in the collected essays in James K. Boyce, Sunita Narain and Elizabeth A. Stanton (eds), *Reclaiming Nature: Environmental Justice and Ecological Restoration* (London: Anthem Press, 2007).

25. Andrew M. M. Samuel, 'Cultural symbols and landowners' power: the practice of managing Scotland's natural resource', *Sociology* 34.4 (2000), 691–706.

26. Alastair Cramb, *Who Owns Scotland Now? The Use and Abuse of Private Land* (Edinburgh: Mainstream Publishing, 1996), 33.

27. Alastair McIntosh, *Soil and Soul* (Edinburgh: Birlinn, 1998).

28. Susan Power Bratton, 'The original desert solitaire: early Christian monasteries and wilderness', *Environmental Ethics* 10 (1988), 31–53.

29. Derwas J. Chitty, *The Desert a City: An Introduction to the Study of Egyptian and Palestinian Monasticism under the Christian Empire* (Crestwood, NY: St Vladimir's Seminary Press, 1997).

30. Ambrose of Milan, *The Story of Naboth*, reprinted in Oliver O'Donovan and Joan O'Donovan, *From Irenaeus to Grotius: A Sourcebook in Christian Political Thought* (Grand Rapids, MI: Eerdmans, 1999), 75–9.

31. Robert Waldron, *Thomas Merton: Master of Attention: An Exploration of Prayer* (Mahwah, NJ: Paulist Press, 2008), 28.

32. Benedict of Nursia, *Rule of Benedict*, 58. 17: online edition http://www.osb.org/rb/ [visited 14 February 2014].

33. Martine Vonk, *Sustainability and Quality of Life: A Study on the Religious Worldviews, Values and Environmental Impact of Amish, Hutterite, Franciscan and Benedictine Communities* (Amsterdam: Omslagontwerp, 2011), 179–80.

34. Vonk, *Sustainability and Quality of Life*, 183.

35. John Klassen OSB, 'The rule of Benedict and Environmental Stewardship', Public Lecture, College of Saint Benedict and St John's University, 2004,

and at https://www.csbsju.edu/SJU-Sustainability/About-Us/Benedictine-Stewardship/Values/Klassen.htm [visited 14 February 2014].

36. Vonk, *Sustainability and Quality of Life*, 186.

37. William Langland, *Piers the Ploughman*, translated by J. F. Goodridge (Harmondsworth: Penguin, 1959), 121.

38. For an incisive account of how the Scottish Land Reform legislation is failing to repeople the Highlands of Scotland, as its architects had once envisaged, see Andy Wightman, *The Poor Had No Lawyers: Who Owns Scotland and How They Got It* (Edinburgh: Birlinn, 2013), Chapter 32.

39. For a critique of the impact of environmentalism on the Scottish Highlands, see James Hunter, *On the Other Side of Sorrow: Nature and People in the Scottish Highlands* (Edinburgh: Mainstream, 1995).

6 Food sovereignty from Joshua to La Via Campesina

1. Ofer Bar-Yosef, 'The Natufian culture in the Levant, threshold to the origins of agriculture', *Evolutionary Anthropology* 6 (1998), 159–77.

2. Kent Flannery and Joyce Marcus, *The Creation of Inequality: How Our Prehistoric Ancestors Set the State for Monarchy, Slavery, and Empire* (Cambridge, MA: Harvard University Press, 2012).

3. Robert J. Wenke, 'Egypt: origins of complex societies', *Annual Review of Anthropology* 18 (1981), 129–55.

4. Ellen Davis, *Scripture, Culture and Agriculture* (Cambridge: Cambridge University Press, 2009).

5. Moses, King David and a number of the Hebrew prophets were also nomadic pastoralists. The ideal of shepherding recurs in the messianic language of the Hebrew prophets and Christ draws on this language in parables and in self-description. Early Christian artists principally depict Christ as the good shepherd.

6. Walter Brueggemann, *The Land: Place as Gift, Promise, and Challenge in Biblical Faith* (Philadelphia: Fortress Press, 1977), 46.

7. Brueggemann, *The Land*, 50.

8. Jonathan Burnside, *God, Justice, and Society: Aspects of Law and Legality in the Bible* (Oxford: Oxford University Press, 2011), 88.

9. See further Burnside, *God, Justice, and Society*, 192–3.

10. Davis, *Scripture, Culture and Agriculture*, 112.

11. Burnside, *God, Justice, and Society*, 195–6.

12. Tom Veerkamp, 'Judeo-Christian tradition on debt: political, not just ethical', *Ethics and International Affairs* 21 (2007), 167–88.

13. On the significance of naming in Genesis see Michael S. Northcott, 'Reading Genesis in Borneo: work, guardianship, and companion animals in Genesis 2',

in Nathan MacDonald, Mark W. Elliott and Grant Macaskill (eds), *Genesis and Christian Theology* (Grand Rapids, MI: Eerdmans, 2012), 190–203.

14. Mike Davis, *Late Victorian Holocausts: El Nino Famines and the Making of the Third World* (London: Verso Books, 2001).

15. Jean Dreze and Amartya Sen, *Hunger and Public Action* (Oxford: Clarendon Press, 1989).

16. Jean Dreze and Amartya Sen, 'Introduction', in Dreze and Sen (eds), *The Political Economy of Hunger: Vol. 1: Entitlement and Well-being* (Oxford: Oxford University Press, 1990), 3.

17. I taught on an MSc in Theology and Development in the 1990s in Edinburgh and every year this problem was raised by African graduate students who had seen the destitution cash crops had brought to their home villages.

18. Aldas Janaiah, 'Hybrid rice for Indian farmers: myths and realities', *Economic and Political Weekly* 37 (2002), 4319–28.

19. Vandana Shiva and Kunwar Jalees, *Farmer Suicides in India* (New Delhi: Research Foundation for Science, Technology and Ecology, 2003).

20. James C. Scott's classic study, *Weapons of the Weak: Everyday Forms of Peasant Resistance* (New Haven: Yale University Press, 1985), reveals rising rural debt, poverty and landlessness associated with the Green Revolution in West Malaysia; his *Seeing Like a State: How Certain Schemes to Improve the Human Condition Have Failed* (New Haven: Yale University Press, 1995) describes the failure of a large-scale government-sponsored agricultural development scheme in Tanzania.

21. Wendell Berry, *The Unsettling of America: Culture and Agriculture* (Berkeley, CA: Sierra Club Books, 1977).

22. James E. Tillotson, 'America's obesity: conflicting public policies, industrial economic development, and unintended human consequences', *Annual Review of Nutrition* 24 (2004), 617–43 and Scott Fields, 'The fat of the land: do agricultural subsidies foster poor health?' *Environmental Health Perspectives* 112 (2004), A821–3.

23. Norman Myers coined the phrase 'shifted cultivator' to describe the destructive effects of enforced migration on developing world forests and ecosystems: see Norman Myers, 'Tropical forests: the main deforestation fronts', *Environmental Conservation* 20 (1993), 9–16. On land theft in Africa, see Jing Gu, 'The last golden land? Chinese private companies go to Africa', Institute of Development Studies University of Sussex, Working Paper 365 (2011), and B. White, S. M. Borras Jr, R. Hall, I. Scoones and W. Wolford, 'The new enclosures: critical perspectives on corporate land deals', *Journal of Peasant Studies* 39 (2012), 619–47.

24. See for example Julian Cribb, *The Coming Famine: The Global Food Crisis and What We Can Do About It* (Berkeley, CA: University of California Press, 2010).

25. Mehul Srivastava and Andrew MacAskill, 'Poor in India starve as politicians steal $14.5 billion of food', 28 August 2012, Bloomberg.

26. C. S. Srinivasan, 'Concentration in ownership of plant variety rights: some implications for developing countries', *Food Policy* 28 (2003), 519–46.

27. Trussell Trust, 'Latest foodbank figures top 900,000: life has got worse not better for poorest in 2013/14, and this is just the tip of the iceberg', Trussell Trust Press Release, 16 April 2014, at http://www.trusselltrust.org/resources/documents/Press/foodbank-figures-top-900,000/foodbank-figures-top-900,000.pdf [visited 17 April 2014].

28. Archbishop of Wales and 600 other religious leaders, 'Open letter to the leaders of the three main political parties about UK hunger', *The Guardian*, 16 April 2014, at http://www.theguardian.com/society/2014/apr/16/open-letter-leaders-three-main-parties-hunger [visited 17 April 2014].

29. Hannah and Dean Chadwick, 'UK hunger crisis laid bare in open letter to PM from professional couple forced to resort to food banks', 16 April 2014, at http://streetdemocracy.wordpress.com/2014/04/16/uk-hunger-crisis-laid-bare-in-open-letter-to-pm-from-professional-couple-forced-to-resort-to-food-banks/ [visited 17 April 2014].

30. Robert F. Harper, *The Code of Hammurabi, King of Babylon about 2250: Autographed Text and Transliteration* (Chicago, IL: University of Chicago Press, 1904).

31. Ernesto Canada, *Food Sovereignty: The People's Alternative* (London: Progressio/Catholic Institute for International Relations, 2006), 18.

32. Michael Redclift, 'Agrarian populism in Mexico – the "via campesina"', *The Journal of Peasant Studies* 7 (1980), 492–502.

33. Redclift, 'Agrarian populism in Mexico', 495.

34. Arturo Warman, 'Andamos arando', *Nexos* 13 (January 1979), cited in Redclift, 'Agrarian populism in Mexico', 498.

35. Antonio Turrent, 'El sistema agricola: un marco de referencia necesario para la planeación de la investigación en Mexico', cited in Redclift, 'Agrarian populism in Mexico', 499.

36. Berry's sharpest critique of the deleterious impacts of land grant university research is in Berry, *Unsettling of America*; however, unlike the Mexicans, Berry does not criticise the land and value accumulation methods of United States banks and agricultural corporations, and this is arguably the biggest weakness in his elegaic defence of the family farm.

37. See further Paul B. Thompson's account of the 'productionist paradigm' in his *The Spirit of the Soil: Agriculture and Environmental Ethics* (New York: Routledge, 1995), 47–71.

38. Jefferson Boyer, 'Food security, food sovereignty, and local challenges for transnational agrarian movements: the Honduran case', *The Journal of Peasant Studies* 37 (2010), 319–51.

39. S. Ryan Isakson, 'O hay ganancia en la milpa: the agrarian question, food sovereignty, and the on-farm conservation of agrobiodiversity in the Guatemalan highlands', *The Journal of Peasant Studies* 36 (2009), 725–59.

40. Isakson, 'The agrarian question'.

41. Raj Patel, 'What does food sovereignty look like?' *The Journal of Peasant Studies* 36 (2009), 663–706.

42. Carl Schmitt, *The Concept of the Political*, translated by George Schwab, enlarged edition (Chicago: Chicago University Press, 2007).

43. 'For the peoples' right to produce, feed themselves and exercise their food sovereignty', Final Declaration of the World Forum on Food Sovereignty, Havana, Cuba, 7 September 2001, cited in Canada, *Food Sovereignty*, 19.

44. For a proper discussion of John Locke's theology of land, see Michael S. Northcott, *An Angel Directs the Storm: Apocalyptic Religion and American Empire* (London: I. B. Tauris, 2004); see also Thompson, *Spirit of the Soil*, 52.

45. Vandana Shiva, *Monocultures of the Mind: Perspectives on Biodiversity and Biotechnology* (London: Palgrave MacMillan, 1993); on evidence for the higher productivity in terms of nutritional outputs of peasant agroecology, see Miguel A. Altieri, 'Agroecology, small farms, and food sovereignty', *Monthly Review* 61 (2009), 102–13, and Michael Windfuhr and Jennie Jonsen, *Food Sovereignty: Towards Democracy in Localized Food Systems* (Rugby: ITDG Pub, 2005).

46. H. J. Massingham, *The Tree of Life* (London: Jon Carpenter, 2003).

47. On the role of local currencies in sustaining local food systems, and promoting community self-reliance and local employment, see further Peter North, *Local Money: How To Make It Happen in Your Community* (Totnes: Transition Books, 2010).

48. Jeffrey Stout, *Democracy and Tradition* (Princeton NJ: Princeton University Press, 2004).

49. I discuss the contest between local and supranational ecclesiologies in Michael S. Northcott, 'Parochial ecology on St Briavels Common: rebalancing the local and the universal in Anglican ecclesiology and practice', *Journal of Anglican Studies* 10 (2012), 68–93.

50. Isakson, 'The agrarian question'.

51. A. V. Chayanov, *On the Theory of the Peasant Economy* (Manchester: Manchester University Press, 1996).

52. Juliet du Boulay, *Portrait of a Greek Mountain Village* (Oxford: Clarendon Press, 1974) and Juliet du Boulay, *Cosmos, Life and Liturgy in a Greek Orthodox Village* (Limni, Evia: Denise Harvey, 2009).

53. Chayanov, *Theory of the Peasant Economy*, 70.

54. On the demise of slavery, and the role of small-scale land ownership in promoting freedom in Western Europe, see Hilaire Belloc, *The Servile State* (London: T. N. Foulis, 1913).

55. Anthony S. Wohl, *The Eternal Slum: Housing and Social Policy in Victorian London* (London: Edward Arnold, 1977), 50–7.

56. See further Daniel Dorling, *Inequality and the 1%* (London: Verso, 2014).

7 The moral geography of sustainable communities

1. Amelia Gentleman, 'No one should die penniless and alone: the victims of Britain's harsh welfare sanctions', *The Guardian*, 4 August 2014.

2. *Social Insurance and Allied Services: Report by Sir William Beveridge* (London: HSMO, 1942), I. 10.

3. Industrial farming is highly oil dependent; it is also highly dependent on mined phosphorous-rich rock. World supplies of this mineral are finite and it is estimated, at present levels of extraction, phosphorus extraction from rock will peak in 2033 and then decline, giving rise to sharp spikes in the price of food: Dana Cordell and Stuart White, 'Peak phosphorus: clarifying the key issues of a vigorous debate about long-term phosphorus security', *Sustainability* 3 (2011), 2027–49, Fig. 4.

4. Clifford Geertz, *Local Knowledge: Further Essays in Interpretative Anthropology* (New York: Basic Books, 1985).

5. On the complicity of many clergy with the Highland Clearances, and the resistance of a minority, see David Paton, *The Clergy and the Clearances* (Edinburgh: John Donald, 2006).

6. Harriet Ritvo, *The Dawn of Green: Manchester, Thirlmere, and Modern Environmentalism* (Chicago: Chicago University Press, 2009), 82–5.

7. Ritvo, *The Dawn of Green*, 165.

8. Robert W. Righter, *The Battle over Hetch Hetchy: America's Most Controversial Dam and the Birth of Modern Environmentalism* (Oxford: Oxford University Press, 2005).

9. John Muir, *The Yosemite* (New York: Century & Co., 1912).

10. Roderick Nash, *Wilderness and the American Mind* (New Haven, CT: Yale University Press, 1967), 177.

11. Righter, *Battle over Hetch Hetchy*, 5.

12. Roger Scruton, *Green Philosophy: How to Think Seriously About the Planet* (London: Atlantic Books, 2012), 340–9.

13. Scruton, *Green Philosophy*, 349.

14. Scruton, *Green Philosophy*, 350–1.

15. Wendell Berry, 'The ecological crisis as a crisis of agriculture', in Berry, *The Unsettling of America*, 17–38.

16. James C. Scott, *Seeing Like a State: How Certain Schemes to Improve the Human Condition Have Failed* (New Haven, CT: Yale University Press, 1988).

17. G. A. Rees, W. A. Doyle, A. Srivastava, Z. M. Brooke, M. A. Crawford and K. L. Costeloe, 'The nutrient intakes of mothers of low birth weight babies – a comparison of ethnic groups in East London UK', *Maternal and Child Nutrition* 1 (2005), 91–9, and M. A. Crawford, W. Doyle, I. L. Craft and B. M. Laurance, 'A comparison of food intake during pregnancy and birth weight in high and low socioeconomic groups', *Progress in Lipid Research* 25 (1986), 249–54.

18. Dennis Hardy and Colin Ward, *Arcadia for All: The Legacy of a Makeshift Landscape* (London: Mansell, 1984).

19. Ward, *Arcadia for All*, 11.

20. Ward, *Arcadia for All*, 13–15. Given the central place of squatters in the formation of the villages and smallholder horticulture of England, it is a sad

irony that the English government has for the first time made squatting in unused dwellings a criminal offence; the offense was introduced in section 144 of the Legal Aid, Sentencing and Punishment of Offenders Act, 2012, and is punishable by six months imprisonment or a maximum £5,000 fine, or both.

21. Gerard Winstanley, *The 'Law of Freedom' and Other Writings*, edited by Christopher Hill (Cambridge: Cambridge University Press, 1973).

22. Belloc notes that this condition came to an end in part because of a law sponsored by landlords and lawyers under Charles II, *'The Statute of Frauds'*, according to which land and dwelling rights – or freehold – were only valid, and not fraudulent, where they were recorded in a legal document paper title, which the majority of yeoman farmers lacked, having inherited their dwellings and lands over many generations before formal legal titles were recorded: Hilaire Belloc, *An Essay on the Restoration of Property*, first published in 1936 (Norfolk, VA: IHS Press 2002), 41.

23. Belloc, *Restoration of Property*, 39.

24. Pontificum Consilium de Iustitia et Pace, *Compendium of the Social Doctrine of the Church* (London: Burns and Oates, 2005), 86–9.

25. See further Martin Shaxson, *Treasure Islands: Tax Havens and the Men Who Stole the World* (London: Vintage, 2012).

26. Bryan S. Turner, 'The enclave society: towards a sociology of immobility', *European Journal of Social Theory* 10 (2007), 287–304.

27. See further Peter Selby, *An Idol Unmasked: A Faith Perspective on Money* (London: Darton, Longman and Todd, 2014).

28. James J. Parsons, 'On "bioregionalism" and "watershed consciousness"', *The Professional Geographer* 37 (1985), 1–6.

29. Peter Berg, 'Strategies for reinhabiting the Northern Californian bioregion', *Seriatim: the Journal of Ecotopia* 1 (1977), 2–8.

30. Mathis Wackernagel and William Rees, *Our Ecological Footprint: Reducing Human Impact on the Earth* (Gabriola, BC: New Society Publishers, 1996), 11–15.

31. Wackernagel and Rees, *Our Ecological Footprint*, 40.

32. Alessandro Gallia, Thomas Wiedmann, Ertug Ercin, Doris Knoblauch, Brad Ewing and Stefan Giljum, 'Integrating ecological, carbon and water footprint into a "footprint family" of indicators: definition and role in tracking human pressure on the planet', *Ecological Indicators* 16 (2012), 100–12.

33. 'World footprint: do we fit on the planet?' Global Footprint Network: Advancing the Science of Sustainability, at http://www.footprintnetwork.org/en/index.php/GFN/page/world_footprint/ [visited 20 January 2013].

34. European Environment Agency, *The European Environment: State and Outlook 2010: Consumption and the Environment* (Copenhagen: EEA, 2010), and at http://www.eea.europa.eu/soer/europe/consumption-and-environment [visited 20 January 2013].

35. See further

36. E. F. Schumacher, *Small Is Beautiful* (London: Sphere Books, 1974), 45.

37. Schumacher, *Small Is Beautiful*, 46.

38. See further Rembert Sorg, *Holy Work: Towards a Benedictine Theology of Manual Labour* (Santa Ana, CA: Source Books, 2003).

39. Rob Hopkins, *The Transition Handbook: From Oil Dependency to Local Resilience* (Totnes: Green Books, 2008).

40. 'Countdown to crisis: eight days that shook Britain', 14 September 2000, BBC News archive at http://news.bbc.co.uk/1/hi/uk/924574.stm [visited 24 January 2013].

41. For an insightful overview of modern logistics, see Alain de Botton, *The Pleasures and Sorrows of Work* (London: Penguin, 2009), Chapter II: Logistics.

42. Hopkins, *The Transition Handbook*, 15.

43. See further Michael Shuman, *Going Local: Creating Self-Reliant Communities in a Global Age* (New York: Routledge, 2000), Chapter 4, 'Financing the future'.

44. http://bristolpound.org, visited 11 November 2014.

45. Annellen Kenis and Erik Mathjis, 'The role of citizenship in transitions to sustainability: the emergence of Transition Towns in Flanders, Belgium', Paper presented at the first European conference on Sustainability Transitions, 'Dynamics and Governance of Transitions to Sustainability', Amsterdam, 4–6 June 2009, at https://lirias.kuleuven.be/handle/123456789/239830 [visited 18 December 2012].

46. Madeleine Bunting, 'A new politics: beyond Westminster's bankrupted practices, a new idealism is emerging', *The Guardian: Comment is Free*, 31 May 2009, at http://www.guardian.co.uk/commentisfree/2009/may/31/reform-transition-a-new-politics [visited 18 December 2012].

47. Justus von Liebig, *Letters on the Subject of the Utilization of the Metropolitan Sewage* (London: W. H. Collingridge, 1865).

48. Bill Mollison and D. Holmgren, *Permaculture One: A Perennial Agriculture for Human Settlements* (Melbourne: Transworld, 1976).

49. David Tracey, *Guerrilla Gardening: A Manualfesto* (Gabriola Island, BC: New Society, 2007).

50. Diane Gibson, 'Food stamp program participation is positively related to obesity in low income women', *Journal of Nutrition* 133 (2003), 2225–31.

51. For an influential analysis of this disconnection, which gave rise to the organic food movement, see Albert Howard, *The Soil and Health: A Study of Organic Agriculture* (London: Devin-Adair 1947).

52. Ailbhe Gerrard, 'Urban agriculture diversity in Britain: building resilience through international experiences', Conference proceedings, 'Innovation and Sustainable Development in Agriculture and Food', 28 June – 1 July 2010, Montpellier, France, at http://www.isda2010.net/index.php/isda2010/layout/set/resume/papers2/urban_agriculture_diversity_in_britain2 [visited 26 January 2013].

53. The lineaments of Marx's analysis of metabolic rift in *Capital* are described in John Bellamy Foster, 'Marx's theory of metabolic rift: classical foundations for environmental sociology', *American Journal of Sociology* 105 (1999), 366–405.

54. The phrase 'society of strangers' was coined by Adam Smith in *Wealth of Nations*.

55. G. A. McKay, *Radical Gardening: Politics, Idealism and Rebellion in the Garden* (London: Frances Lincoln, 2013).

56. Karl Polanyi, *The Great Transformation: The Political and Economic Origins of Our Time* (Boston, MA: Beacon Press, 1944).

57. David Hall, 'Private equity and infrastructure funds in public services', Public Services International Research Unit, University of Greenwich (November 2006), at http://gala.gre.ac.uk/3584/1/PSIRU_9705_-_2006-11-PE.pdf [visited 14 August 2014].

58. See, for example, Naomi Oreskes and Erik M. Conway, *The Collapse of Western Civilization: A View from the Future* (New York: Columbia University Press, 2014).

59. Alasdair MacIntyre, *After Virtue: A Study in Moral Theory* (London: Duckworth, 1981), 154.

60. MacIntyre, *After Virtue*, 115.

61. For a fuller account of Kant's moral epistemology, see Northcott, *Political Theology of Climate Change*, 168–208.

62. See further Alastair MacIntyre, *Dependent Rational Animals* (London: Duckworth, 1999).

63. Carol Gilligan, *In a Different Voice: Psychological Theory and Women's Development* (Cambridge, MA: Harvard University Press, 1982) and Virginia Held, *Feminist Morality: Transforming Culture, Society and Politics* (Chicago: University of Chicago Press, 1993).

64. See further Sophie Powell, *Economic Partnership Agreements: Building or Shattering African Region Integration?* (London: Traidcraft, 2007) and at http://www.traidcraft.co.uk/Resources/Traidcraft/Documents/PDF/tx/policy_EPAs_buildingafricanintegration.pdf [visited 11 November 2014].

65. Thomas Traherne was the first modern author to draw attention to the role of sensory experiences of nature in the formation of morally sensitive human beings; for an excellent account of this, see further the PhD thesis of my graduate student Chad Rimmer, *The moral theory of Thomas Traherne, with special attention to the proformative role of nature in the moral formation of children* (Edinburgh: University of Edinburgh, 2014).

66. Val Plumwood, *Environmental Culture: The Ecological Crisis of Reason* (Abingdon: Routledge, 2002), 231.

67. See the collected essays in Darcia Narvaez, Jaak Panksepp, Alan N. Schore, and Tracy R. Gleason (eds), *Evolution, Early Experience and Human Development* (Oxford: Oxford University Press, 2013).

68. See further Michael. A. Crawford, W. Doyle, I. L. Craft and B. M. Laurance, 'A comparison of food intake during pregnancy and birth weight in high and low

socioeconomic groups', *Progress in Lipid Research* 25 (1986), 249–54, and *The Descent into Negative Welfare: The Zachaeus 2000 Trust's Response to the Public Health White Paper: 'Health Lives, Healthy People'* (London, 2011), at http://z2k.org/wp-content/uploads/2011/09/The-Descent-into-Negative-Welfare-a-response-to-Public-Health-White-Paper.pdf [visited 17 January 2013].

69. Darcia Narvaez, Jaak Panksepp, Alan N. Schore and Tracy R. Gleason, 'The value of using an evolutionary framework for gauging children's well-being', in Narvaez and Panksepp, *Evolution, Early Experience and Human Development*, 3–30.

70. Aldo Leopold, *A Sand County Almanac and Sketches Here and There* (Oxford: Oxford University Press, 1966).

71. Bruno Latour, *We Have Never Been Modern* (Oxford: Blackwell, 1991).

8 Re-placing ethics in the city and the countryside

1. Rudolf Otto, *Idea of the Holy: An Inquiry into the Non-Rational Factor in the Idea of the Divine and its Relation to the Rational*, translated by John W. Harvey (Oxford: Oxford University Press, 1923).

2. Thomas Dubay, *The Evidential Power of Beauty: Science and Theology Meet* (San Francisco: Ignatius Press, 1999).

3. Dubay, *Evidential Power of Beauty*.

4. Mircea Eliade, 'On sacred space', Chapter 1 in *The Sacred and the Profane: The Nature of Religion*, translated by W. R. Trask (New York: Harcourt, Brace and World, 1968).

5. On the importance of beauty and craft in the Temple project, see further the thesis of my doctoral student Jeremy Kidwell, *Drawn into worship: A biblical ethics of work*, PhD thesis, University of Edinburgh, 2013.

6. Margaret Barker, *The Gate of Heaven: The History and Symbolism of the Temple in Jerusalem* (London: SPCK, 1991).

7. Ananda K. Coomaraswarmy, 'The Christian and oriental, or true, philosophy of art', in *The Essential Coomaraswarmy*, edited by Rama P. Coomaraswarmy (Bloomington IN: World Wisdom, 2004), 123–52.

8. See further Colin Richards, *Dwelling among the Monuments: The Neolithic Village of Barnhouse, Maeshowe Passage Grave and Surrounding Monuments at Strenness, Orkney* (Cambridge: McDonald Institute for Archaeological Research, University of Cambridge, 2005).

9. See for example Mark Jturdvejic, 'Civic humanism and the rise of the Medici', *Renaissance Quarterly* 52 (1999), 994–1020.

10. See further George W. Dameron, *Florence and its Church in the Age of Dante* (University of Pennsylvania Press, 2013).

11. On the central role of the guilds in the creation of medieval Florence, see Franklin Toker, *On Holy Ground: Liturgy, Architecture and Urbanism in the Cathedral and the Streets of Medieval Florence* (London: Harvey Miller, 2009).

12. Philip Bess, *Till We Have Built Jerusalem: Architecture, Urbanism, and the Sacred* (Wilmington, DE: ISI Books, 2006), 73–4.

13. Bess, *Till We Have Built Jerusalem*, 75.

14. Bess, *Till We Have Built Jerusalem*, 76.

15. Mike Davis, in *Ecology of Fear: Lost Angeles and the Imagination of Disaster* (London: Vintage Books, 1999), attributes the ills of cities such as Los Angeles to a neglect of their ecological situatedness, and their prioritising of economic function over social justice.

16. Bess, *Till We Have Built Jerusalem*, 91–2.

17. Richard Sennett, *The Conscience of the Eye: The Design and Social Life of Cities* (New York: W. W. Norton, 1990).

18. Gorringe, *Theology of the Built Environment*, 86–9.

19. Saint Augustine, *De Musica*, translated by W. F. J. Knight (New York: Hyperion Press, 1949).

20. John Milbank, 'On complex space', in John Milbank, *The Word Made Strange: Theology, Language and Culture* (Oxford: Blackwell, 1997), 277.

21. Bess, *Till We Have Built Jerusalem*, 130–1.

22. Milbank, 'On complex space', 279.

23. William Cavanaugh, *Torture and Eucharist: Theology, Politics and the Body of Christ* (Oxford: Blackwell, 1998), 214.

24. Cavanaugh, *Torture and Eucharist*, 218.

25. Keith Bladon, '"The gracious gift"; Church of England finances and resources' in Robert Hannaford (ed.), *A Church for the Twenty-First Century: The Church of England Today and Tomorrow: An Agenda for the Future* (Leominster, Herts: Gracewing 1998), 37–79.

26. Oliver O'Donovan, 'The loss of a sense of place', in Oliver O'Donovan and Joan L. O'Donovan, *Bonds of Imperfection: Christian Politics Past and Present* (Grand Rapids, MI: Eerdmans, 2004), 296–321.

27. O'Donovan, 'The loss of a sense of place', 299.

28. O'Donovan, 'The loss of a sense of place', 305.

29. David M. Smith, *Moral Geographies: Ethics in a World of Difference* (Edinburgh: Edinburgh University Press, 2000), 12–21.

30. For a fuller critique of cosmopolitan blindness to geographic boundaries, see Northcott, *Political Theology of Climate Change*.

31. Michel Serres, *The Natural Contract*, translated by E. MacArthur and W. Pawson (Ann Arbor, MI: University of Michigan Press, 1995).

32. Many post-Reformation 'religious' conflicts were proxy wars in the birth pangs of the early modern State: see further William Cavanaugh, '"A fire strong enough to consume the house": the wars of religion and the rise of the state', *Modern Theology* 11 (1995), 397–420.

33. See further Anna Minton, *Ground Control: Fear and Happiness in the Twenty-First Century City* (London: Penguin, 2012); on the alienating effects

of privatisation, see James Meek, *Private Island: Why Britain Now Belongs to Someone Else* (London: Verso Books, 2014).

34. Serres, *Natural Contract*, 49.

35. Robert Costanza, Ralph D'Arge, Rudolf de Groot, Stephen Farber, Monica Hannon Grasso, Bruce Limburg, Karin Naeem, Robert V. O'Neill, et al., 'The value of the world's ecosystem services and natural capital', *Nature* 387 (1987), 253–60.

36. Donald P. Moynihan, 'The normative model in decline? Public service motivation the age of governance', in James L. Perry and Annie Hondeghem (eds), *Motivation in Public Service Management: The Call of Public Service* (Oxford: Oxford University Press, 2008), 247–67.

37. For a literature review of scientific papers on natural places and wellbeing, see Konstantinos Tzoulasa, Kalevi Korpelab, Stephen Vennc, Vesa Yli-Pelkonenc, Aleksandra Kaźmierczaka, Jari Niemelac and Philip Jamesa, 'Promoting ecosystem and human health in urban areas using Green Infrastructure: a literature review', *Landscape and Urban Planning* 81 (2007), 168–78; on political participation and wellbeing, see Charles M. Tolbert, Thomas A. Lyson and Michael D. Irwin, 'Local capitalism, civic engagement, and socioeconomic well-being', *Social Forces* 77 (1998), 401–27.

38. Mark Kirkham, 'An inspirational garden supported by Jo Malone', *EdinburghSketcher*, 16 June 2014, at http://edinburghsketcher. com/2014/06/26/an-inspirational-garden/ [visited 27 August 2014].

39. Vye Wood-Gee, 'Bridgend Allotment Community Health Inclusion Project', Scottish Natural Heritage Health and Natural Heritage Case Studies Report, 31 March 2008, at http://www.snh.gov.uk/docs/C231179.pdf [visited 27 August 2014].

40. *Ormiston Grows Newsletter*, Ormiston Grows, East Lothian, Scotland, February 2014, at http://www.edubuzz.org/whatson/wp-content/blogs. dir/1472/files/2014/01/Newsletter-Feb-2014-FINAL-TO-PRINT.pdf [visited 27 August 2014].

41. Peter Sloterdijk, *In the World Interior of Capital*, translated by W. Hoban (Cambridge: Polity Press, 2013), 12.

42. Peter Sloterdijk, 'Foreword to the Theory of Spheres' *Cosmograms* (2005), 223–41.

43. Bruno Latour, ' A cautious Prometheus: a few steps towards a philosophy of design (with special attention to Peter Sloterdijk)', in Jonathan Glynne, Fiona Hackney and Viv Minton (eds) *Networks of Design: Proceedings of the 2008 Annual International Conference of the Design History Society* (Boca Raton, FL: Universal Publ. 2009), 2–10.

44. Latour, 'A cautious Prometheus', 6.

45. Richard Sennett, *The Craftsman* (New Haven: Yale University Press, 2008), 39–40.

46. Stijn Postema with Tjirk van der Ziel, *Cityside Oasis or How to Bridge the Gap between City and Countryside* (Bunschoten, NL: Eemlandhoeve, 2008), 35.

47. Jan Huijgen, quoted in Postema, van der Ziel, *Cityside Oasis*, 45.

48. Postema, van der Ziel, *Cityside Oasis*, 51.

49. Postema, van der Ziel, *Cityside Oasis*, 56.

50. See, for example, the case studies of local food projects in Willliam A. Shutkin, *The Land That Could Be: Environmentalism and Democracy in the Twenty-First Century* (Cambridge, MA: MIT Press, 2000), and Paula S. Ross, Neil Reid and Jay D. Gatrell, *Local Food Systems in Old Industrial Regions: Concepts, Spatial Context, and Local Practices* (Farnham: Ashgate, 2010).

51. Sloterdijk, 'Foreword to The Theory of Spheres', 223.

52. Peter Sloterdijk, *Bubbles: Spheres Volume I: Microspherology*, translated by Wieland Hoben (Los Angeles: Semiotext, 2011), 335.

53. Arthur J. Taylor, *Laissez-faire and State Intervention in Nineteenth Century Britain* (London: Macmillan, 1983).

54. For a biographical overview of ten Victorian philanthropists and their religious background, see Ian Bradley, *Enlightened Entrepreneurs: Business Ethics in Victorian Britain* (London: Weidenfeld and Nicholson, 1987).

55. Robert Owen, cited in Ian L. Donnachie and George Hewitt, *Historic New Lanark: The Dale and Owen Industrial Community Since 1785* (Edinburgh: Edinburgh University Press, 1993), 49–51.

56. Ian L. Donnachie, *Robert Owen: Owen of New Lanark and New Harmony* (London: Tuckwell Press, 2000).

57. Robert Owen, *A New View of Society Or, Essays on the Principle of the Formation of the Human Character and the Application of the Principle to Practice* (London: Longman, 1817).

58. Lewis Mumford, 'The garden city idea and modern planning', in Ebenezer Howard, *Garden Cities of Tomorrow* (London: Faber and Faber, 1965), 35.

59. Ebenezer Howard, *Garden Cities of Tomorrow* (London: Swan Sonnenschein, 1902), 26.

60. Howard, *Garden Cities of Tomorrow*, 32–4.

61. Peter Katz, *The New Urbanism: Toward an Architecture of Community* (New York: McGraw Hill, 1994).

62. Eric Jacobsen, *Sidewalks in the Kingdom: New Urbanism and the Christian Faith* (Grand Rapids, MI: Brazos Press, 2003).

63. Anna Clark, 'Going without water in Detroit', *New York Times*, 3 July 2014.

64. Bess, *Till We Have Built Jerusalem*, 42–3.

65. Bess, *Till We Have Built Jerusalem*, 49.

66. D. Taylor-Robinson, E. Rougeux, D. Harrisson, M. Whitehead, B. Barr and A. Pearce, 'The rise of food poverty in the UK', *British Medical Journal* 347 (2013), f7157.

67. Thomas Paine, *Agrarian Justice, Opposed to Agrarian Law, and to Agrarian Monopoly, Being a Plan for Ameliorating the Condition of Man By Creating in Every Nation a National Fund* (Paris: Adlard, 1797), 7.

68. See further P. Van Parjis, 'Introduction: competing justifications ', in P. Van Parjis (ed.), *Arguing for Basic Income* (London: Verso, 1992), 3–43.

69. Leo XIII, *Rerum Novarum*, 15 May 1891, at http://www.newadvent.org/library/docs_le13rn.htm [visited 30 August 2014]; on the universal destination of goods, see Manfred Spieker, 'The universal destination of goods: the ethics

of property in the theory of Christian society', *Journal of Markets and Morality* 8 (2005), 333–54.

70. John M. Baldwin, 'The medieval theories of the just price: romanists, canonists, and theologians in the twelfth and thirteenth centuries', *Transactions of the American Philosophical Society* 49 (1959), 1–92.

71. Clark, 'Going without water in Detroit'.

72. Harold J. Massingham, *The Tree of Life* (London: Chapman and Hall, 1943), 74.

73. R. H. Tawney, *The Acquisitive Society* (London: Fabian Society, 1920), 33.

74. Massingham, *Tree of Life*, 98–9.

75. Massingham, *Tree of Life*, 100.

76. Massingham, *Tree of Life*, 104–5.

77. Reinhold Niebuhr, *The Nature and Destiny of Man* (New York: Charles Scribner, 1941), 22.

78. Johan Rockstrom, Will Stefen, Kevin Noone, Åsa Persson, F. Stuart Chapin, Eric F. Lambin, Timothy M. Lenton, Marten Scheffer et al., 'A safe operating space for humanity', *Nature* 461 (2009), 472–75.

79. Naomi Oreskes and Erik M Conway, *The Collapse of Western Civilization: A View from the Future* (New York: University of Columbia Press, 2014).

80. See further James Lovelock, *Rough Ride to the Future* (London: Penguin, 2014), and David Orr, *Down to the Wire: Confronting Climate Collapse* (Oxford: Oxford University Press, 2009); for an inspiring ecofeminist vision of a post-collapse, post-war, ecologically and humanly compassionate, urban-based and technically advanced future, see Marge Piercey, *Body of Glass* (London: Michael Joseph, 1992).

81. For two visionary books on the redesign of the built and urban environments to mimic nature, see Michael Braungart and William McDonagh, *Cradle to Cradle* (New York: Random House, 2008), and David Orr, *Earth in Mind: On Education, Environment, and the Human Prospect* (Washington DC: Island Press, 1994); for a realistic and visionary account of a new economy based on locality, see Molly Scott Cato, *The Bioregional Economy: Land, Liberty and the Pursuit of Happiness* (Abingdon: Routledge, 2013).

82. See further Yoram Levy and Marcel Wissenberg, 'Introduction', in Wissenberg and Levy, (eds) *Liberal Democracy and Environmentalism: The End of Environmentalism?* (New York: Routledge 2004), 1–9.

83. See Chapter 7 of Northcott, *Political Theology of Climate Change*.

84. On the role of ecological collapse in the decline and fall of the Roman Empire, see Clive Ponting, *Green History of the World: The Environment and the Collapse of Great Civilizations* (London: Sinclair-Stevenson, 1991).

85. This is why in the research project I am leading, *Caring for the Future Through Ancestral Time: Engaging the Cultural and Spiritual Presence of the Past to Promote a Sustainable Future*, the research team at the University of Edinburgh are investigating the potential of Ecocongregations, which is a loose affiliation of local churches acting on sustainability, to advance an ecological way of being church that is compassionate to other species and inter-generationally just:

see further http://ancestraltime.org.uk/ [visited 30 August 2014]; the project is jointly funded by UK Research Councils AHRC and ESRC.

86. Thomas Traherne, *Centuries* (London: Mowbray, 1977), 2. 25.

87. See further the thesis of my doctoral student Chad Rimmer, *The moral theory of Thomas Traherne, with special attention to the pro-formative role of nature in the moral formation of children*, School of Divinity, University of Edinburgh, 2014.

88. Traherne, *Centuries*, 3. 11.

89. See further Sam Harrison, '"Why Are We Here?" Taking "place" into Account in UK-Outdoor Environmental Education', *Journal of Adventure Education & Outdoor Learning*, 10 (2010), 3–18, and Giuliano Reis and Wolff-Michael Roth, 'A Feeling for the Environment: Emotion Talk in/for the Pedagogy of Public Environmental Education', *The Journal of Environmental Education*, 41 (2009), 71–87.

INDEX